THE JAZZ AGE

ARNOLD SHAW

THE JAZZ AGE

Popular Music in the 1920's

New York   Oxford

Oxford University Press

1987

OXFORD UNIVERSITY PRESS

Oxford   New York   Toronto
Delhi   Bombay   Calcutta   Madras   Karachi
Petaling Jaya   Singapore   Hong Kong   Tokyo
Nairobi   Dar es Salaam   Cape Town
Melbourne   Auckland

and associated companies in
Beirut   Berlin   Ibadan   Nicosia

Published by Oxford University Press, Inc.,
200 Madison Avenue, New York, New York 10016
Oxford is a registered trademark of Oxford University Press

Library of Congress Cataloging-in-Publication Data
Shaw, Arnold.
The Jazz Age.
Bibliography: p.   Includes index.
1. Music, Popular (Songs, etc.)—United States—History and criticism.
2. Jazz music—United States.   3. Musical revue, comedy, etc.—
United States.   4. United States—History—1919–1933.   I. Title.
ML3477.S475   1987   780'.42'0973   86–33234
ISBN 0–19–503891–6

1 3 5 7 9 8 6 4 2

Printed in the United States of America
on acid-free paper

To my beloved wife
Ghita
with love and admiration

Preface

The 1920s have been the subject of a considerable number of surveys, beginning with the brilliantly analytical and anecdotal *Only Yesterday* by Frederick Lewis Allen. But these studies, including Allen's panoramic view, paid scant attention to the popular music of the time, perhaps because that music was escapist, avoiding serious issues and controversial subjects.

But the twenties were a crucial period in the history of popular music, as significant musically as the fifties were with the advent of the "rock revolution." It was in the Roaring Twenties that a group of new tonalities entered the mainstream, fixing the sound and the forms of our popular music for the next thirty years. Jazz, hot and hybrid, came booming out of the South to prompt the creation of a new-styled dance music and new dances. The blues, also originating with blacks and for a long time transmitted orally, first made their way onto disk and paper, and influenced the songs being written in Tin Pan Alley. Black pianists of the Harlem scene transformed ragtime into stride piano, motivating the creation of bravura pieces known as "piano novelties." The Broadway theater was flooded with revues that were contemporary in theme and, inspired by the heightened tempi and rhythms of jazz, severed its European ties and moved toward the Golden Era of the thirties and forties.

In sum, the twenties were a period when elements of black and white music first achieved a rich and permanent fusion. This book is an attempt to delineate these vast changes, to view them in the climate of the era, and to acquaint the reader with the men and women responsible for them.

Las Vegas, Nevada   Arnold Shaw
September 20, 1986

P.S. It is perhaps not inappropriate to mention here the sheer, lasting appeal of some of the decade's hit songs. If any evidence is required to demonstrate this, Bob Fosse's musical *Big Deal*, which opened on Broadway in April 1986, provides eloquent testimony. After considering a number of eminent show composers, Fosse settled on a group of tunes that were first heard in the twenties: "I'm Just Wild About Harry," "Ain't She Sweet," "Button Up Your Overcoat," and "Happy Days Are Here Again."

   "These tunes had been in my head for years," Fosse explained. "So I ended using old songs that I loved and grew up with. . . ."*

* *New York Times* (April 6, 1986), "Arts & Leisure," 1.

Contents

I

The Jazz Age

✤ 1 ✤

"Flappers Are We"

"Vincent Youmans wrote the music for those twilights just after the war," exulted Zelda Fitzgerald. "They were wonderful. They hung above the city like an indigo wash."[1]

And they possessed that aura of darkness and romance, gaiety and melancholy, that seems a special mark of the Jazz Age. Riding down Fifth Avenue one day in the 1920s, F. Scott Fitzgerald "bawled" because, he later said, "I had everything I wanted and knew I would never be so happy again."[2] That ambivalent sense of exhilaration and foreboding permeates the novels as well as the songs of the era.

A Fifth Avenue bus was the venue also of other emotional displays. Jazz trombonist Miff Mole tells about a day when he and several colleagues gave an impromptu concert on a bus. "Vic Berton, Arthur Schutt, Bix Beiderbecke, Jimmy Dorsey and I," he recalls, "decided that we were going to make the greatest record ever made. We took along two quarts of gin and went up to the Gennett studios. Well, we drank for an hour and a half, played about half an hour, and were told, not too politely, to leave. We hadn't cut any records but we didn't mind. We climbed to the top of a Fifth Avenue bus and played there, all the way home!"[3]

Vincent Youmans, whose music was an expressive accompaniment to those twilights, wrote *No, No Nanette,* creating one of the most popular and imperishable melodies of the twentieth century, "Tea for Two." Moments after the curtain rose on the hit musical of 1925, a bevy of light-limbed girls bounded down to the footlights and chirped airily:

> Flappers are we
> Flappers are we
>   Flappers and fly and free.
> Never too slow
> All on the go
>   Petting parties with the smarties.
> Dizzy with dangerous glee
>   Puritans knock us
>   Because the way we're clad.
> Preachers all mock us
>   Because we're not bad.
> Most flippant young flappers are we![4]

"The postwar world came in," wrote songwriter and actor Hoagy Carmichael, "with a bang of bad booze, flappers with bare legs, jangled morals and wild weekends."[5]

It came in with Scott and Zelda Fitzgerald, who were, in biographer Nancy Milford's words, "the apotheosis of the twenties,"[6] and in poet and anthologist Louis Untermeyer's words, "flaming youth personified."[7] The Princeton dropout and his blue-eyed Alabama belle were married in the rectory of Manhattan's St. Patrick Cathedral in April 1920, just one month after the publication of his seminal novel *This Side of Paradise*. Overnight, *Paradise* became "the undergraduate's bible and its author the acknowledged leader of the Torrid Twenties, laureate of the Jazz Age and its excessive accent on youth."[8] Scott having become a celebrity, the Fitzgeralds went on a roller coaster ride of glamorous Long Island partying, trips to Paris, unbuttoned high jinks, lavish entertaining, and notorious debaucheries that kept Scott emotionally and financially strapped.

Scott undressed at a performance of the *Scandals*, Nancy Milford tells us, "Zelda completely sober dove into the fountain at Union Square,"[9] and when they moved from their honeymoon suite at the Biltmore Hotel to the Commodore, they celebrated by spinning around in the revolving doors for half an hour. They danced the Charleston on restaurant tables and recklessly rang fire alarms. When the firemen arrived and searched for the blaze, Zelda pointed to her breasts and screamed, "Here!" Dorothy Parker recalled first meeting the Fitzgeralds when Zelda was sitting astride the hood of a taxi and Scott was perched on its roof. The reckless exuberance manifested by the Fitzgeralds was typical of a young, affluent generation reacting not only to the tensions of the war just ended but to the emotional reserve of their elders.

Physical pranks were outside the realm in which Dorothy Parker moved, but the verbal prank—the bon mot, the epigram, the wisecrack, and the gag—were integral to her set and to the creative intellectual world of the 1920s. They flourished at the celebrated Algonquin Round Table, widely publicized by, if not actually the creation of, the press agents of the day. Large and round, the table was installed in the Rose Room in 1920 by Frank Case, owner of the hotel at 59 West 44th Street. At long luncheons editors, reporters, drama critics, music critics, and columnists gathered daily. The so-called regulars included *New Yorker* editor Harold Ross, playwright George S. Kaufman, humorist and critic Robert Benchley, novelist Edna Ferber, short story writer and humorist Ring Lardner, drama critic Alexander Woollcott, columnists Heywood Broun and Franklin P. Adams (FPA), Dorothy Parker, and others. The daily game of this legendary circle, or "vicious circle," as they preferred to call themselves, was simply to outdo each other in repartee: who could dazzle the rest with a sparkling display of wit, or come up with the rib-tickling wisecrack, deliver the ultimate bon mot. There may be no connection except a temporal one, but when the martini replaced bathtub gin, at the outset of the Depression, the Round Table went out of existence.

The motivation of this group is partly suggested by a set of parodies of two lines in Cole Porter's famous song "Night and Day" written by Ring Lardner for his radio column. Lardner was obviously concerned to show that he not only could compete but also, perhaps, vanquish Porter at his own lyric game. The two lines he selected for his parodies were:

> Night and day under the hide of me
> There's an Oh, such a hungry yearning, burning inside
> of me.

Lardner pretended the first two variants were written by a young niece of his who lived in Niles, Michigan:

> Night and day under the rind of me
> There's an Oh, such a zeal for spooning, rui'ning the
> mind of me.
>
> Night and day under the peel o' me
> There's a heat that will dree if ye think aucht but a'
> weel o' me.

Now he offers five variants "by uncle himself":

1) Night and day under the fleece of me
   There's an Oh, such a flaming furneth burneth the
   grease of me.

2) Night and day under the bark of me
   There's an Oh, such a mob of microbes making a park
   of me.

3) Night and day under my dermis, dear,
   There's a spot just as hot as coffee kept in a thermos,
   dear.

4) Night and day under my cuticle
   There's a love all for you so true it never would do to
   kill.

5) Night and day under my tegument
   There's a voice telling me I'm he, the good little egg
   you meant.

A number of writers have mistakenly attributed these parodies to humorist Robert Benchley, and they actually appear in a recent anthology *Benchley at the Theatre*.[10]

Tallulah Bankhead was not a member of the Algonquin Round Table. But Alexander Woollcott, the drama critic of the *New York Times*, who was, frequently took her to opening nights. Between the acts of a Maeterlinck play, as they were walking up the aisle, she made the remark, which has often been quoted and which Woollcott duly reported at lunch the following day, "There is less here than meets the eye."

Tallulah grew up in Montgomery, Alabama, where a girl two years her senior became the talk of the town for her beauty and unconventional conduct. Her name was Zelda Sayre, later Zelda Fitzgerald. One does not think of Tallulah Bankhead as a flapper. But her penchant for peeling off her clothes and appearing naked in public, her scatalogical speech, and her readiness to publicize unconventional episodes of her private life—all were typical of the daredevil ways of the flapper coterie.

In a letter to Ernest Hemingway toward the end of the twenties, Fitzgerald wrote of the five years between his leaving the army and finishing *The Great Gatsby* (1919–24): "We were living at top speed in the gayest world we could find."[11] Shortly after the publication of *Tales of the Jazz Age*, Zelda and he decided to forsake Long Island for Europe in order to escape the extravagances, intoxicated excitement, and hullabaloo among which they had dwelt for five hectic years.

The "gayest world," as Scott termed it, figured brilliantly in his short stories and novels, informing and shocking the older generation with the news that its daughters were drinking, flirting outrageously, petting, kissing, experimenting, smoking, and dancing with uninhibited and reckless disregard of what tomorrow might bring.

Of Rosalind in *This Side of Paradise*, whom Zelda regarded as the "original American flapper," a reporter for the *Baltimore Sun* was told: "I like girls like that. I like their courage, their recklessness, and their spendthriftness."[12] To most of their friends and many of Scott's readers, Zelda herself was the prototype of the flapper she eulogized in a piece in *Metropolitan Magazine* in 1922.

Just before they left for Europe in 1924, Zelda Fitzgerald was quoted in a newspaper article: "I'm raising my girl to be a flapper. I like the jazz generation, and I hope my daughter's generation will be jazzier. I want my girl to do as she pleases, be what she pleases, regardless of Mrs. Grundy." And she added, giving us further insight into the outlook of the flapper, "I think a woman gets more happiness out of being gay, light-hearted, unconventional, mistress of her own fate, than out of a career that calls for hard work, intellectual pessimism and loneliness. I don't want Pat to be a genius. I want her to be a flapper, because flappers are brave and gay and beautiful."[13]

The rare writer who mirrored the life of his times as he and his generation lived it, Scott himself described his first book as "a novel about flappers written for philosophers."[14] The description became the title of his second book, *Flappers and Philosophers*, a collection of short stories. By the time Scribner's was ready to release a succeeding collection of stories in May 1922, Scott felt that the word "flapper" had become passé, and opted for the evocative title under which it did appear, *Tales of the Jazz Age*. It would be bought, he wrote his editor Maxwell Perkins, "by *my own personal public* [his emphasis], i.e., the countless flappers and college kids who think I am a sort of oracle."[15] In his intuitive way, Scott gave the era its cognomen when it was scarcely two years old and the music in a state of flux and controversy. (Louis Armstrong did not arrive in Chicago until 1922, really launching the Jazz Age.)

Although Warner Fabian's pseudonymous novel *Flaming Youth* yielded another epithet for members of the "roaring generation"—Duke Ellington wrote and recorded a song of that title in 1929—no one approached Scott and Zelda as far as projecting, embodying, and mythologizing the flapper. Not until 1922 were the pages of the *New York Times* dotted with articles in which churchmen and other guardians of the moral condition either condemned or defended the flapper. Hollywood made only occasional forays into their world; *Variety* dismissed the 1920 film, *The Flapper*, as "the fluffiest of the fluff,"[16] and a 1929 movie, *Exalted Flapper*, was hardly noticed. In 1927, during a sojourn in Hollywood, Fitzgerald attempted a scenario involving a Jazz Age flapper to be played by Constance Talmadge; it never went into production. However, *Our Dancing Daughters* of 1928 presented a vivid portrayal of the flapper, with

Joan Crawford giving an alluring and electrifying performance that included her rousing rendition of the Charleston which projected her from the chorus of the Winter Garden to stardom at Metro-Goldwyn-Mayer.

On Broadway, the flapper made her first appearance in the Rachel Crothers comedy *Nice People*. But Anita Loos drew the definitive portrait in her novel and play *Gentlemen Prefer Blondes* (1926); the musical version of 1949, with a score by Jule Styne, provided Carol Channing with a classic role as Lorelei Lee, the Little Girl from Little Rock. Although Helen Kane played a minor role in *Good Boy* (1925), her coy, squeaky-voiced, "boop-boop-a-doop" delivery of "I Wanna Be Loved by You" was a show-stopper that left an indelible imprint of the flapper sound. The flapper figured in a number of other musicals of the 1920s: *Runnin' Wild*, in which the Charleston was originally introduced; *Dinah*, in which the Black Bottom was first danced—both black shows; *George White's Scandals of 1925* and *Artists and Models of 1925*; *Good News*, the De Sylva, Brown and Henderson collegiate musical; Rodgers and Hart's *The Girl Friend*; and most seductively and successfully in *No, No Nanette*.

"Flapper" made its appearance in a 1926 piano novelty, "Flapperette," by Jesse Greer. But no one song did for the provocative lass what "Collegiate," introduced by Fred Waring's Pennsylvanians (1925), did for the academic flock; Cole Porter's "I'm a Gigolo" in *Wake Up and Dream* (1929), did for the paid male escort; and Rodgers and Hart's weeper, "Ten Cents a Dance," interpolated by Ruth Etting in *Simple Simon* (1930), did for the taxi dancer or dance hall hostess.

The collegian or "cake-eater," as well as the flapper, two emblematic figures of the 1920s, found a brittle and an eye-arresting commentator in John Held, Jr., whose cartoons imparted a "doll-like innocence" to the smart set, with their rolled stockings, short skirts, bobbed hair, and wild parties. There they are in one of his best-remembered cartoons, "The Dance-Mad Younger Set," eight couples, their round-headed sheiks in tuxedos and long sideburns, the long-legged girls in their cropped, shingled hair and scanty skirts, sitting on a long staircase, totally disregarding a small jazz combo, some just chatting breezily and the others involved in various stages of petting and kissing. (Like F. Scott Fitzgerald, whose *Tales of the Jazz Age* he illustrated, Held mythologized the era as it was happening.)

The third emblematic figure of the era, the gangster, made bloody headlines and also made it into the Fox Movietone Newsreels, as Prohibition, in columnist FPA's words, "left a trail of graft and slime, and filled our land with vice and crime."[17] A grisly climax to the war for control of the illegal liquor trade came in a Chicago garage on Valentine's Day in 1929 when four men, two dressed as policemen, lined up seven men, including five members of the Bugs Moran gang, against a wall and pumped bullets from sawed-off shotguns and machine guns into their backs. The world, which had become accustomed to reading of the gangland killings masterminded by mobsters like Al Capone, was shocked by the Valentine Day's massacre.

Operative as of July 1, 1919, the Eighteenth Amendment became a battleground on January 16, 1920, when the Volstead Act made it illegal to sell or transport any beverage containing more than one-half of 1 percent of alcohol. The cast of characters of the "lawless decade," as it has been called, included the Prohibition agent, the rum runner, the bootlegger, the speakeasy owner, the hijacker, the feds and local police grafters, and mobsters like Owney Madden, Dion O'Bannion, Jack (Legs) Diamond, Al Capone, and others. A most unpopular law, Prohibition contributed to the era's loosening of morals, turning millions who had never touched a drop before into drinkers who flouted the law.

Bandleader Vincent Lopez has offered valuable testimony: "The breakdown of law and order, used as an argument by the Drys to peddle Prohibition, materialized the day after it became a national law. Crime and gangsterism, once a smalltime operation, was handed a billion dollar tax free business to organize with blood and bullets.

"No binge in history equaled the one in the Prohibition Era. The

Pekin Restaurant [where the Lopez band played] was a madhouse. People came with baskets and bought liquor by the quart to hoard. That night they used it for shampoos, in their soup, in their finger bowls. . . . Someone brought in a stuffed dummy with a sign pinned on saying, *John Barleycorn.* As he was paraded around the Pekin, the band played *For He's a Jolly Good Fellow.* That was the end of my Broadway career. . . ."[18]

Tin Pan Alley reflected the prevailing attitude in a few songs. "If I Meet the Guy Who Made This Country Dry" by Harry Von Tilzer and William Jerome and "It Will Never Be Dry Down in Havana No Matter What Happens 'Round Here," by William Tracey and Halsey K. Mohr are examples, though neither made an impressive showing. There was also "I'll See You in C-U-B-A," written by Irving Berlin for *Ziegfeld Midnight Frolic* (1920). Initially, American industry believed that Prohibition would be economically beneficial, a delusion shared by Tin Pan Alley. "We were told," music publisher Edward B. Marks has written, "that with Prohibition people would spend more time at home, around the piano. Spending nothing on liquor, they would have money for sheet music. . . . We did not understand that people who stay at home do not get around to hear tunes nor did we realize that depressed, hypocritical people do not sing. The theatrical bunch did not realize how much of the charm of an evening at the theatre consisted in a visit to a good restaurant. They did not know that restaurant patrons would switch to speakeasies, where, plied with jolting liquor, they would remain all evening. Thus many industries which thought they would divide up the brewer's prosperity, found they had merely lessened their own."[19]

Curiously, in this period of "speakeasy morality," the gangster, bloody though his hands were, was not infrequently viewed as a dashing if threatening figure, and not without an aura of romanticism. Consider Jay Gatsby, Duke Mantee (the killer in Robert Sherwood's play, *The Petrified Forest*), Edward G. Robinson, James Cagney, and Humphrey Bogart, among others. The ambivalent sentiment marked the feeling for fictional characters as well as the actors who portrayed them.

The Constitutional Amendment that significantly affected the mood, mores, and modes of the twenties was the Nineteenth, which gave women the right to vote. It was passed on August 28, 1920, after nearly seventy-five years of agitation. To the new feeling of "power," pride, and independence that flowed from this right, sociologists attribute such emancipatory developments as women smoking in public, bobbing their hair (to look more like men), seductively raising the hem of their skirts, rolling their stockings to expose bare knees, and flaunting their sexuality.

These daring and volatile practices quickly acquired musical accompaniment as a group of new sounds invaded the popular consciousness—hot jazz, from New Orleans, the blues, from Mississippi, Memphis, and Texas, ragtime from Missouri, boogie-woogie and stride piano from the keyboards of various piano players, some in Harlem, some itinerant.

All these new sounds were brought to the ears of listeners and to the feet of dancers by phonograph, radio, player-piano, and, toward the end of the era, motion pictures. These media superseded vaudeville, itself born of the nineteenth-century minstrel show which, at its peak, between 1900 and 1925, involved hundreds of performers touring over two thousand theatres. Even before the introduction of talkies, vaudeville was doomed by the motion picture studio, which owned the theatres as well as production companies, and which were more concerned to promote their films than the vaudeville acts to which pictures were initially an appendage.

By 1916, the phonograph, in the form of the Victrola (made by the Victor Talking Machine Company), as well as other brands, was a well-established appurtenance in middle-class homes, where recordings by Caruso, Paderewski, Schumann-Heink, Mischa Elman, Galli Curci, and other concert luminaries enjoyed a great vogue.[20] But it was also through recordings that Americans learned to dance the fox-trot, castle polka, hesitation walk, and other new steps. As for radio, stations began operating in Detroit (WWJ), Pittsburgh (KDKA), and Newark (WJZ) during 1919–20. By 1926, NBC made its inaugural broadcast as a network, and CBS went on the air in

1927, by which time there were over five hundred licensed stations in the country.

Edward B. Marks, writing in 1933, characterized radio as "the most disastrous of all the mechanical developments which have altered Tin Pan Alley. . . . Songs were made into hits in a week, and killed off in sixty days."[21] The decline in sheet music sales, he pointed out, was accompanied by a decline in record sales. "Most pernicious of all was the effect of the new ether toy upon pianos. Home playing practically ceased."[22]

During the twenties, name bands superseded touring vaudevillians as the greatest pluggers of songs and the creators of hits. "And right here," Marks wrote, "there originated an annoyance that has persisted ever since. . . . With the growing interest in syncopation, arranging became constantly more of a trick. . . . Bandsmen decided the publishers' [printed] arrangement [soon known as *stocks*] were not sufficiently exclusive. They demanded special trick arrangements—at the publisher's expense. Otherwise, they refusd to play the number. . . ."[23]

Ragtime, whose vogue was bracketed by two military conflicts— the Spanish-American War and World War I—had passed its prime by the time America entered the latter contest in 1917. That year, Scott Joplin, the major creator of the style—his "Maple Leaf Rag" had inaugurated the craze with a sheet music sale of over one million—died. To his syncopated music, which he regarded as classic American piano music, a generation of dancers had done the cakewalk, turkey trot, and variant steps like the kangaroo, dip, fish walk, snake, grizzly bear, and the two-step. When World War I ended, ragtime sounded passé to a new generation responding to the hot sounds rearing out of New Orleans and Kansas City.

✥ 2 ✥

King Oliver, Jelly Roll, and Satchmo

"The Jazz Age is over," F. Scott Fitzgerald wrote Maxwell Perkins in May 1931. "If Mark Sullivan is going on [with his history of *Our Times: The United States*], you might tell him that I claim credit for naming it and that it extended from the suppression of the riots of May Day 1919 to the crash of the stock market in 1929—almost exactly a decade."[1] He could have added as personal punctuation the mental breakdown of his glamorous, giddy wife in 1930. It was a neat structure that Fitzgerald erected. But the Jazz Age did not begin in 1919. If any year is to be picked, it would have to be 1917. Two events occurred that year, both involving a five-piece combo from New Orleans that became famous as the Original Dixieland Jazz Band (ODJB).

In 1917 the U.S. Navy Department, reacting to wartime moral fervor, shut down Storyville, New Orleans's redlight district—the city was an embarkation point for American troops. With the bordellos shuttered, musicians sought work on the Mississippi riverboats, migrating to port cities like Memphis and St. Louis, and settling in Chicago, Los Angeles, and New York.

The ODJB was not part of the New Orleans diaspora of 1917, most of which consisted of black musicians. The group, which was all white, came north a year earlier, led by a drummer named Johnny Stein, to play the Schiller Cafe in Chicago. While in the Windy City, four of the musicians walked out on Stein to form a new group, and it was this quintet, with Nick LaRocca as the truculent lead cornetist, that became known as the ODJB ("Jazz" at first being spelled "Jass"). After working several Chicago spots and winning acclaim for its fire, drive, and freshness, the ODJB was booked into a prestigious New York restaurant.

Reisenweber's, a three-story establishment on Eighth Avenue near Columbus Circle, occupied a narrow building that later housed Stillman's well known gymnasium, because of the boxers who trained there. Gus Edwards, with a big revue, performed on the street floor; on the top floor high society starting on January 26, 1917, danced to the suave music of Emil Coleman's Band; and the ODJB poured forth its brand of raucous staccato "hot jazz" on the second floor. Aside from LaRocca on cornet, the group included Larry Shields (clarinet), Eddie Edwards (trombone), Henry Ragas (piano), and Tony Sbarbo (drums).

This appearance at Reisenweber's is generally recognized as initiating the Jazz Age in New York. In addition to filling Reisenweber's dance floor with fired-up collegians and adventurous society folk, the ODJB made the first recordings of the new music. The historic occasion came on February 26, 1917, at the Victor studios, when the group cut "Livery Stable Blues," with a whinnying cornet and a mooing trombone, and "Original Dixieland One-Step." The record sold in such surprisingly large numbers that Columbia summoned blues composer W. C. Handy to make competitive versions, which turned out badly.

The impact of the group was not limited to the intrepid dance clientele of the city. It carried over to the top musicians of the day. Bix Beiderbecke was magnetized when he heard them later at the Balconades in New York. James P. Johnson, the inventive stride pianist, and many of his colleagues, were heartened by the acceptance of the new music through the playing of the ODJB. And in 1919, with slightly altered personnel, they took London by storm, creating even more of a sensation than they had at Reisenweber's in New York.

Among the local musicians who went chugging up to Reisenweber's to hear the new music was pianist Vincent Lopez, whose band was then playing at the Pekin Restaurant. "After listening to them," Lopez later wrote, "my first move was to copy them. I listened to their recordings of *Tiger Rag, Fidgety Feet* and the others, and I knew that was for me. After two weeks, we made the switch from schmaltzy music to the drive of Dixieland that does something to the adrenal glands.

"We left Reisenweber's rather early but we stayed long enough to catch the compelling voice of the new star, Sophie Tucker. The event of Dixieland on Broadway changed the entire fabric of the entertainment world."[2]

The ODJB played in a style that was an amalgam of ragtime, march music, and early dance music, with very little black shading (blue notes), and a kind of "pogo-stick" rhythm. Among the numbers they popularized that became dixieland band standards were "Jazz Me Blues," "Ostrich Walk," "Sensation Rag," "At the Jazz Band Ball," and, of course, "Tiger Rag." Fashioned from an old French quadrille, and originally called "Praline," after the New Orleans sweet, by Jack Laine's Ragtime Band, "Tiger Rag" quickly became a classic, with celebrated versions by Chick Webb, Duke Ellington, Louis Armstrong, and the Wolverines, among others.

Vincent Lopez recalled that in addition to "Tiger Rag," "one of the outstanding melodies of the time was Shelton Brooks's *Darktown Strutters' Ball*, which made Joe Frisco popular with his shuffle dance, black cigar and derby hat. A very simple performance but the crowd went for it in a big way! *For Me and My Gal, Indiana, After You've Gone, Ja-Da* were some of the songs you would hear four or five times a night. A pet expression then was *Jazz It Up.*"[3]

The word "jazz" may have come into usage as early as 1915. When Tom Brown's Band, the first white New Orleans combo to go to Chicago, was playing Lamb's Cafe, "that's when people started calling our music *jazz*," according to Arnold Loyacano, who played bass and piano in the group. "The way the Northern people figured it out, our music was loud, clangy, boisterous, like you'd say, 'Where did you get that jazzy suit?' meaning loud or fancy. Some people called it *jass*."[4] According to jazz historian Marshall W. Stearns, "The word 'jass,' later 'jazz,' turned up first in Chicago in the middle teens with an unprintable meaning."[5] Like other words descriptive of musical styles with origins in Negro slang ("boogie," "swing," "rock"), the unprintable meaning was sex or fornicating. Orrin Keepnews and Bill Grauer state that the word had strictly "red-light district meanings."[6]

"When Tom Brown's Band came to Chicago," Barry Ulanov has written, "the word 'jass' had a semi-sordid sexual connotation. Chicago Musicians' Union officials decided that the competition was neither necessary nor tolerable. They thought that labeling this group a jass or jazz band would be a very successful smear. But their attempt to disparage the Brown Band failed; the term caught on and Brown's Dixieland Band became Brown's Dixieland Jass Band, an exciting purveyor of a new kind of music with a new name as virile as the sounds it described."[7]

The Chicago Musicians Union was not the only organization that actively attacked the new music. In Pittsburgh, on November 23, 1921, the head of the union sent a letter to the membership which *Variety* reprinted under the heading, "Death to Jazz." Condemning the craze as "socially demeaning" and "musically immoral," but granting that it was momentarily remunerative, William L. Mayer castigated and caricatured the style, describing the playing of each instrument in ludicrous terms; he downgraded jazzmen for "acting like a bunch of intoxicated clowns" in a passage that had anti-Negro overtones; and he pleaded with his musicians not "to disport themselves as if you had just escaped from your keeper in a sanitarium for the feeble-minded."[8] Commenting on the sounds produced by jazz performers, he complained that the piano, "poor thing, is pulverized with arpeggi and chromatics until you can think of nothing else than a clumsy waiter with a tin tray full of china and cutlery taking a 'header' down a flight of concrete steps."[9]

By contrast, a number of prominent classical musicians, including

Leopold Stokowski, found jazz praiseworthy, as a survey published in *Etude* magazine in August 1924 revealed. A publication of the educational and classical Theodore Presser Company of Philadelphia, *Etude* conducted the survey in response to problems faced by piano teachers—its main readership—whose youthful students wanted to learn about and play the new music. Earlier, on November 23, 1923, the Sioux City *Tribune* printed an interview with John Philip Sousa, in which he applauded jazz and predicted a significant future for it in American music.

The diaspora from New Orleans swelled from 1917 on. By 1920 there were so many jazzmen in Chicago, most of them black, that the center of jazz had shifted. As many as forty outstanding exiles were playing at the Royal Gardens, Dreamland Cafe, De Luxe Cabaret, Red Mill Cafe, the Pekin, and the Vendome Theatre, where Erskine Tate led a band of New Orleans luminaries from 1918 to the end of the twenties. Despite its "vulgar" taint, jazz was spreading to cities on both coasts, with émigrés like cornetist Mutt Carey, trombonist Edward "Kid" Ory, and others settling in Los Angeles, and cornetist Oscar Celestin, clarinetist Sidney Bechet, and a host of others settling in New York.

In 1921, four years after the arrival of the ODJB, the New Orleans Rhythm Kings (NORK), another white group, opened at the Friars Inn on the north side of the city. Formed in 1919, the NORK was led by Paul Mares (trumpet), and included Leon Rappolo (clarinet) and clowning George Brunies (trombone); later Jack Pettis (C-melody sax) was added. Rhythm was supplied by Lew Black (banjo), Steve Brown (bass), Frank Snyder (drums), and Elmer Schoebel, an accomplished pianist and arranger. Playing a peppy, ensemble style close to that of the ODJB, they remained at the inn for two years, making records which later proved an overwhelming inspiration to a group of students at Austin High School in Chicago.

The band that the members of the white ODJB hung around and derived ideas from before leaving New Orleans was led by Joe "King" Oliver, whose group was "the best in New Orleans from

1915 or 1916 to 1918."[10] But it was the playing of the ODJB itself that motivated the Royal Gardens of Chicago to call upon bassist Bill Johnson to supply another band when the ODJB left for the Reisenweber booking in New York. Among those who came to the Windy City early in 1918 was King Oliver, whose chair in Edward Kid Ory's New Orleans band was taken by young Louis Armstrong. When the King took up residence at the Lincoln Gardens (formerly the Royal Gardens) as leader of the Creole Jazz Band, he sent for Armstrong.

Hoagy Carmichael visited the Lincoln Gardens around 1923 with Bix Beiderbecke and other members of the Wolverines, and later wrote in *Sometimes I Wonder:*

> A southside black and tan place, King Oliver's Band was there. This was the solid real jazz. Louis Armstrong played second trumpet. His white teeth showed when Bix gave him the high sign.
>
> Bix said, "That's my boy."
>
> Louis' wife, Lil, was playing piano and she could, too. There was a bass fiddle and clarinet, a regular jazz combo. As I sat down, I lit my first muggle [marijuana cigarette] as Louis and King Oliver broke into the introductory part of *Bugle Call Rag.* Everything was chaos at our table. We smoked and gulped our terrible drinks. Bix was on his feet, his eyes popping out of his head.
>
> Louis was taking a hot chorus. Gene Fosdick [Hoagy's buddy] had a mild spasm, finally overturning the table and sliding off his chair in a fit of stupor, muttering to himself in his strange style.
>
> The joint stank of body musk, bootleg booze, excited people, platform sweat. I couldn't see well but I was feeling all over, "Why isn't everyone in the world here to hear this?"
>
> The muggles took effect, making my body feel as light as my Ma's biscuits. I ran over to the piano and played *Royal Garden Blues* with the band.
>
> Music meant more than flesh just then. I had never heard the tune before, but full of smoke, I somehow couldn't miss

a note of it. The muggles had carried me into another
world. I was floating high around the room in a whirlpool
of jazz.[11]

The use of two cornets in a New Orleans–style combo was a new
idea, but it proved a winner partly because of the masterful interplay
between the two horns and young Armstrong's brilliance as a soloist.
"Oh Boy! Did those two team together," said trombonist Preston
Jackson. "When you saw Joe lean over towards Louis at the first
ending, you would know they were going to make a break in the
middle of the next chorus. And what breaks they made! Louis never
knew what Joe was going to play but he would always follow him
perfectly."[12]

As lead melodist, Oliver more than held his own, producing well-
remembered classics in his versions of "Dippermouth Blues" and
"Sugar Foot Stomp." During 1923–24, the Creole Jazz Band became,
in James Lincoln Collier's estimate, "the most important jazz group
to have its work systematically recorded."[13] The many sides they cut
afford a good overview of New Orleans polyphony, including rags
like "High Society," stomps like "New Orleans" and "Southern,"
and blues like "Royal Garden," "Riverside," "Canal Street," and
"Camp Meeting." Playing in the King's band "probably at its peak
then," said Preston Jackson—were, in addition to Satchmo (as Armstrong later became known), drummer Baby Dodds, bassist Bill
Johnson, and pianist Lil Hardin, with a front line that included
clarinetist Johnny Dodds and trombonist Honor Dutrey.

At the urging of his wife, Lil Hardin, who felt that he was unjustly
overshadowed, Louis Armstrong left the King in 1924 to go to New
York to join Fletcher Henderson's big jazz band. In 1927 Oliver was
offered the Cotton Club job. When he turned it down, Duke Ellington began his historic stand at the famous club. Firmly ensconced as
the kingpin of the Chicago jazz scene, Oliver might have feared the
challenge of the Big Apple. Whatever his reasoning, it proved a dismal turning point for him. By 1928, he was having difficulty main-
taining his band. His career thereafter described a downcurve all too
common among musicians—paralleled, for instance, by Jelly Roll
Morton—and all too typical of the 1920s and dixieland jazz. As a

music of untrammeled revelry, hot jazz was the appropriate accompaniment for a freewheeling time of living it up and letting tomorrow take care of itself, not infrequently with disastrous consequences.

With the onset of the Great Depression in 1929, the cabaret and record business suffered severely. Bandsmen began to balk at traveling; bookers began to take advantage; and the touring Creole Jazz Band was stranded in Kansas City without a job or money. In the changed temper of the times, the New Orleans style began to sound dated.

By the mid-thirties, the King was running a fruit stand in Savannah, and, when that did not prove fruitful, he took a job as janitor in a pool hall. Although he labored from nine in the morning until midnight, he could not make enough to take care of the health problems that now plagued him. Pyorrhea had been causing him to lose his teeth, and high blood pressure was making him short of breath. Struggling to save enough money for a return to New York, he wrote his sister, who lived in the Bronx, that he had finally managed to accumulate $1.60.

In his heyday, the King had been known as a voracious eater—he would consume a dozen hamburgers and a quart of milk at a single sitting. Lil Hardin and others remember him as a happy-go-lucky, easygoing man who was full of jokes, loved baseball, and spent his free time at the pool table. Unlike Jelly Roll Morton, he was not a publicity seeker or an aggressive showman. In one of his letters to his sister, he wrote of bookers, black and white, who had underpaid him and run off with his earnings, and of one who had mortgaged all the band's instruments. He talked of his pioneering work with mutes— "He did most of his playing with cups, glasses, buckets and mutes," said trumpeter Mutt Carey[14]—and of how others had turned their manufacture into profitable businesses. He never returned to New York, except to be buried in Woodlawn Cemetery in the Bronx. He died of a cerebral hemorrhage on April 8, 1938.

"With an ordinary tin mute," clarinetist Buster Bailey recalled, "the King could make the horn talk."[15] And Oliver said to Jelly Roll, "Now, you'll get a chance to see my red underwear," which ostensibly began to show when he blew a steamy chorus and his shirt sprang open over his expanded chest. The "alligators," as the marauders were then known, would sneak in the packed halls and try to steal his riffs. "It was common to see musicians writing on their cuffs in those days," trombonist Preston Jackson said. "Rappolo, the Rhythm Kings' clarinetist, was always writing. In those days, the King was really King, and his boys tore the tops off their music so that no one could see what they were playing."[16] And Louis Armstrong remembered: "King Oliver and I got so popular blending the jive together that pretty soon all the white musicians from downtown Chicago would come there after their work and stay until the place closed."[17] Hangers-on included members of the Isham Jones Band, among various other white groups.

"I don't care to remember him in Savannah, or the funeral," Armstrong said. "I'd rather think about a time like 1928 when I played two nights with Luis Russell's band at the Savoy as a guest. Joe Oliver was there each night, with a new set of clothes, and that Panama hat like he usually wore. And he looked pleased and happy. He was standing right in front of that trumpet. That was a thrill. . . . And he stood there listening with the tears coming right out of his eyes."[18]

"That was my only teacher; the one and only Joe Oliver," Lous Armstrong said of the man who brought him to Chicago in 1922 and put him up in his own home. "There's the man that's responsible for my everything in the world of Swing—Jazz—Hot—Ragtime. . . . I was like a son to him, he said. He sure acted like a father to me."[19] And it was the King who nurtured the kind of melodic improvisation that became an earmark of Louis's style. "You know what King Oliver said to me? 'Play the melody, play the lead, and learn. . . .' Some of that fantastic stuff, when they tear out from the first note, and you ask yourself, 'What the hell's he playing?'—that's not for me."[20] Hoagy Carmichael, who went with Bix Beiderbecke to hear the Creole Jazz Band, later wrote of Armstrong's playing of "Bugle Call Rag": "I dropped my cigarette and gulped my drink. Bix was on his feet, his eyes popping. . . . Every note he hit was perfection."[21]

"I jumped sky-high with joy," Armstrong said of the day he received the telegram from Papa Joe, as he called him, summoning him to the Windy City. "I arrived in Chicago about eleven o'clock the night of July 8, 1922. I'll never forget it. . . . I had no one to meet me. (I did miss the train that the King thought I would be on.) I took a cab and went directly to Lincoln Gardens. When I was getting out of the cab . . . I could hear the King's band playing some kind of real jump number. . . . I said to myself: 'My Gawd, I wonder if I'm good enough to play in that band?'"[22]

Cornetist Francis "Muggsy" Spanier sat on the curbstone outside the Gardens for hour after hour, transfixed by the playing of Oliver and Armstrong, especially by the harmonized "breaks." Drummer George Wettling recalled, "Eddie Condon, Johnny Forton, Floyd O'Brien and other hep kids were all hanging around to hear Joe and Louie."[23]

Too young to be admitted to Lala's Cabaret in New Orleans, Louis later told how he "would delight in delivering an order of stove coal to the prostitute who used to hustle in her crib right next to Pete Lala's . . . just so's I could hear King Oliver play . . . and I'd just stand in that lady's crib listening. . . . And I'm all in a daze. My what a punch that man had. . . . And could he shout a tune . . . like *Panama* or *High Society*. . . . All of a sudden it would dawn on the lady I was still in the crib very silent while she hustled those tricks—and she'd say—'What's the matter with you, boy? What are you still standing there so quiet?' And then I'd have to explain that I was very inspired by the King and his orchestra. . . . And then she handed me a cute one by saying—'Well, this is no place to day-dream. I've got my work to do.' "[24]

Armstrong came from a broken home and an impoverished boy-hood and first encountered the cornet at the Colored Waifs' Home, where he had been sent for harmlessly firing a pistol. He was some-what advanced in years to start an instrument, but his progress was so rapid that shortly after his release he sat in with Kid Ory's band at a picnic. "Everyone in the park went wild," Kid Ory said later, "over this boy in knee trousers who could play so great. . . ."[25] When Joe Oliver left the Kid's band in 1917 to take the Chicago offer refused by the Kid, he "went to see Louis and told him if he got himself a pair of long trousers, I'd give him a job. Within two hours, Louis came to my home."[26] When the call came later from Oliver in Chicago, Armstrong was playing on and off on the riverboats with Fate Marable's Jaz-E-Saz Band. Of Louis's playing on the riverboats, it was said that he would start playing choruses fifteen miles out of St. Louis and would still be finding new things to say when the boat was berthing at the St. Louis dock.

In 1924, the year the Wolverines were formed and made their first recordings with Bix Beiderbecke on cornet, and George Gershwin introduced *Rhapsody in Blue,* Louis married Lil Hardin, King Oliver's pianist, and left for New York to join Fletcher Henderson at the Roseland Ballroom. After that year-plus gig, he returned to Chicago to work with his wife, who had acquired a band of her own at the Dreamland Cafe. In November 1925 Louis began making records as the leader of his own combos, the Hot Five and the Hot Seven; during the next three years the masterful disks he cut brought him world renown and still remain among the most influential of jazz recordings. In them the New Orleans emphasis on ensemble playing (polyphony) is enhanced by Armstrong's solos, with their strong blues feeling. The same shading enriches sides he made with over a dozen blues singers, including, in May 1925, the great Bessie Smith ("Careless Love Blues," "I Ain't Gonna Play No Second Fiddle"). Out of the Hot Five and Hot Seven sessions came such classics as "West End Blues," regarded as the masterpiece of the Hot Seven disks and considered by some critics "the greatest of all jazz records"; also "Muskrat Ramble"; "Gut Bucket Blues" (with appropriate jive talk); "Cornet Chop Suey"; the brilliant and widely copied "Tight Like This," a contemporary erotic blues by Tampa Red and Georgia Tom; "Struttin' with Some Barbecue"; "Potato Head Blues," with Louis's celebrated stop-time chorus; "Twelfth Street Rag"; and "Heebie Jeebies." This last is the side on which Armstrong, employing a flowing stream of nonsense syllables, indulged in the vocal imitation of instrumental style that became known as "scattin'." You can buy or discredit the tale that he dropped the sheet of lyrics while he was singing and in order not to spoil the master (mistakes could not then be edited out, as they can be today on tape, and the number had to be redone from the beginning) simply substituted rhythmic syllables for the words. Among these classic sides, there was also "Skid-Dat-De-Dat," another rhapsodic scat improvisation.

In 1926 while he was working at Chicago's Vendome Theatre with Erskine Tate's "symphonic jazz orchestra"—here he switched from cornet to the larger and richer-toned trumpet—he doubled at the Sunset Cafe with Carroll Dickerson's band. The cafe's proprietor was Joe Glaser, whose respect for Armstrong early found expression in the billing he gave Satchmo: "World's Greatest Trumpet Player." Glaser later formed Associated Booking Corporation, the largest agency devoted exclusively to black artists, and became Armstrong's manager in 1935, a continuing and rewarding relationship for both until Glaser died in 1969. (Glaser's ties with his associates is suggested by an annual trip that Oscar Cohen, who succeeded him as President of ABC, makes to Glaser's grave. Cohen started as Glaser's office boy, and he visits his former boss on the anniversary of his death, to report the progress of the agency during the preceding year.)

As the decade neared its close, Armstrong's renown rose to new heights as a result of two developments. The first was a series of recordings he made in 1929 with pianist Earl "Fatha" Hines and drummer Zutty Singleton. Citing the interplay between Hines and Armstrong in "Weatherbird," "Skip the Gutter," and the classic "West End Blues," as well as in "Basin Street Blues" and "Tight Like This," British critic Max Harrison comments, "Armstrong is now at his most modernistic, the music shaped by a hard, clear virtuosity and full of complex ensembles, furious spurts of doubletimes, unpredictable harmonic alterations and rhythmic jugglery."[27] After these disks, jazz was inescapably a soloist's art.

The second development was Armstrong's appearance on Broadway in a featured role in the revue *Hot Chocolates*, with Leroy Smith's Band, at the same time he was fronting Carroll Dickerson's band at Connie's Inn. It was the proprietor of the inn who produced the revue, which originated as a floor show. The score for *Hot Chocolates*, written principally by Fats Waller and Andy Razaf, contained the imperishable ballad, "Ain't Misbehavin'," which some years ago was the title of a Broadway show composed of songs written by or associated with Fats. Performing first in the pit, Armstrong was moved onto the stage for a vocal as well as instrumental rendition of the ballad, and joined Fats and Edith Wilson in another number in which they were billed as "Three Thousand Pounds of Rhythm." Armstrong recorded the "Misbehavin'" and "Black and Blue," the latter with a vocal chorus that transformed the torch ballad into an impassioned plea for racial equality.

Heard briefly in stop-time vocal breaks on Fletcher Henderson's 1924 recording of "Everybody Loves My Baby," Armstrong made his first recording of a popular hit, Jimmy McHugh and Dorothy Fields's "I Can't Give You Anything But Love," in March 1929. (His first important vocal record was, of course, "Heebie Jeebies," the 1926 Boyd Atkins song on which he did his first scattin'.) Later in 1929, in sessions consisting mostly of songs by black songwriters—"After You're Gone," "I Ain't Got Nobody," "Dallas Blues," and "St. Louis Blues"—he made his inaugural recording of the pop hit "When You're Smiling (The Whole World Smiles at You)." Before the end of the year he introduced on disk a new single by Hoagy Carmichael, "Rockin' Chair," later the theme of Mildred Bailey. And in 1930 he recorded with strings, vocalizing "Song of the Islands." Thereafter, popular songs constantly figured in his recording sessions, and a big band frequently replaced a New Orleans combo as his accompaniment.

Some critics have derogated Louis's turn to popular material. But as far back as 1936 when Armstrong's first autobiography appeared, Rudy Vallee commented in his introduction to the book on Louis's "most extraordinary style of singing—another side of his genius which I feel has not received the recognition it deserves." Vallee added, "That Armstrong's delightful, delicious sense of distortion of lyrics and melody has made its influence felt upon popular singers of our day cannot be denied. Mr. Bing Crosby, the late Russ Columbo, Mildred Bailey and many others have adopted, probably unconsciously, the style of Louis Armstrong. . . . Most of these artists—he antedated them all—who attempt something other than the straight melody and lyric as it is written, who in other words, attempt to 'sing' would admit, if they were honest with themselves, and with their public, that they have been definitely influenced by the style of this master of swing improvisation."[28] Max Harrison likewise takes a positive position: "Having done everything then possible with traditional jazz material, all Armstrong could look to for new challenge was Tin Pan Alley ballads."[29] Harrison names "Body and Soul," "Dinah," "St. Louis Blues," "Some of These Days," and "Ding Dong Daddy" as instances of great solos, culminating in 1930 "in the emotional power, melodic richness, harmonic insight, rhythmic subtlety and superb construction of *Sweethearts on Parade* [Carmen Lombardo's ballad]."

After Armstrong's peak period, 1928–33, which yielded "I Gotta Right to Sing the Blues," later Jack Teagarden's theme, one finds in the 1960s such classics as his rendition of Kurt Weill's "Mack the Knife" and the banal monster hit, "Hello, Dolly." Whatever one may feel regarding the "apostasy" of Armstrong's rejection of pure jazz and the mass appeal he acquired as an entertainer and showman in the fifties and sixties, it is undeniable that his gravel-voiced singing and his appealing recordings greatly enriched the world of popular music. Critic and historian James Lincoln Collier calls him "the first genius" in jazz, an artist whose melodic gift was "simply astonishing"—and there was "no explaining where it came from or how it worked its magic."[30] Add the observation of Dan Morgenstern, of the Institute of Jazz Studies: "It was Armstrong in the main who transformed the working repertory of the jazz musician from traditional materials and ephemeral pop songs to great standards, drawn from the most fertile creative period of American songwriting. He introduced an impressive number of such songs to jazz, and it was to a large extent the jazz players who kept these songs alive and made them evergreens—the jazz players and the legion of popular singers profoundly touched by jazz, and, above all, by Louis Armstrong's magic way with a song."[31]

In 1923, the same year Satchmo made his first appearance on disk—a King Oliver date on Gennett Records which yielded "Chimes Blues," his first recorded solo—Jelly Roll Morton also made his first solo piano recordings. Like Satchmo, Mr. Jelly Roll came from a broken home in New Orleans and also grew up with a feeling of rejection, which perhaps motivated his egocentric and idiosyncratic behavior. "Hustler, pool shark, gambler, pimp, nightclub manager, entrepreneur and high-liver," Collier writes, "Jelly would be worth telling about had he never played a bar of music. He was proud, he was vain, he was arrogant, sensitive, ebullient, a braggart, suspicious, superstitious—but he was, nevertheless, the genuine article, a true artist."[32] He did, of course, make the claim—and more than once—that he originated jazz. "It is evidently known, beyond contradiction, that New Orleans is the cradle of jazz, and, I, myself, happened to be the creator in the year 1902." "Despite his boasting," Collier observes, "and his desire to be the wheeler-dealer, Morton was fundamentally a decent man, honorable in human relations, open with friends, generous towards his family. He simply lacked the character necessary for the bad man."[33]

Jelly Roll was born Ferdinand Joseph La Menthe around 1885, the son of a black Creole father who defected early—his stepfather was a step down socially. Morton never overcame the feeling of being declassed. Being light-skinned, he attempted to pass for white much of the time in order to escape the stigma of being a Creole black. To avoid being called "Frenchy," the label pinned on anyone with a Gallic name, he took the name of his mother's second husband and adopted nicknames with sexual connotations like "Winding Boy" and ultimately "Jelly Roll." As a youthful pianist in the luxurious bordellos of Storyville where he made much money in tips, he was thrown out of the house by the grandmother, who raised him after his mother's death and feared he would be a bad influence on his two sisters. He wandered through a flock of towns on the Gulf Coast and then through the Midwest and along the West Coast, gambling, hustling and conning, all less profitable than music, which he then regarded as a sideline.

His priorities changed when he reached Chicago, where he made about 175 recordings, piano solos or piano rolls of his own compositions. He later arranged and recorded originals like "Milenburg

Joys," "Kansas City Stomps," "Wolverine Blues," "The Pearls," and "Grandpa's Spells" with his famous Red Hot Peppers. These pieces combine ragtime, blues, and the feel of New Orleans marching bands. Just as Armstrong's early fame rested on his Hot Five and Hot Seven recordings, so Jelly Roll's reputation zoomed upward with the disks of the Red Hot Peppers. Starting in 1926 and continuing into 1930, he produced and recorded some fifty sides with the group, some in Chicago and others in New York, where he settled in 1926. He recorded exclusively for Victor Records, the result of a contract negotiated by the Melrose Brothers, Walter and Lester, owners originally of a music store in Chicago, and during the 1920s and 30s important publishers and recorders of black artists. (As they nurtured Morton and hot jazzmen of the twenties, they befriended Big Bill Broonzy and the Urban Bluesmen in the thirties.) With the Red Hot Pepper sides, ragtime blossomed into jazz, and Jelly Roll Morton emerged as a jazz composer, not just an arranger or songwriter.

The personnel of the Armstrong and Jelly Roll combos overlapped. Kid Ory, the Dodds brothers, Johnny St. Cyr, and Zutty Singleton played with the Red Hot Peppers as well as the Hot Seven. But Jelly Roll's sides also included Red Allen and Sidney de Paris on trumpet, J. C. Higginbotham and Wilbur de Paris on trombone, Barney Bigard and Omer Simeon on clarinet, Cozy Cole on drums, and Sidney Bechet on saxophone. "There is no better jazz on record," Max Harrison has said, and he numbers as "supreme" "Black Bottom Stomp," "The Chant," "Smoke House Blues," "Sidewalk Blues," "Deadman Blues," "Steamboat Stomp," "Grandpa's Spells," "Jelly Roll Blues," "Doctor Jazz," and "Cannonball Blues."[34]

As with King Oliver, the impact of the Depression, musically as well as economically, was devastating to Jelly Roll. Although he recorded in the thirties for commercial labels, as well as a series of reminiscences for the Library of Congress in 1939, his career was shot. He drove to Los Angeles in 1940, his Cadillac chained to his Lincoln, and arrived broke. His death in July 1941 passed unnoticed and unsung; even Duke Ellington, who was in Los Angeles at the time, did not attend the funeral.

"The Red Hot Pepper sides of 1926," Collier observes, "swung harder and made more sheer musical sense than anything anybody else was doing by way of band jazz. . . . It seems quite clear that Morton, on these sides, showed Ellington, Henderson, Moten, Basie and Goodman, and the rest, a way that jazz could go."[35] On the one-hundredth-anniversary of Jelly Roll's birth in 1885, the Book-of-the Month Club released a collection of thirty-six sides, including "Courthouse Bump," "Pretty Lil," "Tank Town Bump," "Sweet Peter," "Jersey Joe," "Mississippi Mildred," "The Chant," "Each Day," and "Gambling Jack"—all previously unissued in the USA; the last three masters that had never been issued at all.

3

Bix, Austin High, and Chicago Style

"Bix—he was in school at Lake Forest Academy then—used to sneak down and pester us to play *Angry* so he could sit in," said Paul Mares, cornetist of the New Orleans Rhythm Kings, who were then playing at the Friars Inn in Chicago. "At the time, it was the only tune he knew."[1]

In 1921 in Chicago, a group of white youngsters, after finishing classes at Austin High, regularly went to an ice cream parlor known as the Spoon and Straw to listen to new records. A Victrola gave them contact with disks by Paul Whiteman, Art Hickman, as well as Ted Lewis, who was "supposed to be the hot thing but he didn't do anything to us somehow." Then, one day they found some Gennett records by the NORK. The first tune they played was "Farewell Blues." "Boy, when we heard that," Jimmy McPartland said, "I'll tell you we went out of our minds. Everybody flipped." Everybody included Frank Teschemacher, Bud Freeman, Jim Lannigan, and brother Dick McPartland. "It was wonderful. So we put on *Tiger Rag, Discontented, Tin Roof Blues, Bugle Call,* and such titles. We stayed there from about three in the afternoon until eight at night, just listening to those records one after another, over and over again."[2] And that was the beginning of the famous Austin High School Gang, out of which came not only the jazzmen already mentioned but also Benny Goodman, Eddie Condon, Dave Tough, and others.

The band that inspired and spawned Bix and the Austin jazzmen, though composed of New Orleans white musicians, was formed in Chicago. The NORK, in fact, never played in the Crescent City. According to Paul Mares, who organized the group, people yelled for a substitute when the Original Dixieland Jazz Band left Chicago for New York—so he packed his horn when the offer came to a New Orleans associate who preferred to remain in the cab business. The call from the Friars Inn for a white dixieland band came after he had played at Camel Gardens with Tom Brown, the earliest of the white New Orleans émigrés.

The Friars Inn was a cabaret-styled club in downtown Chicago in a basement of the Loop. Its diner-dancers were influential and moneyed people, including gangsters like Al Capone and Dion O'Bannion. The original personnel of the NORK involved three melody instruments and four rhythm—Jack Pettis (C-melody sax), Arnold Loyacano (bass), Louis Black (banjo), Frank Snyder (drums), and Elmer Schobel (piano). To lure trombonist George Brunies up from New Orleans, Mares sent not only train fare but a new overcoat. What they played was white dixieland, peppy, happy, rip-snorting, two-beat, up-tempo music, much of it arranged by pianist Elmer Schoebel, the only NORK member who could read and write music, and who composed a number of the tunes they recorded and popularized.

Among these were "Farewell Blues," written by Mares, Schoebel, and clarinetist Leon Rappolo, who succeeded Jack Pettis; "Nobody's Sweetheart," interpolated by Ted Lewis in *The Passing Show of 1923* after the New York opening, whose writers included, in addition to Schoebel, Gus Kahn, Ernie Erdman, and Billy Meyers; "Bugle Call Rag," with music by Pettis, Meyers, and Schoebel; and "Tin Roof Blues," with music credited to the NORK (which consisted of George Brunies, Leon Rappolo, Paul Mares, Mel Stitzel, and Ben Pollack). One of their earliest hits, introduced to them by Ted Fiorito, later a pop bandleader, was "Toot, Toot, Tootsie (Goo' Bye)," interpolated by Al Jolson in the musical *Bombo* (1921) after the New York opening and later sung by him in the film *The Jazz Singer*

(1927). "Angry," the tune constantly requested by Bix, was composed by Jules Cassard, Merritt, Brunies, and Henry Bremer of the NORK. Though their earliest disks were cut in 1922 on weekend trips to Richmond, Indiana, home of the Starr Piano Company—owners of Gennett Records—"Angry" was not recorded until 1923. When the NORK recorded they called themselves the Friars Society Orchestra. "We were too young to get into the Friars Inn," Jimmy McPartland explained, "so the only way we could hear the Rhythm Kings was to go down and stand in the doorway and listen. It was great when someone opened the door and one could hear it louder."[3]

Afterward they would got to someone's apartment, "a different one each day because people got tired of us in a hurry. I mean, one had to change flats, otherwise the people downstairs did." They would put on one of the NORK records, "play a few bars, and then all get our notes. We'd have to tune our instruments up to the record machine, to the pitch and go ahead with a few notes. Then stop! A few more bars of the record, each guy would pick out his notes and boom! we would go on and play it. . . ."[4] In that way, with Bud Freeman lagging behind Tesch and the others, all of whom had studied violin for a time, they learned to play nine or ten tunes creditably. After a time, Dave Tough, who came from Oak Park High School in the next suburb, joined the group, and they played at charity meetings, for different frats, and at a gym social in Austin. Since they modeled themselves on the NORK, they called themselves the Blue Friars, after the inn at which the NORK were playing. Cornetist Jimmy McPartland, the loudest member, became the leader who stomped off the group. They landed their first professional job in the summer of 1924. They adopted the name O'Hare's Red Dragons in order to get work at radio station WHT in Chicago, and then became Husk O'Hare's Wolverines, after the band that was becoming known through Bix. Husk O'Hare, a non-playing promoter to whom Jimmy McPartland turned for assistance, found them a gig at the White City Ballroom.

Chicago was the locus of a very energetic jazz scene. In addition to black musicians from New Orleans, there were transplanted white jazzmen who made up the ODJB and, especially, the NORK—and the sounds of these bands gave birth to the Chicago style. Besides the

Austin High group, there were the Wolverines as well as non-affiliated youngsters like Benny Goodman, who at the age of fifteen "blew the hell out of the clarinet, playing about sixteen choruses of "Rose of the Rio Grande," so that Jimmy McPartland "sat there [at Eddie Tancil's in Cicero] with his mouth open."[5] Too young to be hired, Goodman was just sitting in.

Eddie Tancil's was one of the places Al Capone and his mob wanted pushed out of Cicero as they moved into the territory. "One night a bunch of tough guys came in," McPartland later recalled

> and started turning tables over to introduce themselves. Then they picked up bottles and began hitting the bartenders with them, also with blackjacks and brass knckles. It was just terrible.
>
> To us they said: "You boys keep playing if you don't want to get hurt. That's all." And you know who kept playing.
>
> The thugs tore the place apart, beat up all the waiters and barmen and Tancil, too. Eddie was fighting them and he was good, could beat the heck out of any two of those strong-arms. But when they brought out the "billies," he was outclassed.
>
> All over the place people were gashed and bleeding. The mobsters would break a bottle over some guy's head, then jab it in his face, then maybe kick him. They made mincemeat of people. I never saw such a horrible thing in my life. But we kept playing—period.
>
> A couple more nights of work and they came and did it again, much worse. That was the finish. Tancil got rid of the band, and two days later we found out that he had been shot dead. That was the beginning of the mobs' moving in on the night-club business.[6]

Frank Teschemacher (1906–1932), a key figure in the evolution of the Chicago style, is remembered for his oft-copied low register solo on "Darktown Strutters' Ball," made with a Red McKenzie group, the Jungle Kings. Definite examples of Teschemacher's style and of the Chicago style are audible on four sides he made with McKenzie and

Condon's Chicagoans: "Sugar," "China Boy," "Nobody's Sweetheart," and "Liza." Unfortunately, Tesch's very promising future came to an untimely end in 1932 in a car crash; he was just twenty-six years old.

Paul Mares, founder of the NORK, said frequently, "We did our best to copy the colored music we'd heard at home. We did the best we could but naturally, we couldn't play real colored style."[7] What they and the other white combos of the Windy City played was what became known as "Chicago," a largely orchestral ragtime sound with a heavy two-beat march rhythm and a tendency to push ahead of the best. The Chicagoans frequently resorted to "shuffle" in the middle section ("release" or "bridge") of a tune—a figure involving a series of accented eighth notes alternating with weak sixteenths. The "explosion," as they termed it, was a build-up in volume practiced before the repetition of the opening strain of a song. No song or record terminated without a "ride out" in which all the melody instruments clustered for a clambake finish.

Chicago style or dixieland, as it came to be known after a time—the word "Dixieland" at first referred to the South and to New Orleans style—went through a revival in the forties as a reaction against the big band style of the Swing era. At the time, some of the jazzmen sought to restore the authentic dixieland sound of the original New Orleans black pioneers. Others simply sought nostalgically to recall the sounds of their youthful twenties.

In New York City, there were Nick's and Eddie Condon's, two bastions of dixieland, in the Greenwich Village of the 1940s. But there was also Jimmy Ryan's on 52nd Street, which stayed with the sound all through the bebop years. When Swing Street was no more, Ryan's reopened on 54th Street, where it remained a home for the dixieland crowd into the 1980s.

Bix Beiderbecke holds the same fascination for us as F. Scott Fitzgerald. But compared to the torrents of words that have poured forth about Fitzgerald and Zelda, little has been written about Beiderbecke. Of course there was a novel, *Young Man with a Horn,* and a film based on the book. Novelist Dorothy Baker made the disclaimer that her story was not directly about the great musician but "based on Bix's life." The general public had reason neither to suspect nor to be concerned. But the reviewer in *The New Republic*, Otis Ferguson, who knew much about jazz and admired Bix, flatly rejected Baker's denial, asserting that "there was no one else *Young Man with a Horn* could have been about."[8]

Writing in 1938, Ferguson indicates that Bix was "above all men who have made music in this country, already a legend in the seven years since his death (1931)."[9] Bix's reputation was not created by either the novel or the film, as some have suggested. The truth is that Bix was a legend in his own lifetime, brief as it was. He had the kind of talent and personality, and led the kind of life, of which legends are naturally made, all the more so because of his premature though not entirely unanticipated death at the age of twenty-eight.

Leon Bix (not short for Bismarck, as is sometimes asserted) Beiderbecke was born in Davenport, Iowa, on March 10, 1903. His family, going back to his grandfathers, was musically cultivated, and contrary to popular belief, he read music. He also took piano lessons, and when he was only three, according to Hoagy Carmichael, he could play the melody of the *Second Hungarian Rhapsody*. He never became a truly proficient sight-reader, however. As for the cornet, he never took a lesson in his life. Handing him the instrument was like giving a paintbrush to Picasso. In his brief career, he worked with three of the best bands of the day: the Wolverines, the first hot jazz band of white Midwesterners "and more than I could believe," Hoagy Carmichael wrote; the pre-Swing Jean Goldkette band, from Detroit; and the big, elegant, symphonic jazz band of Paul Whiteman. The latter two used sophisticated arrangements, many of them by modernists like Bill Challis, which made heavy demands on laggard sight-readers. What apparently saved Bix was his ear, which was so perfect that he could identify the pitch of a belch, in Carmichael's words.

What came out of his horn brought adulation from his contemporaries. Russ Morgan, who worked with him in the Jean Goldkette Orchestra, never forgot "some of the most beautiful notes you ever heard";[10] when Louis Armstrong heard Bix at a Whiteman concert, he felt Bix's "pretty notes go all through me";[11] when Bix sat in one night with King Oliver—he had a standing invitation—"tears rolled down Oliver's face who said that he was the greatest he had ever heard";[12] and trumpeter Red Nichols frankly said, "Bix made a tremendous impression on me and I'd be the last to deny that his playing influenced mine."[13]

As recently as the 1960s, Philip Larkin, who wrote monthly jazz reviews for the London *Daily Telegraph*, said of listening to Bix, "One is left miserable at the utter waste of the most original talent jazz ever produced. . . . To hear him explode like Judgment Day out of the Whiteman Orchestra (as in *No Sweet Man*) only to retire at the end of sixteen bars into his genteel surroundings like a clock-cuckoo is an exhibition of artistic impotence painful to witness."[14] "Bix's masterworks are *I'm Coming Virginia* and especially, *Singin' the Blues*," James Lincoln Collier writes, "which was memorized by all the trumpet players of the day and recorded note for note by a number of bands, both black and white—Armstrong called the record of *Singin' the Blues* a collector's item—Fletcher Henderson took his *Singin' the Blues* note for note from the Bix and Tram record, with the saxophone section playing the Trumbauer chorus and Rex Stewart playing the Bix chorus."[15]

Apart from the direct and pervasive influence he had on his contemporaries, Bix added new resources to the jazz palette, and actually anticipated later developments in the music. He was a follower of Bessie Smith and Ethel Waters, but had an extensive interest in modern innovators like Schönberg, Stravinsky, Holst, and Eastwood Lane. Paul Whiteman recalled a concert at which Bix was enthralled by Wagner, and Jimmy McPartland remembered a Stravinsky concert to which Bix took him in 1925. "He was the first in Jazz," Jimmy said, "[whom] I heard use the whole-tone or augmented scale."[16] An early instance of this can be heard in "Tia Juana," a Gennett disk made by the Wolverines when they were working as a relief band at the Cinderella Ballroom in Manhattan. Bix's partiality to the whole-tone harmonies of Ravel and Debussy as well as to the modern harmonies of Cyril Scott and Eastwood Lane (especially "Land of the Loon") found expression in a group of piano pieces he improvised and that were transcribed by Bill Challis and other jazzmen. Of the group, which included "Candlelights," "Flashes," and "In the Dark," Bix himself recorded on piano only "In the Mist." Bix was one of the first cornetists to eschew vibrato. These developments have led jazz historians to perceive Bix as a forerunner of the Cool school of Lester Young and Miles Davis, and even of the Third Stream jazzmen who sought in the sixties to develop a fusion of jazz and the classics.

Bix was at his peak as a performer, most critics agree, in the period between February and May 1927 when he made his OKeh recordings with C-melody-saxist Frankie Trumbauer. It was just after they had spent two years with the Jean Goldkette organization and before he, Trumbauer, and Bill Challis joined Paul Whiteman. The classic "Singin' the Blues" was cut in this period, about which Richard Hadlock has observed, "With this record, a legitimate Jazz Ballad style was announced—a method whereby attractive songs could be played sweetly without losing authentic jazz feeling and without sacrificing virility."[17] These sessions also included "Clarinet Marmalade," " a triumph in terms of logical overall structure, melodic symmetry and rhythmic drive, a most extraordinary jazz recording."[18] Hadlock notes that Bix gives color and surprise to the melodic line through the use of ninths, elevenths and thirteenths, and employs scales as substitutes for arpeggios, "a notion that was about three decades ahead of 1927."[19]

What Bix contributed to the legend as a man seems compounded of contradictions, at least in the view of Hoagy Carmichael, who knew him in his formative years and later. He remembers him as well-mannered and clean-cut, his stubborn hair always slicked neatly back. Others have written about the carelessness of his clothes and his laundry. Carmichael, commenting on the novel and movie made of his life, wrote, "He was Bix, the real Bix, not the wild-drinking madman of the legend. He was neat, he was kind, he was low-keyed. He drank but not in the *Lost Weekend* kind of drama; his drinking made him thoughtful, and the mood was always of a man searching, not howling. . . . It is gentleness that is lost in the legend, his ability to charm, to hold friends, to make one feel that it was possible to know and need—and be known and needed by—another human being."[20]

Carmichael does not deny that Bix's slogan was "Don't nurse the bottle, pour!" He indicates that Bix started his journey at the end of the night, latching on to anybody who felt he could keep up with him. Hadlock put it this way: "Bix's consuming passion for music blinded him to the essentials of a healthful life."[21] Everybody agreed, including a girl he saw many times, that he lived in a world of his own, a world made up entirely of music. Carmichael tells us that he always carried the iron mouthpiece of his cornet in his pocket, and when he listened to music, he would finger the melody. "A sweet soul" was Carmichael's epithet, but one who had "a kind of despair about him[22] even in his early years.

By the end of the twenties, it was evident that Bix was physically on the decline, so evident that Paul Whiteman gave him a sabbatical with full salary to regain his health. When he returned, there had been no marked improvement in the alcoholism. Hadlock feels that Bix "spent much of his adult life attempting to reconcile his musical individualism with the demands of the American entertainment industry in the twenties."[23] Working with the Whiteman Orchestra exacerbated this situation, since a weekly radio show, with limited rehearsal time, made tremendous demands on the musicians as sight-readers. Bix was able to cope, largely as a result of his fantastic ear. Nevertheless, it was stressful playing third to several of the top conservatory-trained artists. When they wanted tonal depth and beauty, Whiteman and the arrangers always turned to Bix. On Whiteman's recording of George Gershwin's *Concerto in F*, Bix was chosen for the cornet solo part. After he left Whiteman in October 1929 and returned home to Davenport for the winter, "he could not escape the thoughtless friends," Hadlock tells us, "who wanted to promote and be part of the already forming Beiderbecke legend."[24] Years later, clarinetist Pee Wee Russell said, "In a sense, Bix was killed by his friends. Bix couldn't say no to anybody."[25]

Between 1929 and 1931, Bix worked and recorded sporadically, shuttling back and forth between New York and Davenport. By 1931 he was apparently able to perform only at intervals. He spent his last days in the Queens apartment of George Kreslow, a bassist. He collapsed, and was found to be suffering from lobar pneumonia, which, together with edema of the brain, caused his death at the age of 28.

Whether afflicted with "tragic temperament," as James Lincoln Collier puts it, or the trauma of genius, Bix's doomed journey poses a timeless enigma. Collier has left us with an image that may or may not hold an explanation:

> When he came home sick near the end of his life, he found in a hall closet all of his records that he had proudly sent home—still wrapped in their mailing envelopes. To the Beiderbecke's, their son was a dirty secret and the path he had chosen, abhorrent.[26]

4

Pops and Smack

As handsome, blond, blue-eyed F. Scott Fitzgerald was the public
relations agent extraordinaire for the flapper, portly Paul Whiteman
became the energetic popularizer of jazz, without really playing it,
or, rather, playing what he himself characterized as "symphonic
jazz."

Tall, beefy-necked, with a black, Chaplinesque mustache, and an
easily caricatured oval head, Whiteman (1890–1967) arrived in New
York City in 1920 to lead a band at the Palais Royal at Broadway
and 48th Street and to elevate the stature of popular music and dance
musicians. Son of a noted Denver music educator, with whom he did
not get along but with whom he studied the viola, he had played in
the Denver and San Francisco Symphony orchestras, worked unsuccessfully with a jazz combo, served as bandmaster of the U.S.
Navy's fifty-seven-piece orchestra, and launched the Paul Whiteman
Orchestra in a year's stay at the Alexandria Hotel in Los Angeles,
where he became a great favorite of the movie colony.

The Alexandria booking led to an engagement at the new Ambassador Hotel in Atlantic City (1919–20). During this gig, Whiteman
not only made his first recordings but introduced an innovative style
with which he became associated, "jazzing" the classics. Ferde Grofé,
the pianist he met during his fleeting association with John Tait's
Cafe [Jazz] Band, was the creator of arrangements that attracted Victor Records and led to the first Whiteman platter—a twelve-inch disk

of "Avalon" backed with (b/w) "Dance of the Hours." The latter
came from the Ponchielli opera *La Gioconda*, while the melody of
"Avalon," attributed to Al Jolson and Vincent Rose, was adapted
from the "E Lucevan le Stelle" aria from Puccini's *Tosca*. Legend
has it that it took almost an entire day to make the disk, as the
musicians, unacquainted with recording procedures, ruined master
after master with involuntary exclamations. The disk that established
Whiteman's as the premier dance band of the day was "Whispering"
b/w "Japanese Sandman," whose popularity attracted a sale of over
2 million disks in 1921, in addition to a million copies of sheet
music. Recorded at about the same time in August 1920, "Wang
Wang Blues," written by Whiteman's trumpeter Henry Busse in collaboration with two other sidemen, was released under Busse's name
and racked up a sale of half a million. (Busse, 1894–1955, is also
remembered for his unique hit version of "Hot Lips," recorded by
Whiteman in 1922. In 1927, Busse's trumpet solo on Whiteman's
disk of "When Day Is Done" was credited with launching the vogue
for "sweet jazz").

Known to musicians as "Pops," Paul Whiteman became known to
the world as the King of Jazz, a title reinforced by its use in a Universal 1930 film in which he starred. But Pops himself said, "I know
as much about real Jazz as F. Scott Fitzgerald did about the Jazz
Age." Recognizing that the true kings of jozz were the black creators
of the style, Pops is to be credited for featuring an imposing array
of jazzmen and jazz singers in his large commercial orchestras: Bix
Beiderbecke, singer Mildred Bailey, trombonist Jack Teagarden, the
Dorsey brothers, fiddler Joe Venuti, guitarist Eddie Lang, saxist
Adrian Rollini, singer Johnny Mercer, and the swinging Rhythm
Boys, among others. Spectacularly successful on records, in dance
halls, and nightclubs, over the radio, and on the stage, Whiteman
employed an oversized orchestra to bring an arranged type of jazz,
including improvisatory solos, to the ears of the general public.

No one played as vital a role as he in establishing dance music as
the popular music of the 1920s, a process by which he helped raise
the status of the dance musician. To conductor and arranger Lyn
Murray, Whiteman was "the discoverer of more major singers, or-

chestrators and arrangers than any other impresario of his time; the boisterous ringmaster of a musical circus without whom the jazz-oriented works of Carpenter, Milhaud, and particularly Gershwin, might never have been written."[1] Not the King of Jazz, but surely its unsurpassed publicist. "Paul Whiteman made jazz semi-respectable in 1924," jazz historian Marshall Stearns has said. "That is, jazz became as respectable as high-powered publicity from coast to coast could make it."[2] The Whiteman Orchestra did not play jazz, as the ODJB, Armstrong's Hot Five, or Jelly Roll Morton's Red Hot Peppers played jazz, but its recordings of the day's popular tunes involved arrangements that traded on sounds, harmonies, and rhythms derived from jazz.

The man who initially made these arrangements and was the architect of the Whiteman symphonic jazz sound, was Ferde Grofé (1892–1972), like Whiteman the son of a serious musician. Grofé had also played the viola with a symphony orchestra, the Los Angeles Philharmonic, moonlighting with a ragtime combo. Later the arranger of Gershwin's *Rhapsody in Blue* and himself the composer of one of America's best-known orchestral suites—the popular and pictorial *Grand Canyon Suite*—Grofe was the stylist behind Whiteman's jazzing of the classics.

The phenomenal success of "Whispering," was followed in 1922 by the ardent acceptance of Whiteman's disk, "Three O'Clock in the Morning," the waltz finale of the *Greenwich Village Follies* of that year, and again in 1923 by a million-seller, "Linger Awhile" (by Harry Owens and Vincent Rose), which featured a rousing banjo solo by diminutive Mike Pingatore, a Whiteman sideman for twenty-five years. The sale of over a million copies of sheet music and of 3.5 million disks of "Three O'Clock in the Morning" led Leo Feist, Inc., a publishing company, to sign Whiteman as a "staff writer," a euphemism for a bandleader who was paid an annual stipend to plug all the firm's new hits.

It was a productive association, however; it gave Whiteman a rewarding intimacy with the pop music scene and also access to the best popular tunes of the day. The result was a long list of best-selling hits, including, among others, "Wonderful One" (1922; Dorothy Terriss, Paul Whiteman, and Ferde Grofé, adapted from a theme by Marshall Neilan); "When Buddha Smiles (1921; Arthur Freed and Nacio Herb Brown); Irving Berlin's "What'll I Do?" (1924); Lou Alter's impressionistic "Manhattan Serenade"; and "Ramona" (1928; L. Wolfe Gilbert and Mabel Wayne), sometimes described as the most successful movie theme song of the twenties and introduced during a coast-to-coast broadcast in 1927.

Whiteman's rise in the realm of commercial music made him the most commanding bandsman of the era, far outstripping competitors like Vincent Lopez, Art Hickman, Ben Selvin, Isham Jones, Ted Lewis, and the Casa Loma Orchestra, among others. His bands were almost always double the size of his confreres'. A perceptive judge of good musicianship, he attracted the outstanding white instrumentalists of the day. He was willing to take a gamble, as when he kept alcoholic Bix Beiderbecke on full salary for a period during which the legendary trumpeter took the cure. He had a larger vision than most of his contemporaries, for he sought to elicit ambitious works through commissions from a variety of creative musicians—Duke Ellington, Gershwin, Fletcher Henderson, William Grant Still, Ferde Grofe, and Aaron Copeland, among others.

Despite the scope of his achievement and his immense popularity, Whiteman was not as important or as influential to the cognoscenti of his day as another bandleader—a black bandsman from Atlanta. While Whiteman and his Orchestra were drawing crowds to the Palais Royal, a band led by Fletcher Henderson was holding forth not too many blocks away at the Roseland Ballroom on Broadway. In 1928 Henderson, who played Roseland over a fifteen-year period, paid tribute to Whiteman in a number titled "Whiteman Stomp," cowritten with Fats Waller, who played piano on the Columbia recording. But in the view of John Hammond, veteran record executive, "In the Twenties, the Fletcher Henderson Orchestra was musically the most advanced in the land, but it was revered by a very limited public."

As early as 1921, Henderson was leading the Black Swan Troubadours, a band he organized to tour with Ethel Waters. He had

come to New York from his native Atlanta University to do postgraduate work in chemistry, but almost immediately switched to
popular music. Accepting a job as song plugger at the W. C. Handy
publishing company, he became music director of Black Swan Records when Handy's partner left to organize the first black record
company. By 1924 Henderson was leading the band at the Club Alabam; he then left it for a long-time association with the Roseland
Ballroom.

With his precocious arranger, Don Redman (1900–1964), a pioneer jazz arranger and composer who played virtually every instrument, Henderson formalized the type of freewheeling jazz developed
by the trumpet-clarinet-trombone combos from New Orleans and
Kansas City. Each of these instruments became the lead of a three
or four-man "section," with a three- or four-piece rhythm group
added, and together they embodied the drive, syncopation, and improvisation of the pioneer jazzmen.

Redman worked with the Henderson band from 1924 to 1927
and left to become musical director of McKinney's Cotton Pickers
(1927–31). During the thirties and forties, he led his own band (its
theme was a composition of his own, "Chant of the Weed") appearing on radio in his own series for Chipso (1932) and on television
in his own CBS series. In the early fifties, he served as musical director for Pearl Bailey. As an arranger, he contributed to the libraries
of Count Basie, Louis Armstrong, Jimmie Lunceford, Isham Jones,
Jimmy Dorsey, and Harry James, among others. He also wrote arrangements for Paul Whiteman over a thirty-year-period, which is
not to be overlooked or minimized in considering the jazz coloring
of the Whiteman band's sound. Fletcher Henderson's work developing the big band sound of the thirties benefited greatly from Don
Redman's creativity.

The prestige of the Henderson band among black musicians was
such that his sidemen included at various times virtuoso performers
like Louis Armstrong (who left King Oliver in Chicago to play at
Roseland in Manhattan), tenorman Coleman Hawkins, clarinetist
Buster Bailey, trumpeter Tommy Ladnier, trombonist Jimmy Harrison, saxist Benny Carter, and a host of others. The legacy of recorded

material left by Henderson vies in the number of titles and scope with that of Whiteman and any of the other popular bandleaders of the twenties. The difference is in the material recorded by him. While Whiteman was mainly concerned with the pop hits of the time, Henderson emphasizes blues, stomps, shuffles, and instrumental originals, and when he covered popular tunes like "Ain't She Sweet," "My Gal Sal," or "Somebody Loves Me," he produced a version slanted for the jazz-oriented listener, an approach that might have further limited his public.

Sharing Whiteman's stature—he was six feet, two inches tall—Smack (as he was known to his musicians) was unlike Pops in being somewhat timid, lacking in assertiveness and leadership qualities. His remarkable musicianship and creativity won respect but did not make up for the absence of qualities required of a showman. Nevertheless, his unique style of arranging set the mode for the type of band music that dominated the thirties. Swing was a Fletcher Henderson creation. And it was arrangements that he wrote and played with his own band in the twenties that became the basis of the Benny Goodman library and that brought the Goodman band its initial acceptance. The limited sales of his own recordings of these arrangements was a source of constant irritation to him, peaking in the Swing era when Goodman's versions of these tunes became runaway bestsellers. It was not surprising then that when Columbia Records issued a four-volume retrospective, *The Fletcher Henderson Story*, it subtitled the work, A Study in Frustration.

Henderson's travail might have been somewhat reduced had he been more of a businessman and understood better how his records were promoted, a concern to which jazz critics, including John Hammond, might also have paid more attention. There is a considerable difference in the amount of budget, staff, and muscle that a record company puts behind a pop disk and one directed at a more limited market such as the jazz market. Apart from all other considerations, including the time factor, Smack's disks did not sell as well as Goodman's because Goodman was promoted as pop and Henderson was not.[3] The creator of big band Swing was ahead of his time.

Except for the introduction of talkies in 1927, no pop music event of the twenties compares in significance with the concert presented in New York by Paul Whiteman on Tuesday, February 12, 1924, at Aeolian Hall, located on 43rd Street between Fifth and Sixth Avenues, and a hall primarily given over to classical artists. Whiteman chose it, as Isaac Goldberg has observed, "to justify jazz to the ways of the highbrows,"[4] and glowed when he found in the roster of patrons, such members of the classical establishment as Walter Damrosch, Heifetz, pianist Leopold Godowsky, Fritz Kreisler, John McCormack, Rachmaninoff, critic Pitts Sanborn, Deems Taylor, and others. Before the concert, it was being dismissed by his friends as well as critics as "Whiteman's Folly," an epithet that evaporated when they heard the twenty-second selection on that snowy afternoon's program.

The number was, of course, *Rhapsody in Blue,* performed by its composer, George Gershwin, at the piano, to the accompaniment of Whiteman's enlarged twenty-three-piece band. The concert was almost instantly transformed into legend and soon became universally recognized as a milestone in American music history, classical as well as pop. "It was a birthday for American music," Isaac Goldberg has commented, "even an Emancipation Proclamation, in which slavery to European formalism was signed away by the ascending, opening glissando of the *Rhapsody*."[5]

Sixty years after the event—on February 12, 1984—conductor Maurice Peress recreated the Asolian Hall concert in Town Hall, located on the same street but one block west. "The grand finale was *Rhapsody in Blue,*" the critic of the *New York Post* wrote, "which once again sounded as fresh and original as it did 60 years ago."[6] And in *The New Yorker,* jazz critic Whitney Balliett agreed that the *Rhapsody,* "unwittingly such a shining evocation of New York— sounded bony and exciting and newborn."[7]

The reaction to the premiere sixty years earlier was not quite that unanimous. To be sure, Henry O. Osgood, editor of *Musical America,* rhapsodized that the *Rhapsody* was greater than Stravinsky's *Rite of Spring. Zit's Weekly* observed that Gershwin had succeeded where

Malipiero and Stravinsky and others had failed. Among the New York critics, three were favorably impressed but two wrote thumbs-down critiques.

Olin Downes of the *New York Times* thought the *Rhapsody* revealed an *"extraordinary talent"*: "Its first theme alone, with its caprice, humor and exotic outline, shows a talent to be reckoned with." In the *Sun* and the *Globe*, Gilbert Gabriel thought "the beginning and the end were stunning" and characterized the work as "the day's most pressing contribution." William J. Henderson of the *Herald* praised Gershwin's piano playing and described the *Rhapsody* as a "highly engaging work." In the *World*, Deems Taylor observed that the *Rhapsody* "possessed at least two themes of genuine musical worth" and that it "revealed a genuine melodic gift and a piquant and individual harmonic sense to lend significance to its rhythmic ingenuity."[8]

But even these favorable reviewers dotted their observations with negatives. Downes talked of Gershwin's purpose being "defeated by technical immaturity." Gabriel commented on the work's "formlessness" and thought the middle section "sagged." Deems Taylor thought the *Rhapsody* suffered from "all the faults one might expect from an experimental work—diffuseness, want of self-criticism, and structural uncertainty."[9]

As for Pitts Sanborn: "Although to some ears this *Rhapsody* begins with a promising theme well stated, it soon runs off into empty passagework and meaningless repetition." In the *Tribune*, Lawrence Gilman announced that the work's "gorgeous vitality of rhythm and instrumental colors is impaired by melodic and harmonic anemia of the most pernicious kind."[10] "How trite and feeble and conventional the tunes are," Gilman wrote, "how sentimental and vapid the harmonic treatment under its disguise of fussy and futile counterpoint." And, he urged, "Weep over the lifelessness of its melody and harmony, so derivative, so stale, so inexpressive."[11]

Those were the critics. What about the audience? Observers agree that before Gershwin performed the *Rhapsody*, the audience was becoming "restive, bored."[12] It had sat through over twenty selections: a five-piece-band rendition of "Livery Stable Blues"; a "melodious jazz" treatment of "Mama Loves Papa" by Whiteman's Palais Royal Orchestra of nine pieces; comedy selections, including "Yes, We Have No Bananas"; Zez Confrey romping through "Kitten on the Keys" and other novelties; then some "semi-phonic arrangements of Irving Berlin songs, a Victor Herbert *Suite of Serenades* (written especially for the concert); and a group of popular classics like "To a Wild Rose," played in dance rhythms.

"The overfilled hall was hot," Jablonski and Stewart noted, "standees began to slip through the exits. Of the twenty-three numbers on the program, George was slated to come on in the twenty-second." Then it happened. "George practically darted to the piano on stage, sat down. . . . Whiteman shot a quick glance. Whiteman signaled to [Ross] Gorman, who electrified the entire hall with the *Rhapsody's* opening whoop. . . . When the *Rhapsody* came to the final passage, the hall broke into spontaneous, loud and long applause. George was called upon to take several bows, acknowledging the recognition— the arrival—of himself as a serious composer."[13]

No one could have predicted, not even the most fervent admirer of the piece, how the *Rhapsody* would in time captivate, magnetize, and inflame the world of music, in Europe as well as America. It has been played by virtually every conceivable combination of instruments—by two pianos, by an ensemble of eight pianos, by piano and symphony orchestra, by violin and symphony orchestra, by harmonica and a combo of eight harmonicas, by a mandolin orchestra; it has been background music for a Greek ballet and also for avantgarde dance. In 1930 the Roxy Theater paid Gershwin $10,000 a week to perform the work on stage, and in the same year the Fox film company paid $50,000—the highest fee paid until then for synchronization rights—to include it in a movie. Whiteman adopted the slow, romantic second theme as his permanent theme, played whenever he and his orchestra appeared. When Gershwin's screen biography was filmed in 1946, it bore the title *Rhapsody in Blue*. The Schwann catalog of recorded music lists thirty-seven different versions of the work. It has been estimated that royalties from the sale of sheet music, records, and performances have mounted to a figure of almost $1 million since its introduction in 1924.

Although Aeolian Hall was filled and there were standees, Paul Whiteman lost $7,000 on an investment of $11,000—and that did not include the many hours of overtime expended to rehearse the work after the Palais D'Or (where the Whiteman Orchestra was then playing) had shut down for the night—or the lunches and dinners to which the promotion-minded Whiteman took influentials of the classical world after he had invited them to sit in at rehearsals.

What led Whiteman to approach Gershwin for a "jazz concerto" after he had decided to present "An Experiment in Modern Music"? Until then, Gershwin had contributed tunes to a number of revues, having had a pop hit in "Swanee"; composed a so-so musical, *La La Lucille* (1919), his first complete score; written the music for four editions of George White's Scandals, which yielded the hit, "I'll Build a Stairway to Paradise" in 1922; and was at work on what became the so-so score of *Sweet Little Devil*. It was not, all told, an overwhelmingly impressive record. What made Whiteman believe that Gershwin was capable of creating an extended work was a piece that he and Buddy De Sylva had written for the *Scandals of 1922*. *Blue Monday Blues* (later retitled in concert as *135th Street*), was a twenty-five minute jazz opera. Paul Whiteman's Orchestra was the pit band for the show, and he obviously did not forget the work, despite its being dropped after only one performance.

As the story goes, Gershwin, busily occupied with the score of *Sweet Little Devil*, paid little heed to Whiteman's invitation to write a "jazz concerto." But on a January evening in 1924, while Gershwin and Buddy De Sylva were playing billiards at the Ambassador Billiard Parlor in the theatre district, brother Ira, who was sitting nearby on a stool, spotted an item in the *New York Tribune*, which read, "George Gershwin at work on a jazz concerto." The concert was then just five weeks away.

"Suddenly, an idea occurred to me," George later said. "There had been so much chatter about the limitations of jazz, not to speak of the manifest misunderstanding of its function. Jazz, they said, had to be in strict time. It had to cling to dance rhythm. I resolved, if possible to kill that misconception with one sturdy blow."[14]

Summoned at this time to Boston for the premiere of *Sweet Little*

Devil, "it was on the train [that] I suddenly heard—and even saw on paper—the complete construction of the rhapsody from beginning to end . . . By the time I reached Boston, I had a definite *plot* of the piece. . . ."[15] As for the second theme, it reportedly came to him while he was playing at a party. A week after my return from Boston," he recalled, "I completed the *Rhapsody.* . . . I don't believe that it took more than three weeks to write, on and off."[16]

During this period, Whiteman turned his gifted arranger, Ferde Grofé, over to Gershwin. George's manuscript presented the work in a two-piano arrangement, with some indication of the scoring. Grofé orchestrated the work, practically living at the Gershwin home on 110th Street and Amsterdam Avenue, "drinking Mama's delicious Russian tea," according to Jablonski and Stewart, "engaging in charming *non sequitur* conversations with Pop, and taking George's rhapsody from him practically page by page."[17] On January 25, four days after *Sweet Little Devil* opened in New York at the Astor (the last show to play this theatre before it became a movie house), Gershwin had "more or less" finished the *Rhapsody.* "More or less" because certain piano segments were left open for George to improvise at the performance. Grofé completed the orchestration on February 4. Brother Ira suggested the title under which the work became known.

The startling sound of the opening cadenza, we are told, assumed its character by accident. Gershwin had written a seventeen-note ascending scale, with each note to be tongued separately. During a rehearsal, clarinetist Ross German decided to have a little fun with the figure. Instead of tonguing each note, he played it as a glissando so that it sounded almost like a siren as he ascended from the low register to the upper register. Instead of being annoyed, Gershwin was intrigued and revised his score so that Gorman and all future clarinetists used the glissando approach. "The opening clarinet yawp," David Ewen has appropriately observed, "plunged into the first theme—a brash, impudent, saucy subject that not only set the mood for the entire work but was the voice of the frenetic and convention-shattering 1920s."[18]

As Gershwin proceeded in subsequent years to produce such extended works as *American in Paris, Second Rhapsody,* and especially, *Concerto in F,* it became clear that no one caught the tempo, excitement, nervousness, and frantic drive of the era as did Gershwin. The promise of the *Rhapsody in Blue* was more than fulfilled.

THE COMPLETE PROGRAM
OF THE PAUL WHITEMAN CONCERT
performed at Aeolian Hall, February 12, 1924

I.   True Form of Jazz
    a. Ten years ago—"The Livery Stable Blues"   Baer
    b. With modern embellishment—"Mama Loves Papa". . .

II. Comedy Selections
    a. Origin of "Yes! We Have No Bananas". . .   Silver
    b. Instrumental Comedy—"So This Is Venice". . .   Thomas
       (Adapted from *The Carnival of Venice*)

III. Contrast—Legitimate Scoring vs. Jazzing
    a. Selection in True Form—"Whispering". . .   Schonberger
    b. Same Selection with Jazz Treatment

IV. Recent Compositions with Modern Score
    a. "Limehouse Blues". . .   Braham
    b. "I Love You". . .   Archer
    c. "Raggedy Ann". . .   Kern

V.   Zez Confrey (piano)
    a. Medley of Popular Airs
    b. "Kitten on the Keys". . .   Confrey
    c. "Ice Cream and Art". . .   [no composer listed]
    d. "Nickel in the Slot". . .   Confrey
       (Accompanied by the orchestra)

VI. Flavoring a Selection with Borrowed Themes
    Russian Rose. . .   Grofé
    (Based on the *Volga Boat Song*)

VII. Semi-Symphonic Arrangement of Popular Melodies
    a. "Alexander's Ragtime Band". . .   Berlin
    b. "A Pretty Girl Is Like a Melody". . .   Berlin
    c. "Orange Blossoms in California". . .   Berlin

VIII. A Suite of Serenades. . .   Herbert
    a. Spanish

b. Chinese
c. Cuban
d. Oriental

IX.   Adaptation of Standard Selection to Dance Rhythms
     a. "Pale Moon". . .   Logan
     b. "To a Wild Rose". . .   MacDowell
     c. "Chansonette". . .   Friml

X.   George Gershwin (Piano)
     Rhapsody in Blue. . .   Gershwin
     (Accompanied by the Orchestra)

XI.   In the Field of the Classics
     Pomp and Circumstance. . .   Elgar

II

The Harlem Renaissance

✐ 5 ✐

Duke, Ethel, and the Harlem Scene

On his arrival in Harlem in 1921, the poet Langston Hughes wrote, "I can never put on paper the thrill of the underground ride to Harlem . . . At every station I kept watching for the sign: 135th Street. When I saw it, I held my breath . . . I went up the steps and out into the bright September sunlight. Harlem! I stood there, dropped my bags, took a deep breath and felt happy again." Hughes had come from Mexico, where he worked with his father, ostensibly to study at Columbia University. But as he wrote in his first autobiography, *The Big Sea*, "I really did not want to go to college at all. I didn't want to do anything but live in Harlem, get a job and work there. . . . ."[1]

In those intoxicating years, there was enchantment in the very air of Harlem. It crackled with excitement, with the anticipation of unusual experiences, and the vaulting urge to create something overwhelming. And new poetry, novels, essays, and plays poured from the pens of Countee Cullen, Claude McKay, Jean Toomer, Wallace Thurman, Arna Bontemps, Aaron Douglas, Rudolph Fisher, Alain Locke, Zora Neale Thurston, among others, some inspired by the new spirit of Negro nationalism aroused by Marcus Garvey and his Universal Negro Improvement Association. (The Garvey movement

57

collapsed when he was deported to Great Britain—he was born in Jamaica in the West Indies—after being convicted of mail fraud in connection with his Black Star Steamship Line, whose ships were to be used to repatriate blacks to Africa.)

In the same period that Harlem enjoyed its renaissance, the United States was in the throes of the postwar ferment that saw the emergence of the American novel, of gifted American poets like Edgar Lee Masters, Edwin Arlington Robinson, and Robert Frost, a major playwright, Eugene O'Neill, and a masterful group of Broadway composers. The twenties were the years of Ernest Hemingway's unique prose and T. S. Eliot's *The Waste Land*, a corrosive commentary on modern life and civilization, its engulfing materialism and cultural aridity, which found brooding echoes in novels by Theodore Dreiser (*An American Tragedy, Sister Carrie*), and in Sinclair Lewis's satirical *Main Street, Babbitt*, and *Arrowsmith*.

"Harlem was like a great magnet for the Negro intellectual," Hughes wrote,[2] "pulling an Arthur Schomburg from Puerto Rico, pulling Arna Bontemps all the way from California, a Nora Holt from way out West, an E. Simms Campbell from St. Louis, likewise a Josephine Baker. . . . Dusky dream Harlem rumbling into a nightmare tunnel where the subway from the Bronx keeps right on downtown, where the jazz is drained to Broadway whence Josephine [Baker] goes to Paris, Robeson to London, Jean Toomer to a Quaker Meeting House, Garvey to Atlanta Federal Penitentiary, and Wallace Thurman to the grave; but Duke Ellington to fame and fortune, Lena Horne to Broadway, and [trumpeter] Buck Clayton to China."[3]

But Harlem had an equally powerful hold on liberal white intellectuals, of whom Carl Van Vechten, author of *Nigger Heaven*, became the unacknowledged publicist. Artist Covarrubias caricatured Van Vechten in blackface, titling the drawing *A Prediction*. Andy Razaf's song, "Go Harlem," urged "Go inspectin' like Carl Van Vechten." At almost any Harlem soiree, following Van Vechten's lead, there was an easy mingling of the races that included dancing as well as dining and conversation. The mingling was so convivial that Alain Locke of Howard University's Philosophy department developed the tragic illusion, as did others, that the emergence and rise of black creative people would alleviate racism.

The intellectual and creative ferment quickly found expression in Harlem's entertainment scene. "The world's most glamorous atmosphere!" young Duke Ellington exclaimed when he first visited Harlem in 1923. "Why it is just like the Arabian nights!"[4] "Throughout colored America," James Weldon Johnson wrote in *Black Manhattan*, "Harlem is the recognized Negro capital. Indeed, it is the Mecca for the sightseer, the pleasure seeker, the curious, the adventurous, the enterprising, the ambitious, and the talented of the world; for the lure of it has reached down to every island of the Carib Sea and penetrated even into Africa."[5]

Van Vechten and his wife, Fania, had an apartment (really a salon) on West 55th Street, to which were invited not only white celebrities of the day—Somerset Maugham, Louis Untermeyer, Salvador Dali, Witter Bynner, Horace Liveright, among others—but also the outstanding black creative people. Bessie Smith came one evening with songsmith Porter Grainger and, after downing a tumbler of bootleg gin, sang the blues. Langston Hughes was a frequent guest. And there were exotic visitors like Chief Log Lance, who performed Indian dances, and the Peruvian contralto, Marguerite d'Alvarez, who sang operatic arias and later presented a concert of Gershwin songs. Van Vechten spent much time after hours at the Harlem clubs, about which James Weldon Johnson wrote in *Black Manhattan:* "Within the past ten years, Harlem has acquired a world-wide reputation. It is known as being erotic, colorful and sensuous, a place where life wakes up at night." In a booklet accompanying the long-out-of-print Columbia album *The Sounds of Harlem,* Frank Driggs lists and pictures almost one hundred twenty-five entertainment spots clustered in the dense area between 125th and 135th streets, and between Lenox and Seventh Avenues. In addition to forty or more clubs, whose clientele was basically white, seventeen or more cafes, speakeasies, chicken shacks, cellars, lounges, taverns, rib joints, supper clubs, and bars and grills,—all involved with music and musicians— there were ten theatres and eight ballrooms. The theatres included the Alhambra (Seventh Avenue), Apollo (125th Street), Crescent, Douglas, Harlem Opera House (the oldest, dating back to 1889), Lafayette (Seventh Avenue), Lincoln (135th Street), Odeon and Oriental. The ballrooms: Alhambra (Seventh Avenue), Congress Casino (132nd Street), Garden of Joy (a canvas-enclosed dance pavillion located at the top of a shelf of rock on Seventh Avenue, between 138th and 139th Streets); Golden Gate (West 135th Street); Renaissance Casino (West 138th Street); Rose Danceland (on the second floor at the corner of 125th and Seventh Avenue); and the famous Savoy Ballroom, which occupied the entire block between 140th and 141st on Lenox Avenue.

Many of the small clubs offered outstanding talent. Basement Brownies on West 133rd Street was a favorite hangout of Art Tatum and a gathering spot for stride pianists. At the Elks Rendezvous on Lenox Avenue, Louis Jordan and his Tympani Five worked until hit recordings gave the group national publicity and access to the big midtown clubs. The Campus on 104th and Columbus employed Eubie Blake as house pianist. Van Vechten's hangout was Smalls', where the waiters danced the Charleston while trundling full trays of bootleg whiskey. Smalls' was then located in a Fifth Avenue basement to which Van Vechten and publisher Bennett Cerf took William Faulkner one night, eliciting a sardonic comment from him: "The people up here are soft. They couldn't get along down South." Located at 2212 Fifth Avenue from 1917 to 1925, the Sugar Cane Club (as Ed Smalls called it) was the first Harlem spot to attract the midtown crowd. It was the forerunner of Ed Smalls' Paradise at 2294½ Seventh Avenue, which opened in October 1925 with pianist Charlie Johnson's band, the house unit for ten years. The Paradise continued the audience draw of singing and dancing waiters.

At the height of the renaissance, the Paradise was one of the big three most publicized clubs frequented by high society and the celebrities. Connie's Inn, situated not too far away at 2221 Seventh Avenue, occupied a large basement in a building at the corner of 131st Street and Seventh Avenue. When it opened in November 1921, it called itself Shuffle Inn as a tribute to the Sissle-Blake Broadway hit show, *Shuffle Along*. The orchestra was directed by pianist and songwriter Luckey Roberts. After a short time, the place was bought by George and Connie Immerman, who were in the delicatessen business and who employed Fats Waller as their delivery boy. The Immerman's altered the entrance from the 131st Street side to Seventh Avenue where it opened in June 1923 with the Famous Tree of Hope in front. Like its luxurious competitors, Connie's featured elaborate floor shows. These peaked in 1929 when Louis Armstrong came from Chicago with Carroll Dickerson's Orchestra. *Hot Chocolates,* the floor show written by Fats Waller and Andy Razaf, went to Broadway, yielding such hits as "Ain't Misbehavin'," "Black and Blue," "That Rhythm Man," and "Can't We Get Together."

Of the big three, the Cotton Club was the most opulent, presenting floor shows that vied with Broadway musicals. It was a Jim Crow club, catering to monied whites and gangsters. The recent (1984) film on the club was criticized for its emphasis on the gangster angle, but from 1920 on the club was owned by a group of hoods that included Owney Madden and George "Big Frenchy" De Mange. When their regular bandleader died in 1927, they reportedly commanded Duke Ellington to take the stand "despite all contracts, commitments or desires."[6] An opposition club, the Plantation, opened its doors nearby on West 126th Street, near Lenox Avenue, around 1930, and hired Cab Calloway's band away from the Cotton. The Plantation lasted two nights before Harry Block, a Plantation backer, was found dead and the fixtures, including the bar, found smashed to smithereens in the gutter.

Early Cotton shows were produced by Lew Leslie, later the impresario of the hit musical *Blackbirds,* while songwriting chores fell to young Jimmy McHugh, a Boston tunesmith who later collaborated with New Jerseyite Dorothy Fields of the famous Broadway Fields family. The years at the Cotton Club jelled for these three in *Blackbirds of 1928.*

Whether or not the mob ordered Duke Ellington to take the Cotton Club job in 1927, two men claim a part in bringing the Duke to the club. Jimmy McHugh, who had been listening to Duke's band at the Kentucky Club on Broadway, plugged for the Duke. But other sources credit Irving Mills, who had become the Duke's manager during his Kentucky Club sojourn (and remained with him from 1926 to 1939, getting his name as a collaborator on virtually all of Duke's compositions. Opening on December 4, 1927, with an expanded orchestra, the Duke became nationally known during his five-year stay at the luxurious club. Recognition came largely as a result of nightly coast-to-coast broadcasts—"remotes"—announced by the most elegant voices of the day: Ted Husing, Norman Brokenshire, and David Rose. It was in this period that the band became a jazz band, spurred on by the growl trumpeting of James "Bubber" Miley and the clarinet fluidity of Barney Bigard. Jungle sketches, popular in many of the Cotton Club Parades, as they were called, used Miley's gutbucket growling to great effect.

From the time he was a small boy in Washington, D.C., Edward Kennedy Ellington was a natty dresser, which explains the nickname Duke. During his years at the Cotton, in an atmosphere of opulence, he became a man of sartorial splendor. He developed also his elegant manners and high-flown speech. The period when he produced great standards like "Mood Indigo," "Sophisticated Lady," "Solitude," "Caravan," and others came in the 1930s. But in the Cotton Club years, having composed with Bubber Miley "East St. Louis Toodle-Oo," the band's theme, he wrote "Black and Tan Fantasy," "Creole Love Call" (recorded with Adelaide Hall), and "The Mooch." In 1929 the band doubled in Florenz Ziegfeld's *Show Girl* and appeared in a short film, *Black and Tan Fantasy*.

The spirit of the time is well delineated by drummer Sammy Greer, who recalled that "the last show at the Cotton Club went on at two and the club closed at three-thirty or four. Then everybody would go next door to Happy Roane's or to the breakfast dance at Smalls' Paradise, where the floor show went on at six o'clock in the morning. . . . It was the complete show with 25 or 30 people, including the singing waiters and their twirling trays. Show people from all over New York, white and colored, went there Sunday mornings. It's hard to imagine now, musicians coming out from the breakfast dance at eight or nine in the morning with their tuxedos on, and showgirls with evening dresses on. Or Charlie Johnson's band there, at six or seven in the morning, with maybe twenty-five musicians from the bands all over town, white and colored, playing at one time, all the top names in music business."[7]

For Ethel Waters, as for Duke Ellington, Harlem in the 1920s was the starting point. But her beginnings were hardly as auspicious. Born in Chester, Pennsylvania, to a 13-year-old girl who had been raped, Ethel made her debut at the ramshackle Lincoln Theatre in Baltimore, where she was paid $10 a week as a shake dancer and singer. "On a clear night," she wrote in her autobiography, "you could hear me five blocks away."[8] You could also see her no matter where you sat because she was so tall they billed her as Sweet Mama Stringbean. She became the first women to sing "St. Louis Blues," and when she recorded for Black Swan Records in 1920—the company launched by W. C. Handy's ex-publishing partner, Harry Pace— she became not only the first artist on the label but the very first popular black singer to be recorded.

Yet even after a tour with Fletcher Henderson, arranged by Black Swan, the best booking she could secure was at Edmond Johnson's Cellar at 132nd Street and Fifth Avenue. "It was the last stop on the way down," she later wrote. "After you worked there, there was no place to go except into domestic service."[9] This was Ethel's venue for a number of years, despite accolades from the great Bert Williams and from Sophie Tucker (who paid her for private instruction), and media acclaim as the "Ebony Nora Bayes" (after the reigning queen of vaudeville). The one asset of the Cellar was its pianist, Lou Henley, who helped Ethel expand her repertoire by acquainting her with some of the great show standards. An authentic interpreter of songs by black songwriters like Shelton Brooks, Perry Bradford, Clarence Williams, and others, she soon became adept at handling the sophisticated lyrics and melodies of Harold Arlen, Irving Berlin, and Vincent Youmans.

Ethel's major breakthrough came in the summer of 1925 when Florence Mills, who had starred in *Shuffle Along*, left her headline spot at the well-known Plantation Club and Waters was chosen as her replacement. The Plantation was a high-society, midtown club at

50th Street and Broadway. The score for the floor show was composed by Harry Akst, formerly the accompanist for Nora Bayes,
later for Al Jolson, and eventually the writer of such hits as "Baby
Face" and "Am I Blue?" The Plantation score included "Dinah,"
which became a hit for Ethel and remained in her repertoire.
"Dinah" is sometimes typed as the first evergreen to come from a
nightclub revue; it later served as the theme of Dinah Shore's television show. Touring with the *Plantation Revue,* Ethel elicited from
Ashton Stevens, the tough critic of the Chicago *Herald-American,*
a rave review in which he hailed her as "a new star, the greatest
artist of her race and generation." Another critic of the time commented, "When she sings *Dinah,* she is beautiful. When she sings
Eli, Eli, she achieves greatness. And when she sings *Shake That
Thing,* she is incredible."[10]

In 1927 she was featured on Broadway in a short-lived revue,
Africana. In 1929 she made her first film appearance in *On with the
Show,* popularizing Harry Akst's ballad, "Am I Blue?" In 1933 she
became the headliner at the Cotton Club, where she introduced and
popularized Harold Arlen's imperishable hit "Stormy Weather."
That year she was heard on network broadcasts from the club and
on the CBS network show, "American Revue," backed by the Dorsey
Brothers band. Before the year was out, she was signed by Irving
Berlin as a headliner for his revue *As Thousands Cheer,* becoming
the first black artist after Bert Williams to star in an all-white Broadway show. Her rendition of "Supper Time," the moving anti-lynch
ballad, and of the sizzling "Heat Wave" were high points of the
show. Later, Ethel made her mark in films (*Cabin in the Sky*), and
on the stage with two dramatic, non-singing parts in two plays,
Member of the Wedding and *Mamba's Daughters,* and became the
first black international superstar.

A turning point in the expansion of her artistry came with her
appearance at the Kedzie Theatre in Chicago in the early twenties.
A vaudevillian friend, Earl Dancer, had urged her to reach out to
white audiences: "White people would love you for the rest of your
life. You don't have to sing as you do for colored people."[11] With
great trepidation, Ethel agreed to a booking at the Kedzie. Although

she was certain that she and Earl would flop, they were so well received that they were signed to tours by the Keith-Orpheum circuit. Those who didn't think of her as the "Ebony Nora Bayes" referred to her as the "Yvette Gilbert of her race." As her audience grew, Ethel varied her program, which now included pop and theatre songs as well as blues. She could, as she put it, "riff and jam and growl, but never had that loud approach."[12] A genius at characterization and immaculate in her diction, she sang with a swinging beat or with refinement, according to the demands of the number.

Ethel sang blues, but was not a blues singer. She sang jazz, but was not a jazz singer. She sang pop and show tunes, but was not a pop singer. Her singing was very much like her religion. As a child, she was drawn to Catholicism, but also attended Methodist services and was attracted to the unbuttoned emotionalism of the Holy Rollers and Baptists. From 1957 until her death in 1977, she worked with the Billy Graham Crusade. In song and in spirit, she disregarded categories in order to express her own singular self.

The blues began to develop in the post–Civil War years as an expression of the black man's experiences during Reconstruction; stride piano had its beginnings in ragtime; black musicals were staged on Broadway in the first decades of the twentieth century. But all three of these forms came to fruition and became mainstream phenomena during the Harlem Renaissance. There is no causal relationship between the development of the three forms. However, the atmosphere created by the renaissance permitted all three to evolve. With the onset of the Depression in 1929, the renaissance came to an end. Whites stopped going uptown and the fringe clubs, lounges, grills, taverns, and cabarets began to close, a process hastened when the repeal of Prohibition in 1932 shuttered the speakeasies. Publishers no longer sought books and songs by new black creators. The shutdown of Harlem led to the emergence of 52nd Street as Swing Street and the mecca of jazz. The rise of the nightclub era in the thirties brought Harlem's entertainers and even its rib joints and chicken shacks downtown.

The magic of Harlem during the Renaissance found expression in a number of songs: In 1927 Fats Waller composed "Lenox Avenue Blues," recording it on his favorite instrument, the pipe organ. The following year Charlie Johnson's Paradise Orchestra recorded "Harlem Drag" and Red Nichols recorded "Harlem Twist," written by Fud Livingston, who made the famous arrangement of "Singin' the Blues" for Frankie Trumbauer. The composer for whom Harlem seemed to hold the most special significance was Duke Ellington, who wrote and recorded "Harlem Flat Blues" for the *Cotton Club Days* in 1929, "Harlem Speaks" and "Drop Me Off in Harlem" in 1933, and, with saxist Johnny Hodges in 1938, "Harmony in Harlem." As late as 1940, Harlem still occupied a tender spot in the Duke's memory, as he explained in a vivid commentary on "Harlem Air Shaft":

> You get the full essence of Harlem in an air shaft. You hear fights, you smell dinner, you hear people making love. You hear intimate gossip floating down. You hear the radio. An air shaft is one great big loudspeaker. You see your neighbor's laundry. You hear the janitor's dogs. The man upstairs' aerial falls down and breaks your window. You smell coffee. A wonderful thing, that smell. An air shaft has got every contrast. One guy is cooking dried fish and rice and another guy's got a great big turkey. Guy-with-fish's wife is a terrific cooker but the guy's wife with the turkey is doing a sad job. You hear people praying, fighting, snoring. Jitterbug's are jumping up and down always over you, never below you. That's a funny thing about jitterbugs. They're always above you. I tried to put it all down in *Harlem Air Shaft.* . . .[13]

The roster of Harlem songs would be incomplete without "Harlem on My Mind," which Irving Berlin wrote for and Ethel Waters sang in *As Thousands Cheer* (1933).

⤜∽ 6 ∽⤛

"The Birth of the Blues"

They were the Roaring Twenties, Torrid Twenties, Frenzied Twenties. Every epithet linked the era with a time of untrammeled fun, unconventional living and high excitement. Yet it was in the twenties that the blues entered the mainstream and became part of the tonal fabric of American popular music. The blues evolved as a folk music during the post–Civil War period, embodying the feelings, problems, and experiences of black people as they suffered through the transition from slavery to "freedman." Transmitted orally and "written" and "rewritten" by countless unknown figures, they remained a regional, rural, southern music into the twentieth century. Before the 1920s, a few blues appeared in print, most importantly W. C. Handy's "The Memphis Blues" (1912). Initially written as a song for a Mr. Crump in a Memphis political campaign, the melody was original but two segments of the instrumental version were in classic twelve-bar, three-line, three-chord blues form. Later, one of the most recorded of instrumental blues, "Memphis Blues" made so little impress at the outset that Handy sold the work to a publisher for $50.

Although Handy titled his autobiography *Father of the Blues*, his role was that of adapter, arranger, collector, and popularizer of the folk form, and he admittedly was not its creator. By 1914 he had written and published "St. Louis Blues," "the first commercial blues . . . and the most widely performed and admired blues ever conceived."[1] (Later, in 1926, he compiled one of the earliest anthologies, *A Treasury of the Blues*.[2] Some historians of the Harlem Renaissance see it as a reflection of the Negro search for identity.) "St. Louis Blues" caught on immediately, attracting singers and recordings: Ethel Waters, Sophie Tucker, Gilda Gray, and Ted Lewis, among others. But none of these and not even the infectious song was responsible for the blues explosion that occurred in 1920. The catalyst was a record made by Mamie Smith (1883–1946), a buxom, short, heavy-hipped black vaudevillian and cabaret singer. She was one of the female warblers associated with the group that became known as the Classic Blues Singers, no one of whom, with the exception of Bessie Smith (no relation to Mamie), was really an ethnic blues singer. Born in Cincinnati, Mamie settled in Harlem where she performed in theatres as a dancer and singer, and in clubs like the Garden of Joy. By the time she began recording for OKeh, a Columbia subsidiary specializing in black artists, Mamie was managed by Perry Bradford, a successful black songwriter, publisher, vaudevillian, and bandleader. Born in Montgomery, Alabama (not Atlanta, as some accounts would have it), in 1893 (not 1890), Bradford had worked in minstrel shows as a teenager and in black vaudeville, and also produced several black musicals. When he began writing songs, the country had gone dance crazy, and he specialized in devising dances and writing "dance songs," one of which, "Messin' Around," was featured on an Ethel Waters tour. (In *The Perry Bradford Story*, a recording he made with Noble Sissle as his interviewer, composed of songs, artists and records with which he was associated, the slender, cigar-chomping Bradford claimed to have discovered Bessie Smith, Later, he claimed credit for originating the Black Bottom, a matter for later consideration in this book.)

An amiable and persuasive talker (whom I met and from whom I bought a copy of *The Perry Bradford Story*), Perry convinced Fred Hagar, recording director of OKeh, to cut two of his songs with Mamie Smith. "You Can't Keep a Good Man Down" and "That Thing Called Love," published by Pace and Handy, were recorded in February 1920 with a white house-band headed by Hagar. Mamie was billed as a "contralto" since record companies were then interested only in black "concert" artists. The record sold well enough for Hagar to produce a second session with Mamie in August, this time using a black combo called the Jazz Hounds who employed a "hum and head" arrangement, as Bradford termed the unscored background. "Crazy Blues," the record credited with generating the blues craze, came out of this session. (Stories that disregard the earlier Smith session and that claim Sophie Tucker was scheduled to record "Crazy Blues," with Mamie as a last-minute replacement, are the product of careless or imaginative reporting.) The fact is that "Crazy Blues" sold so spectacularly that every record company quickly set about finding a female blues singer they could sign and, almost overnight, black-oriented labels and subsidiaries sprang up.[3]

Blues were soon being recorded by singers drawn from black vaudeville theatres, among others Victoria Spivey of Houston (1900–1976), Edith Wilson of Louisville, Ky. (1906–1981), Sippie Wallace of Houston (1898–1986). Sara Martin of Louisville, Ky. (1884–1955). Alberta Hunter of Memphis (1895–1984), Ida Cox (uncrowned "Queen of the Blues") of Toccoa, Georgia (1896–1967), Gertrude "Ma" Rainey ("Mother of the Blues") of Columbus, Georgia (1886–1939), Clara Smith (the "World's Champion Moaner") of Spartanburg, South Carolina (1894–1935), and beginning in 1923, Bessie Smith ("Empress of the Blues") of Chattanooga, Tennessee (1894–1937). According to historian Frank Driggs, 211 black women were signed by record companies in this period. In 1921, and again in 1922, at least 50 blues records were issued without nearly meeting the demand. "Between 1920 and 1942," as reported in *Recording the Blues*, "almost 5,500 blues and 1,200 gospel records were released, involving all told about 1,200 artists."[4] When the Fifteenth Infantry Band gave its first concert and dance in 1920 at Manhattan Casino, it included a blues singing contest. Among the four singers who competed for the prize were two who went on to achieve notable careers, Lucille Hegamin of Macon, Georgia (1894–1970), who became known as Harlem's Favorite, and Trixie Smith of Atlanta, Georgia (1895–1943), the Southern Nightingale, who was awarded the Silver

Loving Cup for her performance of an original, "Trixie's Blues." (None of these Smiths was related.)

Trixie was quickly signed by Harry Pace, who had left his publishing partnership with William Christopher Handy to launch a recording company. Black Swan Records, with Fletcher Henderson as its recording director, was the first black-owned record company established in the United States. Although the time seemed ripe for such an enterprise, it was comparatively short-lived (1920–1924), as was Black Patti, founded in 1927 by the former recording director of Paramount Records, which absorbed Black Swan after its demise. Unfortunately, J. Mayo Williams's venture did not last out the year, and he was soon hired as a talent scout by Vocalion Records. A market clearly existed, but these ventures were all underfinanced.

The crossover of the blues brought to the fore at least two major black singers, Ma Rainey and her protégé, Bessie Smith. Born Gertrude Melissa Nix Pridgett, Ma Rainey began performing at the age of twelve as part of a local Columbus, Georgia, show, *A Bunch of Blackberries*. She was married to Will Rainey, and they worked as Rainey & Rainey, "The Assassinators of the Blues." Ma remained a traveling performer for twenty years, playing tent shows, circuses, and black vaudeville theaters through Theater Owners Booking Agency (T.O.B.A.), known among black entertainers as Tough on Black Asses. Of a performance in a little theatre in Pittsburgh, Pa., pianist and arranger Mary Lou Williams said, "Ma was loaded with real diamonds—in her ears, around her neck, in a tiara on her head. Both hands were full of rocks, too. Her hair was wild and she had gold teeth. What a sight! To me, as a kid, the whole thing looked and sounded weird."[5] Ma admittedly also had a penchant for young men.

Ma did not begin recording until 1924, when Paramount described her "as the greatest blues singer ever known" and added, "her records are breaking all records for popularity."[6] With "Moonshine Blues" as her first side, she remained, according to Dixon and Godrich, "a mainstay of the Paramount 12000 series for the next seven years"[7] scoring with numbers like "Don't Fish in My Sea" (words:

Bessie Smith; music: Ma Rainey), Thomas A. Dorsey's "Explaining
the Blues," and her own, "Southern Blues" and "Hear Me Talkin'
to Ya" (used by Nat Hentoff and Nat Shapiro as the title of their
invaluable book).[8] In a five-year period (1924–28), the Mother of
the Blues, as she was billed, cut nearly one hundred songs, recording
at times with downhome hokum bluesmen like Tampa Red and
Georgia Tom, and at other times with top jazz artists like Buster
Bailey and members of a group she called the Georgia Jazz Hounds.

Like Ma Rainey's recording career, Bessie Smith's was almost
wholly a product of the twenties and of the vogue of the blues. From
1923 until the close of the decade, she recorded 180 sides, all for
Columbia. In 1929 when she made a short film, *St. Louis Blues,* she
was at the height of her fame, earning from $1,500 to $2,500 a week.
But by the time she did her final recording session in 1933, her popularity had waned so drastically that her $3,000-a-session fee was
reduced to $50 a side—"and their sales at the time did not even
justify that expense," according to John Hammond, who arranged
the session. She insisted on recording something in a jazz vein because people of the Depression "didn't want to be depressed by
blues."[9] Her assessment was sound, the result of touring the South
for as little as $140 a week when she found that blacks were "turn-
ing to more sophisticated, white-oriented musical values."[10]

But at the height of her career, no blues singer commanded greater
adulation from audiences as well as from other singers and musicians. "Bessie was the Louis Armstrong of the blues singers," said
clarinetist Buster Bailey. "She was terrific!" said Clarence Williams,
who accompanied her on her first recording for Columbia in 1923.
Alberta Hunter, cowriter of "Down Hearted Blues," Bessie's first hit,
and recorded by Alberta a year before Bessie's version, said, "Bessie
made it after it had been recorded on almost all the labels and even
a piano roll. We thought it was exhausted, but she sold 780,000
copies! . . . There never was one like her and there'll never be one
like her again. Even though she was raucous and loud, she had sort
of a tear—no, not a tear but there was a *misery* in what she did. It
was as though there was something she had to get out. . . . Nobody,
least of all today, could even match Bessie Smith. She was the great-

est of all the blues singers."[11] That greatness is still audible on definitive disks such as her version of "Nobody Knows You When You're Down and Out," " 'Tain't Nobody's Business If I Do," "Baby, Won't You Please Come Home," and others.

She was also "probably, the highest paid Negro performer in vaudeville next to Bert Williams," according to Columbia recording director Frank Walker, who managed her bookings and finances. But with fame and top earnings came dissipation, sexual escapades, flagrant spending, unbounded handouts to friends, violence when she was drinking heavily, impulsive and intemperate behavior. She fired Walker and tried unsuccessfully to manage her affairs with the help of a spendthrift husband. "New people were coming along," Walker said, "and Bessie began to lose heart. You might say she didn't have a hitching post to tie her horse to. She began to lose interest in life. She was singing differently and there was bitterness in her. . . ."[12]

By 1933 she was working in a "miserable little ginmill in North Philly as a hostess," John Hammond recalled, "singing pornographic songs for tips. She had given up all hope for a comeback and was drinking more than ever." What became her final session—a departure from her celebrated blues style, despite the autobiographical number, "Down in the Dumps"—did little to revive a faded career. Then, on a dark Mississippi road, on the morning of September 26, 1937, as she was speeding to an engagement, she was in the car crash that ended her life at forty-three. Although the accident inspired the play, *The Death of Bessie Smith*, by Edward Albee, the widely circulated rumor that she bled to death as a result of being refused admittance to a white hospital is false.[13] Of all the great vocal artists I've been lucky enough to produce," John Hammond has said, "including Billie Holiday, Mildred Bailey, Peggy Lee, Joe Turner, and Dinah Washington, Bessie Smith was the most powerful and most original."[14] In 1970 singer Janis Joplin said, "Bessie showed me the air and taught me how to fill it." In the *Philadelphia Inquirer*, a woman inquired in a letter where Bessie was buried. Until then, her grave in Sharon Hill, Pennsylvania, had lain unmarked. Contributions by Janis Joplin, Juanita Green—a registered nurse—John Hammond, and others, led to the placement of a gravestone. The inscription reads: "The Greatest Blues Singer in the World Will Never Stop Singing"—Bessie Smith—1895–1937.

A number of black publishing firms arose in this period, but several, like Handy Brothers (formerly Pace and Handy) and the Perry Bradford Music Company, antedated the twenties, formed generally because black songwriters did not find an open door at the established houses. Clarence Williams Music Company, located in 1924 in the heart of Tin Pan Alley at 1547 Broadway, had its beginnings in Chicago where Williams (1898–1965) peddled his own songs door to door and on street corners, having made an effort to create a demand by performing them in local cabarets and dance halls. After a time, he became one of the first blacks to demonstrate songs in five-and-ten stores, traveling from New Orleans to Texas to New York. Songs of his that gained popularity in the twenties were "Baby, Won't You Please Come Home" (1919), "Royal Garden Blues" (with Spencer Williams) (1918), and "Sugar Blues" (1923), which was adopted by trumpeter Clyde McCoy as his theme. But it was "Squeeze Me," which he wrote in 1925 with Fats Waller that established his and Fats's reputation as songwriters. Williams was a successful recording artist with a group he called his Blue Five, whose hits included "I've Found a New Baby," written by Jack Palmer and Spencer Williams, and "Everybody Loves My Baby, but My Baby Don't Love Nobody But Me" (also by Jack Palmer and Spencer Williams), which featured Louis Armstrong on trumpet and later became a Ruth Etting perennial.

Henry Creamer (1879–1930) was an accomplished lyricist whose collaboration with J. Turner Layton involved songwriting and a vaudeville team. They themselves introduced their bluesy songs, "After You've Gone" (1918), "Dear Old Southland" (1921), adapted from the spiritual "Deep River," and featured later by clarinetist Sidney Bechet; and "Way Down Yonder in New Orleans" (1922). With Bert Williams, Creamer wrote "That's A Plenty" (1909), and with Jimmy Johnson, "If I Could Be with You One Hour Tonight" (1926), and theme song of and bestselling record for McKinney's Cotton Pickers, and later a Ruth Etting favorite. Of "After You've

Gone," identified as "one of the most long-lived jazz standards," Alec
Wilder wrote, "If by this time I haven't conveyed by illustration and
citation what I mean by an American sounding song, *After You've
Gone* should tell you."[15] A founder of the Clef Club of black enter-
tainers, Creamer and his partner, Layton, contributed songs for Bert
Williams to the *Ziegfeld Follies* (1911) and wrote the score for *Strut
Miss Lizzie* (1922).

One of the most successful black songwriters of the twenties was
Maceo Pinkard (1897–1962), who came from Bluefield, West Virginia, and was published by major Tin Pan Alley firms like Robbins
Music and Shapiro and Bernstein, and whose collaborators included
major white songwriters. "Sweet Georgia Brown," probably his big-
gest hit, was introduced by the orchestra of Ben Bernie, whose name
appears on the song as a collaborator, along with Kenneth Casey's.
Other hits included the novelty "Gimme a Little Kiss, Will You,
Huh?" (1926), written with Roy Turk introduced by Guy Lombardo
and his Royal Canadians, and popularized by Whispering Jack
Smith, whose name appears on the song as a collaborator. In 1927
Pinkard produced, with collaborator Billy Rose, "Here Comes the
Showboat," featured in the film of the same title and used as the
theme of *Maxwell House Show Boat*, a popular radio variety pro-
gram of the 1930s. In 1928 he wrote "Don't Be Like That," with
Charlie Tobias and Archie Gottler as collaborators, a song introduced
by the "boop-boop-a-doop" girl, Helen Kane. He composed the scores
for several Broadway musicals, the best-known being *Liza* (1922).

Lovie Austin (1897–1972), born Cora Calhoun in Chattanooga,
wrote the music for Bessie Smith's initial hit, "Down Hearted Blues."
Lovie was the rare college-trained songwriter, attending Roger Williams University in Nashville and Knoxville College. As Austin and
Delaney, she and her husband performed in vaudeville and revues.
Settling in Chicago, she was musical director of the Monogram
Theatre at 35th Street and State for twenty years. For many years
she led a combo known as her Blues Serenaders and made recordings
in her own name and with an impressive list of blues singers, includ-
ing Ma Rainey, Alberta Hunter (her collaborator on "Down Hearted
Blues"), Ethel Waters, and Ida Cox. It was with Cox that she made

her first recording in 1923, collaborating with her on the song, "Weary Way Blues."

"Coot" (for Cutie) Grant came from Birmingham, Alabama, was on the stage with her husband for twenty years, during which they wrote some four hundred songs, and is remembered for "Gimme a Pigfoot," the last title that Bessie Smith recorded. Boyd Atkins came from Paducah, Kentucky, played saxes with Earl Hines at the Elite No. 2 in Chicago (1925) and with Louis Armstrong's Stompers at the Sunset Cafe (spring 1927), and attained a measure of fame with "Heebie Jeebies," which he wrote in 1926. It was recorded by Louis Armstrong and his Hot Five on OKeh and is credited, according to legend, with launching scattin', the vocal style in which the singer simulates a jazzy instrumental style with the use of nonsense syllables instead of the words of the song. After Armstrong, the most noted practitioner of the style is Ella Fitzgerald.

During the twenties, a number of blues were so widely performed and recorded that they became established as standards. " 'Taint Nobody's Business If I Do" (1922), later one of Billie Holiday's most evocative numbers is credited to Everett Robbins and Porter Grainger, the latter an obscure figure but remembered for his piano accompaniments on Bessie Smith records and "as one of the real gentlemen in the business," in Perry Bradford's words.[16] Another obscure figure, Jimmie Cox, accounted for "Nobody Knows You When You're Down and Out" (1922), a widely recorded song that yielded one of Bessie Smith's most poignant recordings.

One of the most recorded of all blues, both instrumentally as well as vocally, is Richard M. Jones's "Trouble in Mind," originally recorded by Chippie Hill. Jones was a New Orleans composer, pianist, and bandleader.

"How Long, How Long Blues" (1929) was the work of lanky, large-handed Leroy Carr of Indianapolis, who died at thirty of alcoholism and arthritis. Despite the brevity of his recording career—a scant seven years—he deeply influenced the style of male blues singing, drawing it away from the raw nasality of the rural blues shouters to a mellow, almost crooning style. Jazz guitarist Scrapper Blackwell, with whom he teamed in 1928, added harmonic and rhythmic subtlety to their performances and to the blues. Unquestionably, their best performance is on "(In the Evening) When the Sun Goes Down," also a Carr song, copyright 1935, the year of his premature death.

What started as a black phenomenon quickly became a white, Tin Pan Alley development, and even invaded the Broadway musical theatre. In fact, the strongest indication of the impact and appeal of the blues was to be found in the number of white songwriters who set about producing pseudo-blues. Among the earliest was show and film composer Jerome Kern, who included "Left All Alone Blues" in the show *The Night Boat* (1920) and "Blue Danube Blues" in the score for *Good Morning, Dearie* (1921). In the revue *London Calling* (1923), Noel Coward presented "Russian Blues," which three years later was interpolated by Gertrude Lawrence in *Andre Charlot's Revue of 1926*. Rodgers and Hart wrote "Atlantic Blues" for the London production of *Lido Lady* (1926), which became "Blue Ocean Blues" in *Present Arms* (1928) on Broadway. Ruth Etting sang "Shaking the Blues Away," which Irving Berlin wrote for the *Ziegfeld Follies of 1927*. Jimmy McHugh and Dorothy Fields, who wrote the hits for *Blackbirds*, produced "When You and I Were Young Maggie Blues," introduced by the popular vaudeville duo, Van and Schenck, and "Out Where the Blues Begin" for *Hello Daddy* (1928).

The Gershwins were attracted early to the blues, beginning with "The Yankee Doodle Blues" in the revue *Spice of 1922*, and continuing with "Half of It Dearie Blues" in the tuneful musical *Lady Be Good!* (1924), where it was sung and danced by Fred Astaire. 1924 was the year that brought us *Rhapsody in Blue*, whose title, tonality, and melodies all reflected the prevailing feeling for the black sound. De Sylva, Brown and Henderson, one of the most successful and prolific songwriting teams of the decade, contributed to the trend in the still widely performed "Birth of the Blues," introduced by strutting Harry Richman in George White's *Scandals of 1926* and later sung by nonchalant Bing Crosby in the film *The Birth of the Blues* (1941).

The scope of the blues trend is suggested by the appearance of

"I've Got the Yes! We Have No Bananas Blues," which parodied the biggest novelty hit of the decade, "Yes! We Have No Bananas," interpolated by ebullient Eddie Cantor in the revue *Make It Snappy* after it was introduced on the radio and in vaudeville by Frank Silver's Music Masters.

A check of Nat Shapiro's *Annotated Index of American Popular Songs for 1920–1929* discloses over two hundred songs with blues titles.[17] In this list, one finds the names of virtually every top Tin Pan Alley songwriter. The number of bestsellers that emerged from this avalanche was surprisingly small. Except for Gershwin, Harold Arlen, Hoagy Carmichael, and a few others, the blues idiom proved elusive. But just as white songwriters responded to the blues, using flatted thirds and fifths and related harmonies in their melodies, black songwriters adapted their themes and tonality to the thirty-two-bar form. The interplay produced the sound that dominated popular music into the mid-fifties and was recognized as uniquely American.

The image of women during the twenties was ambivalent. The new woman, the flapper, was depicted as light-hearted, fun-filled, daring, unconventional. But the female image as it emerges in song and in the musical theatre bears the visage of the tragic muse. Consider Fanny Brice, Ruth Etting, Helen Morgan, and Libby Holman, four of the major singers of the era. Fanny Brice never surpassed her anguished renditions of "My Man." Ruth Etting's repertoire abounded in brokenhearted ballads like "Love Me or Leave Me" and "Mean to Me." Helen Morgan's songs were tear-filled ballads like "Can't Help Lovin' Dat Man," "Don't Ever Leave Me," and "Why Was I Born?" Libby Holman was the impassioned singer of "Moanin' Low." All of these are songs of unrequited love—"torch" songs in music business vernacular—and sometimes described as a white offshoot of the blues. Alec Wilder names Clarence Williams's "I Ain't Got Nobody," published in 1915, as the number with which "the torch song had arrived to stay."[18] He next singles out Raymond Hubbell's "Poor Butterfly"—surely a torcher even if it takes a third-person approach—which made its appearance in 1916.

The personalization of feeling introduced into popular song in the twenties by the blues produced songs exploring many sides of the loss of and longing for love. With music by Sigmund Romberg, Oscar Hammerstein II simply voiced the plea, "Lover, Come Back to Me" (1928). Self-pity figured in torchers like "I'm a Little Blackbird Looking for a Bluebird," sung by Florence Mills in the revue *Dixie to Broadway* (1924); "Nobody's Sweetheart," interpolated by Ted Lewis in *The Passing Show of 1923* and later sung by Rudy Vallee in the film *The Vagabond Lover* (1929); and "Laugh, Clown, Laugh," introduced by Ted Fiorito, who wrote the music and the title theme of the 1928 film.

The memory of lost love was given direct expression in "I Used to Love You but It's All Over Now" (1920) by Lew Brown (words) and Albert Von Tilzer (music), while Irving Berlin said it more tenderly in "The Song Is Ended but the Melody Lingers On" (1926). The Gershwins dealt with the forlorn hope of finding a loved one in the elegant ballad "The Man I Love" (1924). Despair and resignation were the keynotes of songs like "The One I Love Belongs to Somebody Else," introduced by Isham Jones, who wrote the music to Gus Kahn's words; "I'd Rather Be Blue over You (Than Be Happy with Somebody Else)," sung by Fanny Brice in the film *My Man* (1928); and "I'll Always Be in Love with You," sung by Morton Downey in the film *Syncopation*. And there were the torch songs with a vengeance motive: "I Cried for You (Now It's Your Turn to Cry over Me)," introduced by Abe Lyman and his Orchestra with a bestselling record by Cliff "Ukulele Ike" Edwards (1923); "There'll Come a Time When You'll Need Me," recorded by Frankie Trumbauer and his Orchestra, featuring Bix Beiderbecke; and "Day by Day You're Going to Miss Me" (1920).

No commentary on torch songs would be complete without mention of "(I Got a Woman, Crazy for Me) She's Funny That Way," whose lyric was written by Richard Whiting to a beautifully poignant melody by Neil Moret. Most torch songs tended to be written from the woman's point of view, but Irving Berlin contributed at least one magnificently simple ballad to the genre, "What'll I Do?" a song generated by his own wooing of the woman who became his wife despite the opposition of her father.

That there was something desperate in the prolonged binge of the twenties was made most evident, I submit, by the vogue of the blues. It was a response, perhaps, to the loss of limits. There was adventure in turning away from the moral guidelines of the older generation. It was fun and it was exciting. But there was always the morning after—and the letdown and the sense of being on a merry-go-round without destination.

~ 7 ~

"Kitten on the Keys"

Around 1922, Duke Ellington recalled, "Everybody was trying to sound like *Carolina Shout* that Jimmy Johnson made on a player-piano roll."[1] (Stride pianist James P. Johnson was one of the first blacks to make piano rolls in 1916.) What Ellington did to sound like "the king of piano players," as he called him, was to slow down the roll so that he could put his fingers on the depressed keys and learn the piece. As he worked at mastering the stride style, Ellington became part of a group that spent its nights roving Harlem, looking for piano players, and playing wherever they could find an upright piano. In the group were Willie "The Lion" Smith, Fats Waller, James P. Johnson, some members of the Ellington band (drummer Sonny Greer and saxist Toby Hardwicke), and a man known as Lippy, who could "walk up to any man's house at any time at night," Ellington said, "ring the doorbell . . . [and] somebody would wake up and holla out the window about who was it making all the disturbance. Lippy would answer, 'It's Lippy, and James P. is here with me.' These magic words opened anybody's door, and we would sit and play all night long."[2]

House rent parties were a facet of Harlem life even before the Depression. An outgrowth of parlor socials and church suppers held to raise funds for church needs, house rent parties aimed at helping dwellers of Harlem's railroad flats meet rents that skyrocketed monthly. Neighbors brought all kinds of food—fried chicken, baked ham, pig's feet, pork chops, gumbo, potato salad, and more—to which a supply of bootleg liquor was added. An admission was charged, and the piano players supplied the entertainment. "James P. Johnson, Willie "The Lion" Smith and Fats Waller became great favorites," Ellington recalled. "For ten bucks a shot, they somehow made appearances at three or four different rent parties on a good Saturday night,"[3] which did not end until sometime on Sunday.

It has been suggested that the house rent party grew in popularity as a reaction of blacks to their exclusion from Harlem clubs like the Cotton, Connie's Inn, Smalls' Paradise, etc. There was dancing—the bump, grind, monkey hunch. The pianist, assisted at times by a drummer who muffled his traps by covering the head with a blanket, sought to approximate orchestral effects, which, perhaps, helps explain the character of stride piano.

The most direct antecedent of the style was, of course, ragtime, whose bass or left hand was augmented to create a stronger sense of rhythm. The Harlem striders learned much from a group of itinerant piano players who operated as pimps in the 1912 period, and among whom the best known was Jelly Roll Morton. Before Harlem became a thriving entertainment center, these traveling ragtime keyboard players (with curious nicknames like Baltimore's Willie "Egghead" Sewell) performed in saloons in Manhattan's Hell's Kitchen. Barron Wilkins, who operated the Little Savoy on 35th Street, was among the early saloon operators to move to Harlem around 1915, and Luckey Roberts, whom he hired as his house pianist, became one of the first to serve in this capacity.

As a style, stride piano took the bass of ragtime and amplified it by substituting an octave or a tenth on the first beat of a measure and then a three- or four-finger chord in the middle register for the second and fourth beat. You had to have a large or agile mitt to manage the stride and keep the motion going from the tenth and the low fifth on the third beat to the middle register chords. Pianists who had difficulty stretching ten notes would flip their fingers from the low tonic to the tenth. Eubie Blake and Charles Luckeyeth Roberts, who could easily stretch a tenth, included a fifth in the middle of the downbeat tenth chord. As the stride pianist played, the left hand described two arcs in each measure in its movement from the low (one and three beats) to the middle register chord (two and four beats).

The King, the dean of Harlem striders, and recognized as such by his peers, was James P. Johnson (1891–1955), originally a self-taught pianist from New Brunswick, New Jersey, who practiced in the dark, played complicated exercises through a sheet to increase his dexterity, and always performed with a long, fat cigar resting in a tray, close at hand. Johnson was versed in the European classics and in 1927 produced a ballet, *Symphony Harlem*, at the Lafayette Theatre. But he also accounted for such hits as "Charleston," the sensational dance number of the decade, presented in *Runnin' Wild*, the Broadway musical of 1923, which he composed and scored; "If I Could Be with You One Hour Tonight" (1926), the theme song and bestselling record of McKinney's Cotton Pickers; and the classic "Carolina Shout," which dazzled the pianists he himself admired like Luckey Roberts, "the outstanding pianist in New York in 1913" and Eubie Blake, "one of the foremost pianists of all time." He manned the keyboard at Leroy's, Barron Wilkins' and the Clef, among other Harlem spots. He spent his latter years, until he suffered a stroke, leading orchestras, producing, and composing larger works in which he sought to merge Afro-American and European traditions.

Although most of these works have apparently been lost, it is known that he wrote two symphonies, three tone poems, a piano concerto, and five short operas. *Yamekraw (Negro Rhapsody)*, completed in 1927, premiered at Carnegie in 1928. An all-Johnson concert at Carnegie in 1945 heard his *Harlem Symphony*. The second movement of his piano concerto (1934), published in 1947 as "Concerto Jazz-A-Mine," has just been released in an album by pianist William Albright, which also contains *Yamekraw* and "April in Harlem," the second movement of the *Symphony*.

A fat cigar hanging out of his mouth was also a mark of the stride pianist whose full name was William Henry Joseph Bonaparte Bertholoff but who became known as Willie "The Lion" Smith (1897–1973). (James Lincoln Collier claims that Willie got his nickname in France during World War I, when he was cited for courageous action with an artillery battery.) "Jamie [James P. Johnson] gave me the title because of my spunk and enterprise," Willie said. "The Lion named him The Brute. Later we gave Fats Waller the name Filthy. The three of us, The Lion, The Brute and Filthy, and a guy called Lippy used to run all over town playing piano."[4]

When he performed, The Lion sat sideways at the piano so that he could jabber with his audience—he talked freely on his recordings as well. He played all over Harlem—Leroy's, Smalls', Barron Wilkins', and Pod's and Jerry's. Duke Ellington, an admirer, dedicated *Portrait of the Lion* to him. In 1920 he served as the pianist on Mamie Smith's legendary recording of "Crazy Blues." As a teacher in his later years, he taught Joe Bushkin, Mel Powell, and Artie Shaw.

Thomas "Fats" Waller (1904–1943), born in Virginia and raised in Harlem, was overweight from childhood—and his prodigious appetite and endless capacity for good times did nothing to diminish his size. Early on he got a job playing the organ at the Lincoln Theatre in Harlem—where Count Basie literally lay at his feet to watch him pedal—and so impressed J. P. Johnson with his talent that he became his pupil. He was the King's shadow for several years. He made his first piano roll around 1920. Between 1922 and 1929, he recorded at least a hundred sides. He performed frequently in a cocked hat—a derby worn at an angle—and interspersed his playing with jibes, jokes, and jests. He was as accomplished a clown as he was pianist and organist. He was also a prolific and facile melody writer, producing such hits as "Honeysuckle Rose," "Ain't Misbehavin'," "Squeeze Me" (his first publication), "Keepin' Out of Mischief Now," "The Jitterbug Waltz," among others. He was so adept at making hits of songs by others that he is sometimes thought to be the writer of a number of tunes he merely recorded, such as "I'm Gonna Sit Right Down and Write Myself a Letter" (music: Fred Ahlert; words: Joe Young). His eating, drinking, and careless style of living found him perpetually in debt, so he frequently sold songs outright to grab the small sums of money he needed. Rumor has it that some big songs bearing the names of other writers were actually written by him.

In 1927 he settled in Chicago, where he performed with the Erskine Tate Band at the Vendome but played also at the Metropolitan and Royal theatres. With James P. Johnson, he wrote the musical *Keep Shufflin'* (1928), a modest successor to *Shuffle Along*. His most successful show was *Hot Chocolates*, written with Andy Razaf, a frequent collaborator. It started as a Connie's Inn floor show and yielded many of the hits already named, including "Ain't Misbehavin'."

An exuberant personality—at least, outwardly (his overeating and alcoholism have been attributed to the trauma he suffered because of his mother's death)—the only time he was cowed was when he spotted Art Tatum in his Yacht Club audience. "God is in the house tonight," he murmured. Working in the ragtime/stride tradition, he was, perhaps, the greatest combination of musician and comedian America has produced. Had he been able to control a runaway appetite—twenty-four hamburgers at a sitting—and limit his drinking, as he was advised, he might have avoided an untimely death at the age of thirty-nine.

A pioneer of stride piano, Charles Luckeyeth ("Luckey") Roberts (1887–1968) participated in the transition from ragtime to jazz piano, together with J. P. Johnson, Fats, and The Lion. During the twenties, however, he was widely known as a society bandleader who catered to the millionaires who frequented Newport and Palm Beach. He was, in fact, the first black to play regularly at the exclusive Everglades Club in the Florida resort. When he first came to New York from Philadelphia, where he was born a Quaker and, as a child, worked in a bicycle and juggling act, he played the piano at the Little Savoy Club and at Barron Wilkins' in Harlem. His first published composition was "Junk Man Rag" (1913), but his better known piece is "Pork and Beans (One Step, Two Step, Turkey Trot)," also a 1913 copyright. His "Ripples of the Nile," a demanding rag, yielded the melody that, with a lyric added, became "Moonlight Cocktail," a hit for the Glenn Miller Band in 1941. Though he himself did not drink or smoke, in the forties and fifties he owned a popular bar, the Rendezvous, on St. Nicholas Avenue in Harlem, where he frequently performed at the keyboard "with vast hands," in the words of Rudi Blesh and Elsie Janis," that introduced tenths and twelfths into the ragtime bass. . . . His mercurial playing was a thing of almost overpowering brilliance." Earlier, in the twenties, he was among the first group of black pianists engaged to cut piano rolls for Quality Reigns Supreme (QRS), a group that included James P. Johnson, Fats Waller, and Clarence Williams, among others.

Initially, he played by ear and, like Irving Berlin, in the key of F sharp—the black keys on the piano. Later in life, like J. P. Johnson, he composed extended works and performed in Carnegie Hall (1939), Town Hall (1941), and Robin Hood Dell (1944), where he played his *Whistlin' Pete—Miniature Syncopated Rhapsody*, for piano and orchestra. He also composed the scores for more than a dozen black musical comedies, including *Go-Go* and *Sharlee*, both produced in 1923 at Daly's 63rd Street Theatre. When the Prince of Wales visited the United States, Roberts played for him for nine consecutive nights and thereafter served as his adviser in selecting records for his "hot" collection.

Art Tatum (1910–1956), about whom it was said, "No one can imitatum," brought the art of popular and jazz piano playing to a peak it has never quite attained again. In his playing, one hears a summation of ragtime, stride, pop, and jazz styles, raised to a level of rare brilliance by prodigious technique and mastery of harmonic variation. But the twenties were his apprentice period, spent in his native Toledo, before appearance at Chicago's Three Deuces and on New York's Swing Street made him a supreme artist whose performance drew the greats of classical music as well as of jazz. It was not only his colleagues but virtuosi like Vladimir Horowitz and Sergei Rachmaninoff who marveled at the impeccable precision and aureate beauty of his playing, and applauded the creativity and originality that produced whirlwind arpeggios, surprise alterations of chords and tempi, startling harmonic modulations, and a seemingly endless variety of improvisations. No one could "over-ratum." As John Lewis, leader of the Modern Jazz Quartet, has said recently, "Tatum was the greatest player that Jazz has produced and maybe the greatest of all jazz pianists."[5]

Ragtime and stride piano were both black-originated styles. During the twenties, white songwriters and pianists developed a derivative music that became known as "piano novelties." Some of these epitomized a stride bass, but the essence of the style was a fleeting, fluid right hand, attractive melody, and up-tempo performance. Nacio Herb Brown wrote "Rag Doll," "Wedding of the Painted Doll," and "Doll Dance," the latter popularized by Vincent Lopez and his Band. Jesse Greeg wrote "Flapperette," also a favorite of Lopez, whose repertoire included "Parade of the Wooden Soldiers." Rube Bloom wrote and introduced "Soliloquy." But the two most popular and impressive of the genre remain "Nola" and "Kitten on the Keys."

"Nola" was the work of a New York–born composer, Felix Arndt (1889–1918), who had previously written special material for such vaudevillians as Nora Bayes and Gus Edwards. Named after Nola Locke, to whom he was engaged in 1915, "Nola" is a syncopated, modulating piano piece that requires a nimble right hand. On publication it attracted the notice of Vincent Lopez, who adopted it as his theme when he began an engagement at the Hotel Pennsylvania and thereafter played it throughout a long career on stage, in the showrooms of New York hotels, and in the 1945 film *That's the Spirit*. Arndt was himself an accomplished pianist and is said to have made as many as three thousand piano rolls for all the leading companies of the day, including QRS, and Duo-Art. Many of these were of his own rag-influenced piano novelties: "Monette," "Toots," "Soup to Nuts," and others. But none attained the acceptance and popularity of "Nola." It is said that George Gershwin was inspired to make piano rolls as a result of listening to Arndt, and even tried his hand at a piano novelty, "Rialto Ripples," written in 1916 in collaboration with Will Donaldson.

The most prolific and versatile writer of piano novelties was Zez Confrey of Peru, Illinois (1895–1971). Working initially in the ragtime idiom, Confrey ultimately wrote ninety piano novelties, all published by Mills Music. "Twaify's Piano," among those not put into print, was based on the old instrument in Twaify's store in LaSalle, Illinois. Confrey was able to imitate the out-of-tune keyboard, flapping piano roll, and the wheezes. It was this composition that led to his making piano rolls for QRS and Victor. The high point in his career came in 1924 when he was featured, along with George Gershwin, at the legendary Aeolian Hall concert of February 12. Paul Whiteman and his Palais Royal Orchestra introduced the delightfully discordant "Kitten on the Keys" as well as the *Rhapsody in Blue.* Although none of Confrey's numerous novelties approached "Kitten on the Keys" in popularity and sales, "Dizzy Fingers" was a very engaging piano novelty and the pentatonic "Stumbling," a song using virtually only the black keys on the piano, became a hit.

~~ 8 ~~

Shuffle Along

In 1980 when an old-time revue, *Black Broadway*, played briefly at New York's Town Hall, *Newsweek* was moved to recall "the almost forgotten era: the exuberant Black Broadway of the 1920s—a bubbling cauldron of creativity, a melting pot of black and white, old and new, vaudeville and operetta, burlesque and musical comedy."[1] The flame under the bubbling cauldron was a show that opened on May 23, 1921, at an old lecture hall on West 63rd Street, converted into a theatre later called Daly's. *Shuffle Along*, which launched the era of black theatrical creativity, was also the culmination of two decades of experimentation.

As far back as 1898, a New York theatre patronized exclusively by whites housed the all-black musical, *Clorindy: or the Origin of the Cakewalk*. It was the work of Will Marion Cook, one of a group of black composers, lyricists, bookwriters, and arrangers who helped bring the black musical out of the womb of the minstrel show and vaudeville. Among other blacks who participated in this transformation were Bob Cole, J. Rosamond Johnson, Joe Jordan, Ernest Hogan, Will Vodery, and Eubie Blake. Many of these contributed their talents to the musicals starring (Bert) Williams and (George) Walker, who were crucial in advancing the growth of the black musical theater.

Vodery (1885–1951), who became the first black arranger to invade the Hollywood musical scene, served in that capacity for *Shuf-*

fle Along, recently described by *Newsweek's* Jack Kroll as "the thermo-nuclear fusion of vaudeville, operetta and musical comedy that Eubie Blake and Noble Sissle brought to Broadway."[2] At its outset in 1921, the show was hardly regarded in the glowing terms used by Kroll, a fact suggested by its inability to secure a Broadway theatre. The "choice" of the 63rd Street was indicative of the early difficulties and stringencies faced by *Shuffle Along*, celebrated later as the "critical influence . . . in the rush to Harlem for entertainment."[3] The musical was born when two black vaudeville teams met by accident in Philadelphia. Comics (Flournoy) Miller and (Aubrey) Lyles came up with the idea of the libretto, and songwriters (Noble) Sissle and (Eubie) Blake with the score. Operating with scant financing, they dressed the cast in costumes bought from a folded 1919 black musical (*Roly-Boly Eyes*). Their "previews" were one-night stands in New Jersey and Philadelphia theatres, with the threat of foreclosure hanging over their heads.

It is no wonder, then, that in November 1921, seven months later, *Variety* observed that the show was "one of the surprises of the season," and expressed astonishment that on the completion of its Broadway run, it would play no less than a "Loop" theatre, the prestigious Olympic, in Chicago.[4] *Shuffle Along* had established itself—it ultimately ran for 504 performances—and was to affect the style of succeeding musicals, white as well as black. *Shuffle Along* had three important elements going for it: talent, in the starring performances of Florence Mills, Josephine Baker, and Hall Johnson, among others; a tuneful, memorable score; and whirlwind dancing. Among the unusual number of appealing melodies, there were "I'm Just Wild About Harry," the big hit; the love ballad "Love Will Find a Way"; and the festive "Bandana Days." The dancing had verve, excitement, and drive, with its tap routines, buck and wing, soft shoe that set a standard for black shows but also proved a challenge to white musicals. Until then black dancers had worked to a ragtime or cakewalk beat. *Shuffle Along* brought the sound of jazz, or what was regarded as jazz, onto the musical comedy stage. Henceforth, white musicals veered from the stately movements of the Ziegfeld statuesque beauties to the more rhythmic steps of music with a jazz beat. With the change in rhythm and sound came a change in outlook: sentimentality tended to yield to cynicism. The musical was beginning to keep step with the tenor of the time.

Composer Eubie Blake (1883–1983), who died a week after his one-hundredth birthday, was born in Baltimore to freed slaves. At fifteen he began playing ragtime piano in Baltimore bordellos, composing "The Charleston Rag" at sixteen. In 1907, after touring with a medicine show, he started playing in Baltimore for eight years, mainly at the Goldfield Hotel. Noble Sissle (1889–1975), who came from Indianapolis, formed his first band there in 1914. Working with Bob Young's Band in Baltimore, he met Eubie Blake and Lucky Roberts, each of whom occasionally manned a second piano in the band. After leading his own band at the Cocoanut Grove in Palm Beach, Florida, he joined Jim Europe's Society Orchestra as a guitarist and vocalist, touring with it after a stint in the Army, until Europe's unfortunate death in 1919. (He was stabbed to death during an altercation with his drummer.) It was then that Sissle joined forces with Blake, with whom he produced and wrote *Chocolate Dandies* (1924) and *Shuffle Along*. Florence Mills (1895–1927), who achieved stardom by singing "I'm Just Wild About Harry," died suddenly at the untimely age of thirty-two. Her funeral brought Harlem into the streets. A flock of blackbirds was released over the hearse bearing her coffin, in tribute to her epithet, "The Little Blackbird."

As might be expected, the fabulous acceptance of *Shuffle Along* created a thriving market for black musicals. Between 1922 and the end of the decade, there were as many as twenty different all-black musicals and revues on "Broadway." (Fifty-seventh Street marked the northward boundary of Broadway, but most of the black shows played at the Colonial or Daly's, both farther uptown.) Of the twenty, only four approached *Shuffle Along* in popularity or quality. The others failed after short runs—and these failures included two efforts by Sissle and Blake: *Elsie* (1923) and *Chocolate Dandies* (1924), the latter closing after sixty-six performances and being slammed by some critics as suffering from "too much white man."[5] While this criticism might be interpreted as a call for black originality, some saw it as a suggestion that the black artist ought to stay in his place and not try "to emulate witty, white mountings."[6] Among the black shows that flopped were Henry Creamer and Turner Layton's *Strut Miss Lizzie* (1922); *Plantation Revue*, whose cast included Florence Mills, Will Vodery, and Shelton Brooks, who was the writer and performer of two great standards, "Some of These Days" and "The Darktown Strutters' Ball"; Maceo Pinkard's *Liza* (1922); *Dixie to Broadway*, Florence Mills's last starring role before her death; Porter Grainger's *Lucky Sambo* (1925); and *Africana* (1927), starring Ethel Waters.

The black musical that came closest to duplicating *Shuffle Along*'s success was *Runnin' Wild* (1923), with a book by Miller and Lyles that reworked the old Williams and Walker formula of the sharpie and the schlemiel. What gave the show its wallop was the dance song "Charleston" by Cecil Mack and James J. Johnson, which was a "gawky, zesty, and obviously irresistible"[8] high-stepping dance. *Black- birds of 1928*, a smash hit in 1928, boasted an "all-white" score by Dorothy Fields and Jimmy McHugh, performed by an exuberant all-black cast. At least three numbers emerged as full-fledged hits: "I Can't Give You Anything But Love," sung by Aida Ward and then by Lois Deppe and Adelaide Hall; the rhythmic "Diga Diga Do," belted out by Hall; and "Doin' the New Low-Down," elegantly tap-danced by nimble-footed Bill Robinson. Almost a decade elapsed before another revue equaled its 518 performances.

Before it came into the Hudson Theatre in June 1929, *Hot Choco- lates* entertained diners at Connie's Inn. The floor show was the work of Andy Razaf and Fats Waller, who had been part of a quartet of writers who did not quite make it with *Keep Shufflin'* (1928). But "Ain't Misbehavin'," later the title of a 1980s musical based on the career of Fats Waller, gave *Hot Chocolates* one of its most pleasur- able and enduring moments. Young Louis Armstrong who was in the pit orchestra, came on stage for one solo. Audiences had a sweet tooth for *Hot Chocolates* for over six months.

A curious work that should not be overlooked was *Deep River* (1926), with a book by Lawrence Stallings (author of the play *What Price Glory?*) and Frank Harling, a musician with abilities as a pop- ular writer ("Beyond the Blue Horizon"), and also a serious composer. *Deep River* was set in New Orleans in 1835 when elite Creoles each picked the most beautiful dancer at the Quadroon Ball as their mistress. A thirty-piece oversized orchestra was used in the pit, and singer Jules Bledsoe, later of *Show Boat*, brought the house down with his rendition of a minor number. A somber work, more of a native opera than a musical, it lasted only four weeks, with critic Burns Mantle regretting that "the opera-going public would not come down to it nor the theater people rise to it."[9]

In the last year of the decade, three other black musicals went through revolving doors, opening and closing almost immediately. *Deep Harlem,* a revue with a flimsy story line, written and performed by unknowns, opened on Monday, January 7, and closed the following Saturday. *Messin' Around,* an April revue boasting several show-stopping dances and a boxing bout between two women, folded after four weeks. *Bamboola,* a June book musical, also ran for four weeks, despite a tour-de-force salute to Bill Robinson in which twenty hoofers imitated Robinson's well-known routine of tapping his way up and down a staircase. Reviews of these folded musicals and other black shows found the critics guilty of a curious kind of racism. *The Evening Journal* wrote, "The Negro IS funny. He's very funny when he's allowed to be funny in his own way."[10] More than one critic took the position, as Gerald Bordman pointed out, "that black revues should be distinctly black in their vitality, tackiness and naivete!"[11]

Flops or smashes, black musicals were an effervescent expression of the high-flying spirit of the Roaring Twenties and the Harlem Renaissance. According to Langston Hughes, "Manhattan's black Renaissance . . . began with *Shuffle Along, Runnin' Wild* and the Charleston. . . . It was the musical revue, *Shuffle Along,* that gave a scintillating sendoff to the Negro vogue in Manhattan. . . . It was a honey of a show. Swift, bright, funny, rollicking and gay, with a dozen singable, danceable tunes. . . ." And, he added, "It gave just the proper push—a pre-Charleston kick—to that Negro vogue of the 20s, that spread to books, African sculpture, music, and dancing."[12]

III

Tin Pan Alley

9

"Dardanella"
(1920)

New Year's Day 1920 dawned cloudy and rainy in New York after a night that was, according to the *New York Times,* "gay in hotels but quiet in the streets, with an abundance of liquor in dining rooms, brought in packages by the guests."[1] The night of the "dismal sixteenth," when the Volstead Act was to take effect, was yet to come, "the night of incredible sadness, of silly high jinks . . . of gaiety with overtones of mockery,"[2] as Stanley Walker of the *Herald-Tribune* phrased it. But the Eighteenth Amendment, making it illegal to sell or transport any beverage containing more than .5 of 1 percent of alcohol, had become law on July 1, 1919. Prohibition was in—and the country was beginning to go "dry."

The day after New Year's, readers of *Variety,* "the bible of show business," were startled by its front page. Instead of the typical headlines and news stories, there was a full-page advertisement. It read like a sign posted to warn poachers against trespassing, only it was concerned not with land (or liquor) but with a song. "WARNING," said the top line, followed by equally large capitalized words, "THIEVES AND PIRATES!" The third line, in small upper-and-lower letters, "*and* those who live on the efforts of other people's brains." Then, capitals again: "DON'T IMITATE, COPY OR STEAL," small letters, "any part of" (in letters three inches high) "DARDANELLA, The Biggest Musical Hit of the Past 20 Years." The succeeding paragraph stated that "we will

95

prosecute . . . criminally and civilly, any infringement on the melody or lyric of *Dardanella*. . . ." The ad was signed by copyright owners, McCarthy and Fisher, Inc., of 124 West 46th Street, Nathan Burkan, Attorney.

Although the reference in the ad was to a possible infringement on "melody or lyric," what concerned the copyright owners was really the song's bass line, a novel adaptation of an eight-to-the-bar boogie figure with an ascending chromatic melody. It was different, had an identity of its own, and added to the attractiveness of the song by giving the melody line a memorable underpinning. Whether or not they anticipated an infringement, the fact is that two years later, they had occasion to bring suit—and not against an unknown composer.

From its beginnings, the song had a curious history and involved two strange and eccentric people. Of its publisher, Fred Fisher, who also wrote the words, it was said that when he became nervous he pulled paper money out of his pockets and tore up the bills; also that he was one of the few publishers who brought a wastepaper truck to his door to dispose of an overstock of unsalable copies of a "dog" song, lest he be crowded out of his limited office space. Of German descent, Fisher never lost his accent but mastered the language and musical idiom of his adopted country well enough to cowrite a long list of hits, including "Peg O' My Heart" (1913), "There's a Broken Heart for Every Light on Broadway" (1914), "Ireland Must Be Heaven for My Mother Comes from There" (1916), and "Chicago (That Toddlin' Town)" (1922), originally popularized in vaudeville by Blossom Seeley.

The writer who brought "Dardanella" to Fisher was Johnny Black, a vaudevillian whose great hit was "Paper Doll," originally identified with Tommy Lyman, which went on to sell 6 million records for the Mills Brothers in 1942. Reports have it that Edward B. Marks turned the "Doll" down when he first heard it, but finally in desperation accepted it when Black played it repeatedly on a violin with a trained canary perched on his shoulder chirping along. The title under which Fisher first heard "Dardanella" was "Turkish Tom-Tom," a piano instrumental without a lyric or chorus. Fisher's ear was caught by the novel bass. When Black returned with a lyric as requested, Fisher agreed to publish, and called it "Dardanella," a word derived from the Dardanelles, a strait in Turkey that figured prominently in World War I.

Shortly after the song appeared in print, another vaudevillian, Felix Bernard, came to Fisher and claimed he was the composer. The problem was resolved when Black agreed that Bernard's name should appear on copies as co-composer. Apparently an arrangement by Arthur Lange gave the song an appeal that made it sell and that led to a recording by violinist Ben Selvin and his Novelty Orchestra. (Selvin reportedly made nine thousand disks during a career that stretched from 1919 to 1963, recording under thirty-nine different names for as many different companies.) Listed in *The Book of Golden Discs* as the first pop dance disk to sell over a million copies—Whiteman's "Whispering" b/w "Japanese Sandman" was listed second—Selvin's "Dardanella" is reported to have sold 6.5 million records without the benefit of any radio or film plugs, and over 2 million copies of sheet music. It was Fred Fisher's biggest hit. Boasting that he grossed over $1 million, he awarded Johnny Black a year's contract and gave bonuses to the members of his staff, three of whom promptly left and opened a rival publishing company. (The fourth, Jack Mills, later launched the giant Mills Music Company with his brother, Irving.)

"Dardanella" 's history includes two lawsuits, both won by Fisher. The first involved Felix Bernard, who sold his interest in the song to Fisher for $100 before it became a hit, and then sued afterward, claiming he had been deceived. The second suit was initiated by Fisher and it involved the celebrated show composer, Jerome Kern. Claiming infringement, the suit was occasioned by a song called "Ka-lu-a," composed by Kern for the 1922 musical, *Good Morning, Dearie*, produced by Charles B. Dillingham and published by T. B. Harms, headed by the venerable Max Dreyfus—all highly legitimate professionals.

What was at stake, of course, was not the melody but the "unique" bass figure that had originally intrigued Fisher. In the course of the trial, the defense lawyers introduced testimony by such formidable figures as conductor Leopold Stokowski, Metropolitan Opera music director Arthur Bodanzsky, and operetta composer Victor Herbert.

All rejected the claim that the "Dardanella" bass was original. To support his claim, Fisher presented an eight-piece band performing "Dardanella," with added solos on the ukulele by May Singhi Breen and on the piano by himself. To demonstrate further that the bass line had a unique identity, Fisher played the hymn, "Nearer My God to Thee" "against the harem thump and wriggling rhythm of "Dardanella" 's bass."[3]

Presiding Judge Learned Hand, who felt that the suit was "trivial pother . . . and a waste of time for everyone," as he said in his verdict, called a meeting in chambers. Fisher offered to settle the suit for a suit of clothes. Whatever Kern's reasoning—ego, insult to his reputation, confidence in his witnesses—he rejected the offer. Judge Hand thereupon ruled in Fisher's favor, asserting that the bass material was "essential and substantial"[4] and awarded him the minimum sum of $250 in damages.

With "Dardanella" selling in quantities that spelled hit, Fred Fisher attempted to piggy-back a new song on its popularity. In the *Variety* of January 24, 1920, a large ad devoted to celebrating the success of "Dardanella," including a reprint of its lyric, carried the announcement of a new Fred Fisher song, "Daddy, You've Been a Mother to Me," which became a moderately popular ballad. It is sometimes remembered because of a gag that a fellow publisher perpetrated on Fisher, who never forgave Joe Goodwin for it. After Prohibition, the Globe Cafe on Broadway near 47th Street was turned into a freak exhibition hall, with freaks stationed on platforms selling photographs, and performing similar tasks. When Fisher was about to release "Daddy You've Been a Mother to Me," Joe Goodwin purchased a photograph of the bearded lady and sent it to Fisher with the suggestion that he use it as the illustration on the song cover.

Another major copyright became a source of controversy early in 1920. There was no issue of plagiarism, but two major songwriters and publishers were involved. The conflict surfaced as the result of advertisements in *Variety* on February 20 and 27. The earlier ad came from Harry Von Tilzer, who identified the problem as one involving songs with "almost identical titles"—"When My Baby Smiles"

and "When My Baby Smiles at Me." Claiming that his publication—
the latter—was written first and first placed on the market, Von Tilzer
told the story of how he had heard this piece of music one evening
"early in September 1919," at Rector's. Learning that it was unpub-
lished, he approached the pianist, who was also the song's composer,
and in the course of the evening suggested the title, "When My Baby
Smiles at Me," improvising lyrics to the rest of the chorus, which the
orchestra proceeded to play and sing not only that evening but throughout the month of September. In December 1919, after he had spent
about $4,000 for copies, song-and-dance orchestrations, and advance
advertising, Von Tilzer learned that Irving Berlin had written a song
with a similar title. He proposed a conference at which the two songs
were played, and everyone agreed that they were entirely different except for the titles. Berlin's pianist, Harry Akst, thereupon suggested
that a coin be tossed to decide which firm would retain the original
title. Berlin refused the ploy—and there the matter rested.

But in the following week's *Variety*, an advertisement signed by
Berlin's professional manager, Saul H. Bornstein, included a repro-
duction of a letter from MPPA (Music Publishers Protective Association) stating that "When My Baby Smiles" was registered with the
organization on November 14 and the Von Tilzer song, "When My
Baby Smiles at Me," later on December 22. E. C. Mills, Secretary to
the Executive Board, indicated that the organization's regulations
barred from registration "only such titles as were IDENTICAL with
titles previously registered." In his ad Bornstein further sought to for-
tify the priority of the Berlin song by reproducing a note from the
Library of Congress indicating that the Von Tilzer publication was
deposited on December 31, 1919, "upon the publication January 2,
1920."

Innuendoes were now tossed about, with Bornstein accusing Von Tilzer of being guilty in another case of title duplication (involving his
own brother). He terminated the ad by sneering at a statement attributed to Von Tilzer: "My imprint on a song means a great more
to the music buying public, than his [Irving Berlin's] ever will." If
Von Tilzer made the statement, it was gratuitous and out of line. Although Von Tilzer did write such hits as "My Old New Hampshire

Home," "A Bird in a Gilded Cage," "Down Where the Wurzburger Flows," "Wait Till the Sun Shines Nellie," and others—he was not in Berlin's class. Nevertheless, when it came to the two songs at issue, it was the Von Tilzer publication, not Berlin's, that became the hit, doubtless because of the constant use of "When My Baby Smiles at Me" as a theme song by Ted Lewis, the clarinetist who performed in a battered stovepipe hat, half-talked the words of songs, and made a byword of his onstage query, "Is everybody happy?"[5]

By 1920 Irving Berlin, born Israel Baline in Temun, Russia, in 1888, had already published over one hundred songs, including such hits as "Alexander's Ragtime Band," "Everybody's Doing It Now," "Play a Simple Melody," and "A Pretty Girl Is Like a Melody." He was about to launch the *Music Box Revues* in his own theatre, initiating a series of sparkling show and film scores that prompted the writer of a recent *New York Times* article headed, "Irving Berlin at 98 Is Still the Greatest," to say: "It would be impossible to celebrate Christmas or Easter, salute the flag, march in a parade or serve in the armed forces without paying homage to Irving Berlin. . . . He is our most virtuosic songwriter, a title he always preferred to that of composer."[6] The writer was thinking of such everlasting songs as "White Christmas," "Easter Parade," and "God Bless America," among others, to which one might add "Say It with Music," "There's No Business Like Show Business," "Blue Skies," "Puttin' on the Ritz," and the hit-filled scores of *Annie Get Your Gun* and *Call Me Madam,* among others. Berlin is one of the few American songwriters who wrote both words and music, served as his own publisher, and was remarkably successful not only as a hit Tin Pan Alley writer but as a sophisticated film and theatre writer. In his probing book, *American Popular Song,* composer, arranger, and songwriter Alec Wilder calls Berlin "the best all-around overall songwriter America has ever had."[7]

Despite the unconventional format of both "Dardanella" and "When My Baby Smiles at Me," the popular song form became quite stylized in the 1920s—and the form was maintained until the advent of rock in the mid-fifties. Thirty-two bars were the set number, divided into four segments of eight bars each. The most common arrangement was $A^8 \ A^8 \ B^8 \ A^8$, with the B segment known as "the bridge,"[11] "release," or "channel." Among the hundreds of songs that fit into this framework are "Avalon" (1920), "The Man I Love" (1924), and "My Heart Stood Still" (1927). Variations of this setup include $A^8 \ B^8 \ A^8 \ C^8$ ("April Showers," 1921), "Carolina in the Morning" (1922), and "I'm Just Wild About Harry" (1921), which added four bars to the C segment. Another variant is $A^8 \ A^8 \ A^8 \ B^8$ ("My Blue Heaven," 1927). The *AABA* form is used far more often than the others. (In passing, let it be said that the rock era, when its songs did not adhere to the twelve-bar blues progression, brought a wide variety of forms into popular music, frequently involving a verse-chorus arrangement, which had been quite common during the eighteenth and nineteenth centuries but largely disappeared during the twenties, except in show, production, and film tunes.) The thirty-two-bar form was both a boon and a challenge, supplying the songwriter with a usable and acceptable form but challenging his creativity to achieve freshness within its restrictions.

Tin Pan Alley—it never was an alley—acquired its name by accident some time in the early twentieth century. As a locale where song publishers, songwriters, entertainers, and related businesses—theatres, clubs and restaurants—clustered, it existed in Manhattan during the 1880s and 1890s. It was then focused around Union Square at East 14th Street. When M. Witmark and Sons had its first hit, "The Picture that Is Turned toward the Wall," in 1891, it was situated on the corner of 13th Street and Broadway, across from the Star Theatre. (Its first complete building was at 8 West 29th Street, and in 1903, it rented a building at 144–46 West 37th Street.) By the time the alley acquired its cognomen, it was largely located on West 28th Street between Broadway and Fifth Avenue in a group of five-story buildings. Here, according to legend, a songwriter named Monroe Rosenfeld, who was also a freelance journalist, concocted and used the colorful phrase in articles he wrote. The cacophony of different tunes being

banged out by song pluggers on tinny upright pianos, was nicely suggested by the reference to tin pans. Hence Tin Pan Alley, a phrase
that quickly caught on between 1903 and 1910, and that remains in
use today.

By the 1920s, Tin Pan Alley had left 28th Street and moved uptown, settling in buildings in the West 40s. Broadway Music and
Jack Mills Music were on West 45th Street. Jerome Remick, Harry
Von Tilzer, and Fred Fisher were on West 46th. Shapiro, Bernstein were at Broadway and 47th, M. Witmark at 1582 Broadway,
Irving Berlin at 1587 (the corner of 47th Street), and Waterson, Berlin and Snyder were in the Strand Theatre Building. The incentive to
move came from three developments: the building of new theatres
along West 44th, 45th, and 46th streets, the location of the major network studios, and the opening of new hotels and restaurants. By the
1920s, eighty theatres existed in the Broadway area, and forty or
fifty musicals were produced each year. When CBS was incorporated
in 1927, it settled in a building at 52nd Street and Madison Avenue,
while NBC put its offices and studios at 55th Street and Fifth Avenue.

When World War I came to an end, the impulse to break loose led
people to dine out and dance more and more frequently. As a result,
all the major hotels in Manhattan opened large dining rooms, usually
with a bandstand and dance floor. For soft summer nights, there were
the cabaret roofs at the Astor, St. Regis, and Commodore, among
others, offering dining and dancing under the stars.

Opening nights at these major hotels, like Broadway premieres,
were covered by the society reporters. On June 6, 1928, for example,
Cholly Knickerbocker, the *New York American*'s columnist, carried
the following account of the summer opening of the St. Regis Roof:

> Society's newest aerial dining and dancing rendezvous
> opened last evening in a gala blaze of colorful surround-
> ings, people, and the strains of Vincent Lopez's music. So
> great was the demand for resservations that more than a
> thousand guests were turned away after accommodations
> for 500 were exhausted, with the result that another open-
> ing will be held tonight. . . .

Nothing quite so magnificent as the St. Regis Roof has ever been attempted, and to the famous Joseph Urban goes the credit for providing Mayfair with the most beautiful place in New York.

The columnist proceeded to name the prominent members of society who attended (the Tony Biddles, Dan Toppings, Cornelius Vanderbilts, among others), as well as the political bigwigs (Mr. and Mrs. James Walker, Mr. and Mrs. Franklin D. Roosevelt). "Strangely, though," he added, "the only representative of show business I spied was Marie Dressler. . . . Let me give warning that the strict rule is dinner dress. Even the most conservative blue suit isn't enough at the St. Regis this season. . . ."

Dance bands were, of course, the main feature of these dining rooms, composed generally of nine- to eleven-piece groups—like Vincent Lopez's Hotel Pennsylvania Orchestra: three brass (two trumpets, trombone), three reeds (sax, clarinet, and flute), and four rhythm (piano, bass, banjo, and drums). But at the St. Regis Roof, where he settled for several years, Lopez led a band of eighteen, including two violins and a quartet that doubled on Latin rhythm instruments (bongos, claves, maracas). Some of the bands took their names from the hotels where they played, such as Abe Lyman's California Ambassador Orchestra, Gus Arnheim's Cocoanut Grove Orchestra, and others. They played fox-trots, waltzes, and at times, Latin-American dances like the tango, and later the rhumba, cha-cha, etc. They were sometimes known as "Society bands," and later to the more sophisticated musicians, as Mickey Mouse bands. In major cities like New York, Chicago, and Los Angeles, these hotel bands, especially those heard over the radio, became the focus of the music business, with publishers and songwriters turning to them for plugs and hit-making. The number of dance bands increased tremendously around the country so that by 1929 *Variety* carried the routes of over seven hundred bands, noting whether they were playing ballrooms, cafes, dance halls, hotels, parks, restaurants, or theatres.

Among the most popular bandleaders of the time, in addition to those already mentioned, were Isham Jones, Paul Specht, George Olsen, Ted Lewis, Art Hickman, Jean Goldkette, Hal Kemp, Meyer Davis, Fred Waring, and Ben Bernie (1891–1943), who was born Benjamin Anzelwitz, referred to himself as the Old Maestro, and was known for his sense of humor. He formed his band in 1922 after playing in vaudeville as a monologist and violinist and then in a partnership with comedian Phil Baker. Using the moody "It's A Lonesome Old Town" as his theme, he delivered vocals in a style that was one part singing and seven parts talking. "Yowsah" was one of his favorite expressions. He carried on a fabricated feud with tabloid columnist Walter Winchell, the basis of two films in which they costarred in the thirties, *Wake Up and Live* and *Love and Hisses.* "Sweet Georgia Brown" (1925) and "Who's Your Little Who-zis?" (1931) were among the songs on which he appeared as cocomposer. He closed his radio broadcasts with "Au Revoir, Pleasant Dreams."

The "romancing" of orchestra leaders instead of vaudevillians came at a time when, as in 1921, seventy or more vaudeville houses closed, reduced the number of acts on a bill, or switched to a straight motion picture policy. The film companies accelerated the phasing out of vaudeville since they not only produced the films but owned the theatres as well at the time.

As the era progressed and the Charleston became the most popular dance, bands tended to play in an up-tempo, staccato, one-step style. A tuba frequently burped its basement notes on the first and third beats of a four-beat measure while the drummer sounded an after-beat on a crackling cymbal. Stop-time choruses were not unusual, with a muted trumpet, "smear" trombone, squealing clarinet, syncopated piano, or even the rackety banjo taking a break.

The major Tin Pan Alley songwriters of the 1920s came mostly from the East and Midwest. Not surprisingly, New York accounted for the largest number, with at least seven successful tunesmiths coming from Manhattan (Fred Ahlert, Sammy Fain, and Bert Kalmar), four from the Lower East Side (Harry Akst, Con Conrad, Harry Ruby, and Billy Rose), and four hailing from Brooklyn (J. Fred Coots, Walter Donaldson, Harry Warren, and Mabel Wayne). One possible explanation as to why the Lower East Side was a breeding ground of songsmiths is suggested by something Harry Ruby once told Max Wilk. "In the days when I was growing up on the Lower East Side," he said, "you've got to remember that all the families around us were poor. But *they had pianos*. Waters, I think they were called; you could buy one for a hundred dollars and pay it off on time payments. They'd hoist it up to the apartment on a rope. I lived on the same block as the Gershwins—Eldridge Street—that's how the piano came into their house.

"These people, who had barely enough to eat and pay the rent— for some reason they wanted their children to *learn* something. Everybody got lessons in the hope that it would lead to something. . . . "8

Outside New York, Massachusetts gave us the Tobias brothers (Harry, Henry, and Charles) from Worcester, Harry M. Woods from Chelmsford, and George W. Meyer and Jimmy McHugh from Boston. Two songwriters came from Ohio: Cliff Friend (Cincinnati) and Isham Jones (Coaltown). Chicago produced Milton Ager; Philadelphia sent Joe Burke. Baltimore was the birthplace of Abel Baer, and Newark of Ted Fiorito. From the Far West, Joseph Meyer came from Modesto, California. Jay Gorney, Sam H. Stept, and L. Wolfe Gilbert came from Russia, as did Irving Berlin, while Jack Yellen was a Polish émigré.

Quite a number came from musical families in which the mother usually played the piano. But very few indulged in formal study, Sammy Stept and Mabel Wayne being notable exceptions. Before they became songwriters, many were involved in completely unrelated activities. Jack Yellen worked as a reporter. Con Conrad and Walter Donaldson both served as pages on the Wall Street Stock Exchange. Joseph Meyer and George W. Meyer came to Tin Pan Alley from the dry goods business. There were a certain number who spent their time leading bands—Ted Fiorito, Sammy Stept, and Isham Jones, among others. Some toured the country as vaudevillians—Con Conrad, Sammy Fain, Cliff Friend, Mabel Wayne, Harry Woods, and the Tobias brothers, among others. A considerable number served apprenticeships as song pluggers and/or staff pianists. Milton Ager and Fred Ahlert worked at Waterson, Berlin and Snyder; and Harry Akst and Billy Rose, at Leo Feist. For a time, Richard Whiting ran the Detroit office of Jerome H. Remick. In Boston, Jimmy McHugh was one of twenty-two men employed to promote Irving Berlin songs. To get around, he and his associates used bicycles, supplied by Berlin.

In the scramble to create hit songs, Tin Pan Alley publishers and songwriters sometimes tried to associate a song with an important event or celebrity. Lyricist Dorothy Fields once told how on her first meeting with Irving Mills of Mills Music, he asked her to write a song about Ruth Elder, who was about to attempt a flight across the Atlantic. "I'll give you fifty dollars to do this," he said, "if you can do it by tomorrow. I'll even give you a title—*Our American Girl.* The two lines of verse you have to use are, 'You took a notion to fly across the ocean.'" Miss Fields eyed Mills coldly, observing, "You don't 'take a notion.'"[9]

Event songs were more prevalent in the twenties than in later years, perhaps because they seldom developed into hits. In 1920, "Alla" was dedicated to movie star Alla Nazimova; "Bebe" by Sam Coslow (words) and Abner Silver (music) to Bebe Daniels (1923); "The Beggar" by Irving Kahal, and Francis Wheeler (words) and Ted Snyder (music) to Pola Negri, whose film, *The Secret House* (1928), it served as the theme. "Ching, Ching, Chinaman," with music by the distinguished composer, Louis F. Gottschalk, was inspired by Lon Chaney's role in the film *Shadows* (1922). Among other events, the wreck of a dirigible in Ohio in 1925 was memorialized in "The Wreck of the Shenandoah," words and music by Maggie Andrews (pseudonym of country singer Carson Robinson). None of these became bestsellers, nor did any of the songs, some by successful writers, about Lindberg's sensational flight.

A major hit of 1920 was "Margie," introduced by the Original Dixieland Jazz Band and used later as the title of a 1946 motion picture starring Jeanne Crain. It brought to the fore Con Conrad (his name was actually Conrad K. Dober), who collaborated on the music with J. Russell Robinson. Inspired, it is said, by Eddie Cantor's five-year-old daughter Marjorie, the words were by Benny Davis. Cantor sang the song at a Sunday evening concert at the Winter Garden in New York City, and later included it in the film *The Eddie Cantor Story* (1954). Benny Davis recalls that Sophie Tucker sang it at the old Edelweiss Gardens in Chicago when he and Russell Robinson demonstrated it for her.

For Benny Davis (1895–1979), "Margie" was his first bestseller, launching a career as a Tin Pan Alley lyricist that spanned more than forty years. He started in show business as a vaudevillian at the tender age of fourteen, later touring the circuits with Benny Fields as an accompanist to lusty singer Blossom Seeley (1891–1974). He was performing in vaudeville as late as 1925 when he introduced his song, "Oh, How I Miss You Tonight," a collaboration with Joe Burke and Mark Fisher. In succeeding years he wrote such hits as "Yearning," "Baby Face," "Carolina Moon," and "I Still Get a Thrill." He wrote the lyrics for the Broadway musical *Sons O' Guns* (1929), three editions of the Cotton Club, and the title song for the film *Follow the Boys* (1963).

Con Conrad (1891–1938), for whom "Margie" was one of his first hits, did most of his composing for the stage and films. Before he migrated to California with the exodus of Tin Pan Alley songwriters in 1929, Conrad scored with "Barney Google" (1923), a novelty based on a popular comic strip, and with "Lonesome and Sorry" (1926). When the Motion Picture Academy added "Best Song" to its annual awards in 1934, "The Continental," composed by him to lyrics by Herb Magidson for *The Gay Divorcee*, won the first Oscar in that category. "The Continental" was interpolated into the Cole Porter score, and was danced by Fred Astaire and Ginger Rogers.

In 1920 the famous Roseland Ballroom opened its doors, making it possible for any single or lonely man to dance with a girl of his choice by purchasing a ten-cent ticket. The girl's plight found expression some ten years later in a touching ballad in the show *Simple Simon*. Written in a minor mode, "Ten Cents a Dance" by Rodgers and Hart proved a magical vehicle for Ruth Etting. (Incidentally, in 1985, its sixty-fifth year, Roseland reinstated its dance hostess routine on Thursday nights, though the tariff was raised from ten cents to one dollar.) In the year that Roseland went into business, Rodgers and Hart wrote their first little-noticed, complete music score for *Poor Little Ritz Girl*. They thought their score was complete until they attended the opening and found that, without their knowledge, eight songs had been interpolated by Sigmund Romberg and Alex Gerber.

Some of the year's most popular songs emanated from Broadway musicals. The season's smash, *Sally*, with incandescent Marilyn Miller as its star, yielded "Look for the Silver Lining," music by Jerome Kern and words by B. G. DeSylva. "Alice Blue Gown" came from *Irene*, a hit musical with songs by Joseph McCarthy and Harry Tierney. And "The Love Nest," words by Otto Harbach and music by Louis A. Hirsch, outclassed the title song of the show, *Mary*. All three of these musicals, titled with a girl's name and exploiting the Cinderella theme of the poor girl who makes it rich, possessed a kind of homely domesticity that gave no clue as to what was about to happen to the morality and psychology of the American people with the proliferation of speakeasies and their Judas holes, secret passwords, and cocktails served in coffee cups.

Through the twenties and later, Tin Pan Alley functioned on a . plane of superficial escapism that evinced little concern for the amorality, cynicism, and hypocrisy of the times—themes treated by novelists like Theodore Dreiser and Sinclair Lewis (who won the Nobel Prize in 1930) and by poets like Edgar Lee Masters and T. S. Eliot. The garish sentimentality of the early twenties found expression even in trade advertising. When publicity-minded publisher Jack Robbins got married, he inserted an ad in *Variety*, naming some of the hits he had picked and presenting "his latest and biggest hit"—a photograph of his bride.[10] One of the most colorful personalities of the Big Ballad era, Robbins later prided himself on his rhumba dancing and his way with women. He was widely publicized inside the music business as Mr. Music.

The devastating impact of radio and records on the active piano-playing generation—with its swains gathered around the upright for an evening of songs, played by the belle of the house—was forecast by the slump in sheet music sales in April 1920. Whether or not *Variety* was reacting to the problem or rising paper costs, also troubling music publishers, on April 16, 1920, it broke with a fourteen-year-old tradition and appeared for the first time without its green cover.

Among the solo interpreters of popular song, Nora Bayes made a hit of "I'll Be with You in Apple Blossom Time" by Neville Fleeson (words) and Albert Von Tilzer (music), and in vaudeville popularized "The Japanese Sandman," words by Raymond B. Egan, music by Richard A. Whiting; Fanny Brice scored a hit in two *Ziegfeld Follies*, singing "I'm a Vamp from East Broadway" by Bert Kalmar, Harry Ruby, and Irving Berlin, and "Rose of Washington Square" by Ballard MacDonald and James F. Hanley; Van and Schenck popularized "Down by the O-HI-O (O-My!-O!)," (words) Jack Yellen and (music) Abe Olman, in the *Ziegfeld Follies of 1920*, a song that Lou Holtz also sang in *George White's Scandals of 1920;* Eddie Cantor signed an exclusive deal with Emerson Records, guaranteeing him $220,000 over a five-year period; and Mabel Mercer, later the doyenne of 52nd Street, left for Paris to star at Brick Top's.

On January 9, 1920, Al Jolson recorded "Swanee" on Columbia, a song by Irving Caesar (words) and George Gershwin (music) he had interpolated in *Sinbad* after trying it out on one of his Sunday night concerts at the Winter Garden. The idea for the one-step-styled song was born when the two songwriters, then unknown, were lunching at Dinty Moore's. Riding on a Fifth Avenue bus to Gershwin's apartment on Washington Heights, the idea was developed and the song was completed in Gershwin's living room. That afternoon it was auditioned before friends who had been playing poker in an adjoining dining room, "with Papa Gershwin providing an obbligato by whistling into a comb wrapped in tissue paper. "Although it was presented in October 1919 by Ned Wayburn in a sumptuous stage production at the newly built Capitol Theatre on Broadway and 51st Street—sixty chorus girls with electric bulbs glowing on their slippers danced to its rhythms on a darkened stage—it did not catch on until Jolson performed and recorded it. Then "Swanee" became a nationwide popular hit, launching Caesar and Gershwin on their distinguished songwriting careers.

While the older generation was dining and dancing to the elegant music of Paul Whiteman in 1920, and humming hits he created like "San," "Whispering," "Japanese Sandman," and "I Never Knew I Could Love Anybody," the younger set was trekking up to Harlem to hear Mamie Smith and her Jazz Hounds and other black artists, or buying records by the snappy Original Dixieland Jazz Band, which introduced songs like "Palesteena," and "Singin' the Blues (Till My Daddy Comes Home)."

10

"The Sheik of Araby"
(1921)

In 1921 American women began going to the movies to make love. The object of their affection was a young man with long sideburns and dreamy eyes named Rudolph Alfonso Raffaele Pierre Filibert Guglielmi di Valentina d'Antonguolla, who became known as Rudolph Valentino. In two films, *Four Horsemen of the Apocalypse* and especially *The Sheik*, Valentino established himself as the acme of masculine sex appeal sweeping women off their feet and, in their fantasies, into the bedroom. Popular music quickly reacted to this development. Mills Music published "The Sheik of Araby," which became an overnight hit. The line "into your tent, I'll creep" produced unprintable parodies and countless jokes by the day's comedians.

Ted Snyder, who wrote the catchy melody, and later accounted for "Who's Sorry Now?" (1923), published one of Irving Berlin's earliest songs, gave Berlin a job as staff lyricist at $25 a week, collaborated with him on several songs, including "That Beautiful Rag," appeared with him in a Shubert revue, *Up and Down Broadway* (1910), and joined publishing forces with him in the very successful publishing operation, Waterson, Berlin and Snyder.

Valentino's overpowering hold on the ladies was short-lived—he died in 1926 of a perforated ulcer—but it reached a sensational and hysterical peak in his funeral, characterized by Frederick Lewis Allen

111

as "a striking demonstration of what astute press-agentry could do to make a national sensation."[1] His lying in state at Campbell's Funeral Parlor on Broadway "would hardly have attracted a crowd which stretched through eleven blocks," Allen wrote, "if his manager had not arranged the scenes of grief with uncanny skill, and if Harry C. Klemfuss, the undertaker's press agent, had not provided the newspapers with everything they could desire—such as photographs, distributed in advance, of the chamber where the actor's body would lie, and posed photographs of the funeral cortege. . . . With such practical assistance, the press gave itself to the affair so wholeheartedly that mobs rioted about the undertaker's and scores of people were injured."[2]

Tin Pan Alley did not allow the occasion to go unnoticed. Mills Music published "There's a New Star in Heaven Tonight," by J. Keirn Brennan, Jimmy McHugh, and Irving Mills, with a dedication to Rudolph Valentino. (The bathetic lyric was developed in somewhat different form on the death of the great classic tenor, Enrico Caruso; in 1921 George A. Little and Jack Stanley titled their maudlin opus, also published by Mills Music, "They Needed a Songbird in Heaven, So God Took Caruso Away.")

1921 was disinguished by the appearance of *Shuffle Along*, the black musical that shook up the American musical theatre; the novelty instrumental "Kitten on the Keys," featured three years later by Paul Whiteman at the celebrated Aeolian Hall concert; and "Wabash Blues," a recond that sold nearly 2 million copies and made the world aware of the Isham Jones band.

Although Isham Jones (1894–1956) was a noted bandleader, he was equally outstanding as a songwriter, composing more than a dozen popular standards. Among the two hundred songs he wrote are such hits as "Swingin' Down the Lane" (1923), "I'll See You in My Dreams" (1924), "My Castle in Spain" (1924), "It Had to Be You" (1924), and "The One I Love Belongs to Somebody Else" (1924). Jones organized his first band at the age of twenty, playing dances in various Michigan cities. But after advanced study in Chicago, he was booked into such top Chicago spots as the Green Mill, the million-dollar Rainbow Gardens, and the College Inn, where he performed for six years. His arrangers included Gordon Jenkins, later a Sinatra favorite, and among his instrumentalists was clarinetist Woody Herman, who also sang. As the leader of one of the outstanding dance bands of the era, he went on to gain fame abroad as well as in this country. His recording of "Wabash Blues"—Dave Ringle (words), Fred Meinken (music)—was one of the biggest hits of 1921–22. A trumpet solo by Louis Panico contributed greatly to its success, as Henry Busse's trumpet solo helped make Paul Whiteman's "Wang Wang Blues" a hit that year.

One of the few hits of the twenties born outside Tin Pan Alley, Broadway, and even vaudeville was the zesty "Down Yonder," introduced by lyricist and composer L. Wolfe Gilbert at the Orpheum Theatre in New Orleans in 1921. Having scored in 1912 with the snappy "Waiting for the Robert E. Lee"—music by Lewis F. Muir—he proceeded to publish the song with his own short-lived firm. It made no great impact. An aggressive promoter, he succeeded in having it performed by such top vaudevillians as Jolson, Cantor, Belle Baker, and Sophie Tucker, still without achieving a hit. "Down Yonder" did, however, become a hit, but not until a dozen years later when it was recorded by Gid Tanner and His Skillet Lickers, a hillbilly quartet that sold an unbelievable 4 million records. In 1951–52, "Down Yonder" once again became a million-selling record, this time on a disk by country pianist Del Wood.

L. Wolfe Gilbert (1886–1970) came from Odessa, Russia, at the age of one, and grew up in Philadelphia. A successful vaudevillian and cafe performer, he was playing at the College Inn, a Coney Island cafe, when "Waiting for the Robert E. Lee" became one of his big numbers. So impressed by his presentation was a group of British showmen that they tried to book him in England, a move opposed by his publisher, Mills Music. But it is said that the Englishmen took the number back with them, launching the ragtime craze in Great Britain. Prolific as a lyricist, Gilbert accounted for such hits of the twenties as the Austrian, "O Katharina," German words by Fritz Lohner and music by Richard Fall; it was introduced during the run of Balieff's *Chauve-Souris* revue, which also presented "I

Miss My Swiss Miss, My Swiss Miss Misses Me," by Gilbert and Abel
Baer. In 1928, he scored two hits, "Ramona," the theme song of the
film *Ramona*, with music by Mabel Wayne, and "Jeannine," I Dream
of Lilac Time," the theme song of the film *Lilac Time*, with music by
Nathaniel Shilkret. The following year, "My Mother's Eyes," with music by Abel Baer, was introduced by George Jessel in the film *Lucky
Boy*.

During the early thirties, Gilbert became involved with a number
of Cuban songs that made the rumba popular with American dancers.
"The Peanut Vendor" by Cuban composer Moises Simons was found
in Havana on his honeymoon by Herbert E. Marks, son of music
publisher Edward B. Marks. Gilbert collaborated on the American
lyric with Marion Sunshine, wife of the Cuban bandleader, Don Az-
piazu. There were popular recordings by Paul Whiteman, Guy Lombardo, and Xavier Cugat. It was followed by "Mama Inez," music
by Eliseo Grenet, which was introduced to the public by Maurice
Chevalier. Gilbert wrote the lyrics also for "Maria My Own," music
by Ernesto Lecuona, the composer of "Malagueña," and for "Marta,"
composed by Moises Simons. "Marta" became the opening and closing
radio theme of Arthur Tracy, who was known as the Street Singer.

In 1921 two new theatres opened their doors in New York. The
Jolson Theatre on 59th Street and Seventh Avenue, built by the Shuberts in honor of their Winter Garden star, made its debut with
Jolson in *Bombo*. Although the score was by the Shubert musical work-
horse, Sigmund Romberg, the three hits that emerged were interpolations by other songwriters that became Jolson favorites: "Toot, Toot,
Tootsie," "April Showers," and "California, Here I Come." The last
two were added so late that they were not listed in the program, but
"April Showers," words by B. G. De Sylva, and music by Louis Silvers, stole the show on opening night, October 6, 1921. None of these
quite matched "My Mammy," the song that Jolson sang on one
bended knee with hands outstretched—the pose most associated with
Jolie. (Although he first presented "My Mammy" in *Sinbad* in 1918,
the song was not copyrighted until 1921, and was not written for
him, the initial performances being by William Frawley in vaude-

ville.) But as reviewer Pearl Sieben wrote, "In the sparkling new theater, which immortalized his name . . . when Jolson sank down on one knee and beseeched his mammy to forgive him, the whole nation jumped to its feet to applaud."

The other theatre, "a new, exquisitely beautiful" one,[3] was located at 239 W. 45th Street. The Music Box, as it was called, was built by Irving Berlin in association with Sam Harris, George M. Cohan's former partner. The initial production was the *Music Box Revue*, written and produced by Berlin. Among the songs in the first edition was the lovely "Say It with Music," which became the theme of the series. Before he set the song in the revue, Berlin had it played down at the Sixty Club in New York. It caught on so fast and drew so many requests for repeat plays that Berlin became concerned lest it lose its impact as a new ballad in the show. His worry proved groundless for most reviewers shared Percy Hammond's description of it as "a molten masterpiece." Berlin wrote four *Music Box Revues* before the theatre was opened to outside productions.

Chicago also boasted a new, impressive theatre, much larger than either Manhattan's Jolson or the Music Box. Called simply the Chicago, it was a giant movie palace that seated 3,800 patrons. Opening on October 26, 1921, it presented the superfilms and superstars of the twenties and thirties, but deteriorated with the nationwide decline of movie palaces and of State Street as Chicago's affluent thoroughfare. Almost torn down by the Plitt Theater owners in the early eighties, it was saved by a community-minded group of investors who bought the theatre for 311.5 million in October 1985, refurbished it at a cost of $3.5-million, and reopened it in September 1986 as a showcase for touring Broadway shows, top talent concerts, and touring orchestras—à la New York City's Radio City Music Hall.

Not too many songs gave expression to the incipient freewheeling, devil-may-care spirit of the times. But in 1921 lyricists Gus Kahn and Raymond B. Egan came up with the title, "Ain't We Got Fun," to which Richard A. Whiting set an infectious gang melody. George Watts, now forgotten, introduced it in vaudeville, where it attracted the well-known team of Van and Schenck, who proceeded to popularize it and generate a sale of over a million copies. It was not until the middle of the twenties that several dance songs like the Charleston and Black Bottom gave expression to the unbuttoned sexuality of the period. In 1921 women were still having fun at their social teas and at lunch in some restaurants where they could play mah-jongg, or with Ouija boards.

Richard A. Whiting (1891–1938), who wrote the spirited music for "Ain't We Got Fun," hailed from Peoria, Illinois, and moved into songwriting after being stage struck in his youth. For a time he worked to develop a vaudeville act—it never came off—with Marshall Neilan, a Pierce Arrow chauffeur who later became a well-known movie director. On a visit to Detroit, where Jerome H. Remick bought three of his songs at $50 apiece, he was offered the post of "Professional Manager," which he declined at first, but accepted when the salary was upped to $25 a week. He supplemented the meager take by playing piano for $10 a week at a local hotel backed by six native Hawaiians. What was probably the biggest hit of his career was also nearly his first—"Till We Meet Again" (1918)— a great group song that reportedly sold over 5 million copies. During his two years in Detroit, he collaborated with Ray Egan and Gus Kahn, who came from Chicago expressly to work with him. Efforts to persuade Kahn to go to New York to write shows failed. Whiting, nevertheless, went to New York and was almost immediately handed a train ticket for Hollywood by a music publisher. His first film contract was with Paramount, but after scoring two Broadway musicals in 1931 he returned to tie up with Fox and then with Warner Brothers, collaborating with Johnny Mercer.

During the 1920s he produced a series of top songs: "Japanese Sandman" (1920), recorded by Nat Brandwynne, Russ Morgan, and Ray Noble; "Sleepy Time Gal" (1924), recorded by Harry James, Art Lund, Buddy Cole, and Paul Weston; "Ukulele Lady" (1925); "Breezin' Along with the Breeze" (1926), and the torch song "She's Funny That Way" (1928), recorded by Connie Haines, Martha Stewart, and, after a time, Frank Sinatra. Ray Egan was the lyricist on "Japanese Sandman" and "Sleepy Time Gal," while Gus Kahn authored "Ukulele Lady," and Neil Moret, a pseudonym for Charles N. Daniels, wrote the plaintive lyric of "She's Funny That Way." Richard Whiting's legacy also includes daughter Margaret Whiting, a superlative vocalist who at sixteen sang her father's song "Too Marvelous for Words" on Johnny Mercer's NBC morning program and secured a regular spot on the show. When Capitol Records was established in 1942, Margaret made "My Ideal," another of her father's ballads and one of the label's first bestsellers.

Few singers have become so identified with a single song as Fanny Brice (1891–1951) was with "My Man." Born Fanny Borach on New York's Lower East Side, the daughter of a saloon keeper, she won an amateur contest in a Brooklyn theatre at 13, and early began working in vaudeville, circuses, and burlesque houses. Her rendition of Irving Berlin's "Sadie Salome, Go Home" (1909)—she used a Yiddish accent—caught the attention of Ziegfeld, who starred her in the *Follies* of that year (the great black comic Bert Williams made his debut in the same edition). She was involved thereafter with a dozen editions of the *Follies,* including the final two in 1934 and 1936. In her debut, she sang "Goodbye Becky Cohen," Berlin's first song for Ziegfeld, again in dialect. On opening night, she stopped the show with "Lovie Joe," a ragtime love song by Will Marion Cook and Joe Jordan, and reportedly was called back for twelve encores. It was not until the edition of 1921 that Miss Brice revealed an unsuspected facet of her talent.

"Mon Homme" was originally a French song, with words by Albert Willemetz and Jacques-Charles, and music by Maurice Yvain, introduced in the revue *Paris Qui Jazz* (1920) by Mistinguett. An American adaptation was made by Channing Pollock for Mistinguett's debut in the *Ziegfeld Follies of 1921.* During rehearsals, Ziegfeld was unimpressed by Mistinguett and dropped her from the show. In the previous edition of the *Follies* (1920), Fanny had again stopped the show with three numbers: "I'm a Vamp from East Broadway" (Berlin with Bert Kalmar and Harry Ruby), "I Vas a Floradora Baby" (Ballard MacDonald and Harry Carroll), and "I'm an

Indian" (Blanda Merrill and Leo Edwards). She was the dialect comedienne without peer.

Nevertheless, Ziegfeld chose her to sing "My Man" in place of Mistinguett. During rehearsals, Miss Brice sang the torch ballad, dressed in a formal evening gown. According to reports, Ziegfeld leaped on stage during one rehearsal, ripped off the gown, substituted the shabby dress of a street urchin and instructed her to sing the number while leaning against a lamppost. Singing with a poignancy that brought down the house, Fanny Brice made the song her own, partly because of events in her own life. "In my mind," she said of her tearful rendition, "I think of Nick [her husband] leaving and the tears just come." Nick was Nicky Arnstein, a gangster to whom Brice was joined in an unhappy marriage that ended in divorce. During her career, Fanny Brice recorded three different versions for Victor, and sang it in three different films: her talking picture debut, *My Man* (1928); *The Great Ziegfeld* (1936); and *Rose of Washington Square* (1939). Later, attaining fame and popularity on the radio as Baby Snooks, Fanny inspired the title role of the Broadway musical, *Funny Girl* (1964). Barbra Streisand, who starred in both the stage and film version (1968) of the musical, recorded a number of Fanny's hits, including "Second Hand Rose," which was also interpolated in the *Ziegfeld Follies of 1921*. (This revue included a tribute to entrancing Marilyn Miller, then the queen of Broadway musicals, "Sally, Won't You Come Back to Me?" She starred in *Sally* (1920–21), written by Gene Buck [words] and Dave Stamper [music], and introduced by Van and Schenck.)

At least three jazz-blues classics were added to the standard instrumental repertoire in 1921. In addition to "Wabash Blues," popularized by Isham Jones and, to a lesser extent, by the Benson Orchestra of Chicago, there were "The Wang Wang Blues" and "Jazz Me Blues," commercial, not ethnic blues. "Wang Wang" was popularized by Paul Whiteman and his virtuoso trumpet player, Henry Busse, cowriter of the tune. "Jazz Me Blues" began its celebrated career with recordings by classic blues singer, Lucille Hegamin, and by the Wolverines, who cut it on the first session the great Bix Beiderbecke made with the group.

By 1921 the illicit liquor business was in full swing. Outside the three-mile limit of the Atlantic seaboard, Rum Row (as it became known) flourished with fleets of speedboats smuggling contraband liquor; luxury liners made excursions to sea for jet setters who could afford to pay for a cocktail with a hundred-dollar bill. Chicago, Boston, New York, and other cities were rife with hijackings, sawed-off shotguns, and bloody confrontations. Other cities occupied themselves with various activities: Atlantic City, with its first Miss America bathing beauty contest, concocted by local businessmen to promote tourism after Labor Day; Jersey City, with the Jack Dempsey-Georges Carpentier heavyweight prizefight, the first major boxing match broadcast over the radio.

∾ 11 ∾

"Three O'Clock in the Morning"
(1922)

"In the real dark night of the Soul," F. Scott Fitzgerald wrote in an oft-quoted sentence, "it is always three o'clock in the morning." The feeling of despair and foreboding was echoed in saloon singer Frank Sinatra's recollection of a lost love ("In the Wee Small Hours of the Morning"), later in a more frantic frame, "Help Me Make It Through the Night" by Kris Kristofferson, and in a blues of yearning by B. B. King, "Three O'Clock Blues." The ballad that Paul Whiteman and his Orchestra recorded in 1922, and that became a million-seller, sounded an entirely different concept of 3:00 A.M. His "Three O'Clock in the Morning" was a lilting waltz ballad whose opening lines projected an image of two people falling deeply in love: *"It's three o'clock in the morning . . . We've danced the whole night through . . ."* The sentiment was as timeless as the melody itself.

The song began, curiously, as a piano solo by Julian Robledo, published originally in New Orleans in 1919. The following year it was republished, still without a lyric, in London and Germany. In the 1921 edition of *The Greenwich Village Follies*, it was interpolated with the lyrics by Dorothy Terriss that established it as the standard it became. In the Follies it was heard in the final scene as a duet by

Richard Bold and Rosalind Fuller, sung in front of a plain-blue curtain and danced to by Margaret Petit and Valodia Vestoff, ballet dancers, who served as the chime ringers in the triple-bell effect of the song. In its middle strain, the waltz made use of the famous Westminster chimes of London's Big Ben. The romantic ballad proved the most memorable song to come out of the seventh edition of the *Greenwich Village Follies*, a strange turn considering the revue's vaunted reputation for cynicism, mockery, and sophistication.

Dorothy Terriss was not really the name of the lyricist, but a pseudonym for Theodora Morse, the wife of Theodore F. Morse (1873–1924), a successful turn-of-the-century songwriter and publisher who was the author and/or composer of "Keep on the Sunny Side," "M-o-t-h-e-r," and "Hail, Hail, the Gang's All Here," this last written to the music of the "Pirate's Chorus" in Gilbert and Sullivan's comic opera *The Pirates of Penzance*. Theodora Morse's best-known lyrics were written to Ernesto Lecuona's "Siboney," popularized by Grace Moore in the film *When You're in Love* (1929), and to the Paul Whiteman-Ferde Grofé tune, "Wonderful One," a 1922 musical adaptation from a theme by film director Marshall Neilan.

Another giant song of 1922 with exotic origins was "Parade of the Wooden Soldiers." Originally a German instrumental, Léon Jessel's "Die Parade der Holzsoldaten," published in 1911, it was introduced in the Russian cellar revue *Chauve Souris*, which was a hit in London, displayed its charm when it was presented at the Forty-ninth Street Theatre in Manhattan, and became a box-office smash when it moved to the Century Theatre. The great attraction was its master of ceremonies, Nikita Balieff, whose English pronounciation convulsed audiences "Phooden Soldjurs") and the effectiveness of whose role thereafter made M.C.'s a *must* in revues. Edward B. Marks, its publisher, wrote:

> As a show number, the *Parade of the Wooden Soldiers* was a great success, but it sold few copies. Who wanted a precision march at home in the living room? It seemed a great plug gone to waste. But I swore I would make the tune a best seller as well as a stage hit. "What?" roared my neighbors. "It's just a Dutch march!"

The number of arrangements I had made, I do not care
to remember. The lyrics I caused to be written would fill
a book. But finally J. Bodewald Lampe made a danceable
arrangement. And that started a vogue for fast marches as
dance music, which extended right through *Valencia* and
The Maine Stein Song.[1]

Recorded by both Paul Whiteman and Vincent Lopez, "Wooden Soldiers" became the theme song of Willie Creager and his Orchestra.

Two days before the opening of *Chauve Souris*, the pages of the
country's newspapers were blazoned with the murder of suave movie
director William Desmond Taylor, found shot to death in his South
Alvarado Street apartment. The murder became not only one of the
film industry's most tantalizing unsolved mysteries but also one of
its most unsavory scandals, wrecking the careers of Mary Miles Minter, a rival of Mary Pickford, and of comedienne Mabel Normand.
In a 1986 book, *A Cast of Killers*, by Sidney D. Kirkpatrick, the
killer is identified as the mother of young Miss Minter—a woman
who was apparently successful in bribing three district attorneys to
escape prosecution. "Hollywood was just climbing into long pants,"
author Kirkpatrick has said in a comment about the 1920s. "Virtually, overnight, you had former circus actors, vaudevillians, nickelo-
deon owners becoming millionaires. It was an incredibly volatile
time and the Taylor murder epitomized what was going on."[2]

The popularity of both the schmaltzy waltz and of the foreign revue
suggested that the taste in popular music was hardly homogenous.
The sounds of jazz and the blues, heard in cabarets, ballrooms, and
on hotel dance floors, and in new songs by Tin Pan Alley imitators
of the blues style, were largely embraced by the young generation.
But the middle and older generations were still hearkening and responding to the music of their early years—and both producers and
publishers were not unaware of this nostalgic market.

In 1922 operetta composer Sigmund Romberg had two new musicals on the stage—*The Blushing Bride* and *Springtime of Youth*,[3]—
with an effort being made to Americanize the settings. Although Victor Herbert's *Orange Blossoms* was his final operetta in a richly pro-

ductive thirty-year-career, it yielded one of his most memorable and performed songs, "A Kiss in the Dark," with a lyric by Buddy De Sylva. "A Kiss in the Dark" was another of the waltz hits of the year, which included an English version ("Love Everlasting") by Catherine Chisholm Cushing of operetta composer Rudolf Friml's "L'Amour Toujours L'Amour." Even Walter Donaldson, composing to a lyric by Gus Kahn, found appeal in the waltz rhythm, setting the popular "My Buddy" in a ¾ signature. And one of the biggest record-sellers—on a pioneer jazz label, Gennett—was "Dreamy Melody," a waltz by Ted Koehler, Frank Magine, and C. Naset, recorded by Art Landry and his Call of the North Orchestra. When Landry, whose sale of "Dreamy Melody" brought him a Victor Records contract, first recorded it for Gennett, it was with the Syncopated Six! Estimates place the sale of "Dreamy Melody" at 1.5 million disks.

Although the Americanization of the musical progressed apace during the twenties and jazz came to dominate the music of the era, the operetta continued to command an audience, and, in fact, achieved a period of peak revival between 1924 and 1928. In addition songs entered into the American music scene from foreign countries, introducing sounds indigenous to Mexico ("Cielito Linda," 1923), France ("Titina," 1925), Austria ("My Little Nest of Heavenly Blue," 1926), Germany ("Where Is My Meyer—Where's Himalaya," 1927), Cuba ("Malagueña," 1928), and other places. The number of such successful compositions seemed to grow through the decade. Even the songs coming from England, which accounted for the largest number of importations, were frequently in a nostalgic style out of the past.

Humorous songs, or novelty songs, as they became known in the music business, were not uncommon in the zany atmosphere of the twenties. In 1922–24 Billy Rose accounted for two, "Barney Google" and "Does the Spearmint Lose Its Flavor on the Bedpost Over Night?" Although "Barney Google," with a catchy melody by Con Conrad, was written for "Banjo Eyes" (Eddie Cantor), it was popularized and became identified with two madcap comics, Olsen and Johnson, and proved one of the biggest noisemakers of the year. The chewing gum novelty, whose collaborators included Marty Bloom (words) and Ernest Breuer (music), was the butt of many jokes and became a record hit thirty-three years later during the Skiffle craze in England when it was recorded by Lonnie Donegan. (Another novelty, from 1920, was titled "Who Ate Napoleons with Josephine When Bonaparte Was Away?")

The big novelty song of the year—more of an audience-raiser than a gang song—was "Mr. Gallagher and Mr. Shean," popularized in the *Ziegfeld Follies of 1922* by Gallagher and Shean. Although the pair supposedly wrote the patter song, publisher Isidore Witmark has stated that songwriter Ernest Ball contributed much to it as an act of friendship.[4] The construction of the song made it easy to insert names and jokes so that it became a long-standing favorite at parties and conventions.

By 1922 the Algonquin Round Table was flourishing, as were Broadway revues. Two theatre-oriented regulars among the wits who met daily for the wisecracking luncheons in the hotel's Rose Room, George S. Kaufman and Marc Connelly, became prime movers in putting together a revue. They called it *The 49ers,* for no reason except that it opened at the minuscule Punch and Judy Theatre on 49th Street. Concerned to present a revue that "eschewed spectacle and vaudeville vulgarity," they offered a burlesque of current operetta, parodies, and satiric sketches. The contributions were by celebrated figures like Dorothy Parker, Ring Lardner, Heywood Broun, FPA, Robert Benchley, and other Round Table jokesters. Opening on November 7, 1922, *The 49ers* "bombed out" after an abbreviated run of two weeks. In critic Burns Mantle's words, "the multitude sniffed and would have none of it."[5] Obviously, it took more than wisecracks, bon mots, and epigrams to mount a successful Broadway show, as proved by the success of *The Grand Street Follies,* which had similarly elevated aims, but more substance.

The two novelty songs named above are hardly an index of Billy Rose's talents or scope. Born on the Lower East Side, like Fanny Brice, to whom he was married for a time, he became a fifty-yard dash champion while attending Public School 44—it was a matter of being beaten up by the local bullies or outrunning them. In high school, he turned his command of speed to shorthand, winning the New York City student title for speed and accuracy in his sophomore year; later, under the tutelage of the inventor of the Gregg system, he was acclaimed world's champion. He could take better than two hundred words of dictation a minute and could write forward and backward with either hand. As a stenographer for the War Industries Board of World War I, he became head of the clerical staff. When he decided to become a songwriter, having heard of the large royalties on hits, he spent five months in the New York Public Library methodically analyzing past hits while he lived in a $5-a-week room and ate doughnuts and coffee for his three meals a day. Persistence brought him a collaboration with a staff pianist at Leo Feist, Inc., and the publication in 1920 of a novelty song, "You Tell Her— I Stutter," with a melody by Cliff Friend.

During the 1920s he was associated with a long list of hit songs: "A Cup of Coffee, a Sandwich and You" (1925); "Don't Bring Lulu" (1925); "Clap Hands! Here Comes Charlie" (1925); "Me and My Shadow" (1927); "Back in Your Own Backyard" (1928); "There's a Rainbow 'Round My Shoulder" (1926); and the songs in the Vincent Youmans show *Great Day*. His success carried into the thirties with "Cheerful Little Earful" and "Would You Like to Take a Walk" in *Sweet and Low* (1930); "I Found a Million Dollar Baby (in a Five and Ten Cent Store)" in Billy Rose's *Crazy Quilt* (1931); and "It's Only a Paper Moon" in the film *Take a Chance* (1933).

Rose did not limit his activities to songwriting; he also became a busy and highly successful producer and nightclub owner. In 1924, with Joe Frisco as M.C., he opened the Back Stage Club in a second-story loft over a 56th Street garage; Helen Morgan was the headliner, singing in a Prohibition club so crowded she had to park herself on the grand piano to be seen and heard—Scotch and champagne sold for $25 a bottle. There followed a Fifth Avenue Club sans liquor, directed at the High Society crowd, with a floor show written by Rodgers and Hart and a chorus that included Nancy Carroll, who later became a film star. In 1933 he opened the Casino de Paree, offering an eight-course dinner and a ninety-minute show for $2.50

with no cover charge. Then came the Diamond Horseshoe, the world's most famous nightclub, with Twentieth Century-Fox paying $175,000 for the use of the name in the film starring Betty Grable.

In 1935, determined to outdo the great Ziegfeld as a super show-man, he produced *Jumbo* at the New York Hippodrome, the last show to play that famous house of giant spectacles before its closing. Paul Whiteman and his Orchestra starred with comic Jimmy Durante, and the musical score was by Rodgers and Hart, who accepted the assignment despite, as Rodgers wrote later, Rose's failure to pay them for a previous assignment. In 1944 Rose reopened the Ziegfeld Theatre as a legitimate playhouse, presenting *Seven Lively Arts*, with a score by Cole Porter. On opening night, he served vintage champagne to all his patrons.

Meanwhile, he had become the creator of colossal outdoor spectacles, including the Fort Worth Frontier Days Celebration in 1936–37 (for which he received a flat fee of $100,000), the Great Lakes Exposition at Cleveland in 1938 (also for a $100,000-fee), and the New York World's Fair Aquacade (1939), which never grossed less than $100,000 a week.

Pint-sized, physically unattractive, tending toward surliness, and characterized by Richard Rodgers as a man "who never parted with a dime if he didn't have to,"[6] Billy Rose parlayed a small advance on his first song into a $5-million fortune. He took a genuine interest in the status of songwriting as a craft and in the plight of songwriters, as evidenced by his role as instigator of the Songwriters Protective Association founded in 1931. This organization (now known as The Songwriters Guild of America) compelled music publishers to adopt a contract that guaranteed certain royalties and rights previously denied to writers.

Chicago's influence in popularizing jazz and its central position in the Prohibition gang wars brought it more and more into the news and also made it a focus of literature and music. Carl Sandburg's famous poem celebrating the expanding energy of the city found a popular echo in Fred Fisher's "Chicago (That Toddlin' Town)."

In 1922 the impact of jazz and blues, and the songs of black songwriters like Clarence Williams, Spencer Williams, Perry Bradford, Creamer and Layton, and others, was beginning to be heard in imitative songs penned by Tin Pan Alley tunesmiths. By 1922, there were close to twenty-five titles listed by Nat Shapiro in his *Annotated Index of American Popular Songs*, pseudo-blues with titles like "Great White Way Blues" and "Doo Dah Blues (Sweet Cryin' Babe)." Jimmy McHugh co-authored "When You and I Were Young Maggie Blues." Little-known William Tracey (words) and Dan Dougherty (music) produced "You Can Have Him, I Don't Want Him, Didn't Love Him Anyhow Blues!" England joined the trend, exporting "Limehouse Blues," pseudo-Chinese as well as pseudo-blues, introduced in the United States by Gertrude Lawrence. In Broadway musicals, audiences heard Jerome Kern's "Blue Danube Blues" in *Good Morning Dearie* and George Gershwin's "Yankee Doodle Blues" in the *Spice of 1932*.

As early as 1922, during the infancy of radio, manufacturers began to sponsor radio programs. Most were musical, with a steady band, orchestra, or singing group bearing names associated with the product. Atlantic and Pacific had its "A & P Gypsies," whose theme song was a Russian gypsy folk song, "Two Guitars," arranged by their leader, Harry Horlick. There were the Clicquot Club Eskimoes, who popularized "Mexicali Rose" (1923), later a Bing Crosby standard. Interwoven had its Interwoven Pair, while the Happiness Candy Company had the Happiness Boys, Billie Jones and Ernie Hare. Their theme was "How Do You Do?" and they were successful in popularizing novelty numbers such as "What Ever Became of Hinky Dinky Parley Voo?" (1924), "Thanks for the Buggy Ride" (1925), and "I Love to Dunk a Hunk of Sponge Cake" (1928).

George Gershwin had already produced a classic in "Swanee" (1919) when "I'll Build a Stairway to Paradise" emerged from his score for the *George White Scandals of 1922*. Originally known as "A New Step Every Day," it acquired its new title when Bud De Sylva worked on the lyrics with Arthur Francis (the pen name used by George's brother Ira). Employing bluesy notes (flatted thirds and sevenths) in his melody, Gershwin enhanced the song's impact with

rhythmic jazz accentuations. Winnie Lightner and a chorus introduced the hit to the accompaniment of Paul Whiteman's pit band.
Zez Confrey produced a hit in "Stumbling," whose tricky melody
was developed on the pentatonic scale—the black notes of the piano.
A number of other songs that year embodied unusual tonal or
rhythmic gimmicks. In "Carolina in the Morning," Walter Donaldson set Gus Kahn's words—"Nothing could be finer than to be in
Carolina . . ."—to a pair of notes, a minor third apart, repeated
seven times. Employing schottische rhythm, the song was introduced
in vaudeville by William Frawley and interpolated successfully in
The Passing Show of 1922 by Willie and Eugene Howard. In "Way
Down Yonder in New Orleans," a bright, dixieland-styled tune,
J. Turner Layton (music) and Henry Creamer (words) took the
stop-time device and incorporated it into the song. When the lyric
read, "Stop!—Oh, would you give your lady fair . . . ,"—the melody paused after the word "stop." The device was repeated in the
succeeding line: "Stop!—You bet your life . . ." Dropped from the
short-lived show, *Strut Miss Lizzie,* "Way Down Yonder" became
known through the *Spice of 1922.*

The year saw the rise of Ager, Yellen and Bornstein, a very successful publishing firm, among whose first hits was "Lovin' Sam, the
Sheik of Alabam," written by Ager and Yellen, and introduced by
Grace Hayes in the musical *The Bunch and Judy.* Among songwriters
for whom 1922 brought the first rays of recognition, there were composer Harry Warren with "Rose of the Rio Grande"; composer
J. Fred Coots with "Time Will Tell," interpolated in *Sally, Irene and
Mary;* composer Ray Henderson, whose first collaboration with lyricist Lew Brown yielded "Georgette"; and lyricist Gus Kahn, whose
first joint effort with Walter Donaldson produced the classic tear-
jerker, "My Buddy," popularized by the ubiquitous Al Jolson.

J. Fred Coots (1897–1985) started his career as a song plugger
and then performed in vaudeville and nightclubs. He composed his
biggest hits in the thirties: "Love Letters in the Sand" (Nick and
Charles Kenny), which became the theme of George Hall and His
Orchestra; "Santa Claus Is Coming to Town," written with Haven
Gillespie, with whom he also collaborated on "You Go to My Head,"

introduced by Glen Gray and the Casa Loma Band, and adopted as his theme by Mitchell Ayres and His Orchestra. Coots achieved recognition initially in the twenties through his contributions to many Broadway shows, although he accounted for no major hits. After *Sally, Irene and Mary* (1922), his songs were heard in two editions of *Artists and Models* (1924–25), *June Days* (1925), and *A Night in Paris,* among other productions. In 1928 he produced two hits, both in films: "A Precious Thing Called Love," introduced Nancy Carroll in *Shopworn Angel,* and "I Still Get a Thrill," was included in the score for *Ripples.*

Bert Williams, regarded by many as the greatest comic of his time, died in 1922 after catching a cold that developed into pneumonia. A transfusion he received from his friend, arranger Will Vodery, was not effective in preventing his death on March 8 at the early age of forty-eight. After starting as a banjo player in minstrel shows, Williams joined forces with George Walker and the two became famous. From playing vaudeville in blackface, Williams and Walker moved successfully into black musicals, starring in *In Dahomey* (1903), *Bandana Land* (1908), and others. By the time of *Mr. Load of Koal* and the death of George Walker, Williams was more than ready for the bigtime.

In 1910 he became the first black featured in an all-white Broadway musical when Florenz Ziegfeld starred him in the *Follies* of that year despite opposition from white cast members. Thereafter, Williams starred in eight successive *Follies,* winning plaudits from fellow comics as well as from critics and audiences. His last appearance was in *Broadway Brevities of 1920,* a George Le Maire production in which he performed "The Moon Shines on the Moonshine" and "I Want to Know Where Tosti Went (When He Said Goodbye)." He recorded the former, one of more than seventy sides he cut from 1901 into 1922, all for Columbia except for eight sides made for Victor in 1901.

Although his talent was theatrical—he was a superb actor and comic—from the early days of his partnership with George Walker, Williams wrote songs that the pair used in their vaudeville appearances. His most important tune, encapsulating the role of the downer he generally played on stage, was "Nobody," with words by Alex Rogers, first performed in 1905. It became the song most identified with him, and he recorded it at least three times. Throughout his career Egbert Austin Williams, born in the British West Indies in 1874, suffered not only from the indignity of being compelled to perform in blackface but also from the prejudice rampant even in theatrical circles. "I am what I am," he wrote in an article in *American Magazine*, "not because of what I am, but in spite of it. . . . Every time I come back to America, this thing they call race prejudice follows me everywhere I go. . . ."[7]

At times, people walking along 125th Street in Harlem were amazed to see what looked like a reel of film rolling along the street. In fact, it was movie film, set in motion by employees of a movie house exhibitor who was a rival of theatre owner Leo Brecher. Brecher made projectionists go downtown to get the films shown in the many Harlem movie houses he owned. Finally, Frank Schiffman, a former schoolteacher, established a delivery service that did away with the hijacking; he thus became a Brecher theatre manager and associate. In 1922 the two took over the Harlem Opera House, just down the block on 125th Street from the Apollo Theatre. "They developed a successful format," Ted Fox observed in *Showtime at the Apollo,* "of stage comedies and musicals featuring stars and stars-to-be, among them, Al Jolson, the Four Marx Brothers, and a stock company presenting Ann Harding [the future film star]. For a time, their operation included running girlie shows at the Loew's Seventh Avenue on 124th Street and operating Harlem's Lincoln Theatre. However, the Lafayette became the capital of their theatrical empire. . . ."[8] In 1934 they took over the Apollo, making it the legendary theatre for black performers.

The shimmy was a ragtime dance whose major performers included Gilda Gray, Bea Palmer, and Ann Pennington. It involved a sinuous shaking of the hips and shoulders and was celebrated in songs like "I Wish I Could Shimmy Like My Sister Kate" and " 'Neath the

South Sea Moon," the latter a Gilda Gray show-stopper in *Ziegfeld Follies of 1922*. The frantic gyrations of the shimmy caught the tempo of the time just as the song "Runnin' Wild," by A. Harrington Gibbs (music) and Joe Grey and Leo Wood (words) mirrored the madcap exuberance of the era's young people. Popularized by Art Hickman and His Orchestra, "Runnin' Wild"—unrelated to the black show of the same name that was a hit in 1923—became a favorite of Red Nichols and His Five Pennies.

✐ 12 ✐

"Yes! We Have No Bananas"/ "Charleston"
(1923)

Songwriters have frequently drawn ideas for songs and titles from conversations, heard and overheard. It was an unknown Greek fruit peddler whose ambiguous handling of affirmatives and negatives inspired one of the most successful novelty songs of all time. His reply to a customer who asked whether he had any bananas, was the legendary, "Yes! We Have No Bananas."

As the basis of a song, the expression was brought by Irving Conn (né Cohen) and Frank Silver to Waterson, Berlin and Snyder, who rejected it along with Conn's request for a $1,000 advance. Louis Bernstein of Shapiro, Bernstein liked the idea but wanted the specimen lyric rewritten. What emerged, according to Douglas Gilbert, was "a perfect job of collaboration by virtually the entire Shapiro, Bernstein office. The late James Hanley contributed the line, 'There's a fruit store on our street,' and Elliott Shapiro offered, 'It's run by a Greek,' and Lew Brown, later of De Sylva, Brown and Henderson, finished the verse. The lyric of the second verse was touched up by

Ballard Mac Donald—everybody had a fist in it."[1] As for the music, it was "as lovely a bit of bastardy as was ever seminated in the Alley." Sigmund Spaeth, who had a radio show as a tune detective, pointed out that "its chorus melody was borrowed, consciously or unconsciously, from Handel's *Hallelujah Chorus,* the finale from *My Bonnie, I Dreamt That I Dwelt in Marble Halls* (the middle strain), and *Aunt Dinah's Quilting Party* (by way of Cole Porter's *An Old-Fashioned Garden*)."[2]

Worried about the possible infringement of the Porter bars, the composers took the song to Max Dreyfus, Porter's publisher, who refused permission for its use. But scanning the sheet, he made a slight change: "But if you do it this way, it is O.K." They returned to the Shapiro office and had Bob King smooth the melody. Then somebody recalled that the title had been used as a catch line by the cartoonist Ted Dorgan. Investigation disclosed that the title was not original even with Dorgan, and that veterans returning from the Philippines to San Francisco were "full of yarns about a fabulous fruit vendor in Manila whose pidgin English included the sentence Bernstein had accepted for the song title."[3] If one sang the original words to the several melodies from which the song was borrowed, the result would go, according to Spaeth, as follows: "Hallelujah, Bananas! Oh, bring back my Bonnie to me. I was seeing Nellie home to an old-fashioned garden; but Hallelujah! Bananas! Oh, bring back my Bonnie to me."[4]

The first successful performance was by Eddie Cantor after the writers had introduced it in a New York restaurant to a lukewarm reception. Starring in *Make It Snappy,* a revue playing Philadelphia prior to its Broadway opening, Cantor was moved to try the novelty at a matinee. Audience reaction was so strong that he not only added the zany song to the show score but made it a permanent part of his repertoire. His Victor recording, a bestseller, was one of many recorded versions. In Irving Berlin's *Music Box Revue* of the year, it was parodied à la the sextet from *Lucia di Lammermoor* in mock grand operatic style.

Derivative in title and melody, "Yes! We Have No Bananas!" became one of the biggest novelties of the decade, a song and an expression that swept the world. When F. Scott Fitzgerald met Ernest Hemingway in Paris in 1924, Hemingway's favorite expressions, according to biographer Nancy Milford, were "Parbleu!" and "Yes, we have no bananas!"[5] It was played, sung, talked about, and joked about to such an extent that it eventually led to the writing of "Yes! We Have No Bananas Blues." Foreign publishers bid for the rights, even though translating the title and retaining the ridiculous ambiguity was virtually impossible. A Viennese firm first tried a literal rendering: "Ja, Wir Haben Keinen Bananen." Good German, but it did not have the humorous impact. In despair, they settled for "Angerechnet Bananen!," which meant, "Of All Things! Bananas!"

On October 29, 1923, a black musical titled *Runnin' Wild* opened at the Colonial Theatre. It was the only show to approach the success of *Shuffle Along*. A hoofer named Elizabeth Welch danced a fast, high-stepping fox-trot, swinging her legs behind her and to the side, to a song titled "Charleston." Written by Cecil Mack (a pseudonym for Richard D. McPherson) and stride piano king James P. Johnson, "Charleston" became the dance that, in Gerald Bordman's words, "ultimately expressed and symbolized the whole gaudy era about to explode. It pronounced the beat for the 'lost generation' and liberated the whole jazz movement."[6]

It quickly elicited a commentary in "Charleston Crazy" by Porter Grainger and Bob Ricketts, recorded by Fletcher Henderson and his Orchestra on Vocalion. Clarence Williams likewise reacted quickly and with Thomas Morris and William Russell, wrote "Original Charleston Strut," recorded by Thomas Morris's Past Jazz Masters on OKeh. The fad grew apace, peaking in 1924 when a Charleston Marathon held at Roseland Ballroom in New York City lasted almost twenty-four hours. In Boston, the floor of the Pickwick Club collapsed during the dancing of the Charleston, killing fifty. In George White's *Scandals of 1925*, the popularity of the dance was documented in a performance by Tom Patricola, aided and abetted by no fewer than sixty girls.

Clarence Williams was also a collaborator on "Just Wait 'till You See My Baby Do the Charleston Dance" (1925), recorded by his

Blue Five on OKeh. In 1925, two Alley songwriters produced the tame "I'm Gonna Charleston Back to Charleston." Paul Whiteman reacted to the dance's popularity, introducing "Charlestonette" by himself and Fred Rose, later of Acuff-Rose, the country's leading publisher of country music. The following year, Louis Armstrong and Paul Barbarin wrote "Don't Forget to Mess Around When You're Doing the Charleston," which Louis later recorded with his Hot Five on OKeh. As late as 1928, Charlie Johnson's Paradise Band recorded a jazz instrumental, "Charleston Is the Best Dance After All," with music by Arthur B. Porter and Charles Johnson. The decade produced other popular dances—the Varsity Drag, Shimmy, Black Bottom, and others—but even today the Charleston remains the ineluctable symbol of the era.

1923 was a year of significant beginnings. Duke Ellington made his debut at the Kentucky Club in mid-Manhattan, a gig that led to his opening the following year at the Cotton Club, where he gained national status. The Cotton Club opened its mob-controlled doors in 1923, as did the House That Jack Built (Mills Music, Inc.), which formally inaugurated the Jack Mills Building in October 1923 on 46th Street, next door to *Variety*. (Its manager was Jimmy McHugh, later a hit songwriter whose songs were published by Mills.) In 1923 the Empress of the Blues, Bessie Smith, began her historic recording career, and Grace Moore, later of the Metropolitan Opera, made her Broadway debut in Irving Berlin's *Music Box Revue*. Her songs included "An Orange Grove in California," during which the audience was sprayed with the scent of oranges, and "Tell Me a Bedtime Story." She performed the latter sitting in an enormous wicker chair surrounded by girls in their nighties. Critic Alexander Woollcott wrote, "Hats were thrown in the air and cheers resounded from one end of Broadway to the other, and a new star was born."

The year also brought the first recordings of hillbilly music (later known as Country and Western) when OKeh Records sent a team of producers into the hills of Tennessee, Kentucky, Virginia, and the Carolinas on horseback, on mule, in Tin Lizzies, and on foot. Among the country artists they discovered were "Fiddlin'" John Carson

(1868–1949), whose record of "Old Joe Clark," and Henry Whittier Dalhart (1883–1948), whose disks of "The Wreck of the Old '97" and "The Lonesome Road Blues," each sold about a million copies. Other disks that went into the so-called Gold Record class that year were Wendell Hall's "It Ain't Gonna Rain No Mo'," Ted Weems's "Somebody Stole My Gal" and Paul Whiteman's "Linger Awhile." The Whiteman disk was a hit largely because of the banjo strumming of Mike Pingatore, a hunchback who worked with Whiteman for a quarter of a century.

Ted Weems (1901–1963), one of the most popular bandleaders of the pre–World War II era, formed his first band after leaving the University of Pennsylvania. His arrangements frequently featured whistling. He is best remembered, perhaps, for hiring as his vocalist a Pennsylvania barber, named Perry Como, who went on to enjoy a long and legendary career. The success pattern of "Somebody Stole My Gal" was repeated at least twice in Weems's career. Written in 1918 by Leo Wood, the song did not become a hit on Weems's disk until 1923. And much later, when the Big Band era was history, a disk jockey in Charlotte, North Carolina, dug Ted Weems's 1933 disk of "Heartaches" out of the files—it featured whistling by Elmo Tanner—and spun it into a 1947 hit.

Wendell Hall (1896–1969) known as the "Red-Headed Music Maker," was a multifaceted talent, an accomplished composer, author, poet, singer, guitarest, actor, and radio and TV artist. After working in vaudeville and with an orchestra, he served as a staff artist on Chicago radio station KYW, starting at $25 a week. He introduced and popularized a new instrument, the four-stringed ukulele, which originated in Hawaii. On "It Ain't Gonna Rain No Mo'," based on an old country tune, Hall accompanied himself on this exotic instrument. The Victor disk reportedly sold 2 million copies.

Considering the desperate spirit of dusk-to-dawn high jinks and high living that marked the twenties, the number of popular songs that stressed reassurance and optimism may come as something of a surprise. "It Ain't Gonna Rain No Mo' " was one such song. Others were "Waiting for the Sun to Come Out" (1920), "Pucker Up and

Whistle Till the Clouds Roll By" (1921), "Put Away a Little Ray of Sunshine for a Rainy Day" (1924), "Looking at the World Through Rose-Colored Glasses" (1926), "My Blackbirds Are Bluebirds Now" (1928), "Watching the Clouds Roll By" (1928), and "Painting the Clouds with Sunshine" (1929). It seemed as if uninhibited sex, defiance of conventions, and boisterous, self-indulgent fun were all part of an effort to escape premonition of disaster.

Some of these "optimistic" songs came from revues, of which there seemed to be a plethora in 1923: *Greenwich Village Follies, George White's Scandals, Shuberts' Passing Show, Earl Carroll's Vanities, Shuberts' Artists and Models, Topics of 1923, Nifties of 1923,* and looking forward—but not for long—*Fashions of 1924.*

Some songs go through stages before they achieve a form that appeals to the public. Rudolf Friml's "Chansonette" went through three incarnations in seventeen years before it emerged as a hit. In its original form it was a piano teaching piece, titled "Chanson" and published, not by a Broadway publisher, but by a major "classical" house, G. Schirmer. In 1923 musicologist, historian, and tune detective Sigmund Spaeth urged Friml to make his teaching piece a pop song. Spaeth was joined in the undertaking by two people, neither one of whom seemed a natural collaborator for Friml: Dailey Paskman, a minstrel show buff, and ace lyricist Irving Caesar. The revamped "Chanson" emerged with words and the title "Chansonette." The melody was so attractive that Paul Whiteman included it in his Aeolian Hall concert of February 12, 1924, under the heading "Adaptation of Standard Selections to Dance Rhythm." But it was not until 1937 that it finally became a major hit. In that year, Rudolf Friml's debut American operetta sensation of 1912, *The Firefly,* was made into a film. It featured a new song, "Donkey Serenade," with music by Herbert Stothart and lyrics by Chet Forrest and Robert Wright.

Among the most popular songs of 1923 was "Bambalina," from the musical *Wildflower,* the season's biggest hit, and the rhythm ballad that brought Vincent Youmans recognition as a composer. A song about an eccentric country fiddler who delighted in confusing square dancers by halting suddenly at unexpected moments, it made use of a short attractive melodic phrase repeated several times over changing harmony—a device that became characteristic of a number of Youmans's hits, including "I Want to Be Happy" and "Tea for Two."

"Barney Google," another 1923 hit, was a novelty written for Eddie Cantor by Con Conrad, but it became an Olsen and Johnson vaudeville vehicle when lyricist Billy Rose persuaded them to use a routine in which they pranced up and down the aisles of the theatre in the getup of a horse while another actor, made up like the cartoon character Barney Google, played the jockey. That year, Con Conrad and Billy Rose also accounted for a blues-oriented ballad popularized by the "Last of the Red Hot Mamas," Sophie Tucker: "You've Got to See Mamma Ev'ry Night (Or You Can't See Mamma at All)."

Three musicals were singled out in *Variety's* columns. Although the *Ziegfeld Follies* of that year was regarded as a "step down" by some, the usually acidulous George Jean Nathan's encomium of the series in *Judge* magazine concluded, "It has set a revue standard for the world. . . ." The piece was reprinted in a *Variety* advertisement captioned "Ziegfeld and His Follies Win International Reputation."[7] The *Music Box Revue* of that year also won a rave from *Variety:* "Opulence and grandeur, the novel and the beautiful, creations that are original and wonderful . . . true of the first two [revues] and applicable to the third . . ."[8] The Shuberts' *Artist and Models* elicited a tribute to its "rawness." Observing that the girls were bare from the waist up and thinly covered below, *Variety* characterized the show as "the smartest, fastest, dirtiest revue in American history."[9]

Among the songs introduced in 1923 by the popular vaudeville singing duo Van and Schenck, was "Who's Sorry Now?," a weepy hit revived in 1957 by Connie Francis at the start of her singing career. The melody was by Ted Snyder, and the words were by Bert Kalmar and Harry Ruby. It was their first hit, a productive collaboration that lasted a quarter of a century. When the partnership was severed by Kalmar's death in 1947, Ruby, who outlived his collaborator by more than twenty-five years, virtually stopped writing.

They were a colorful pair. Both were born in New York City and both nursed ambitions that had nothing to do with songwriting. Bert Kalmar (1884–1947), ran away from home at the age of ten to become a magician in a tent show, and never gave up the desire to be a performing magician. Harry Ruby (1893–1974) developed in his youth an overpowering love of baseball, and throughout his life would have preferred, in the words of a fan, "to hit homers rather than write the nation's hits."[10] Max Wilk tells the story of a lunch-time discussion in the MGM commissary in which Joseph L. Mankiewicz said to Ruby, "Let's assume you're driving along a mountain road. You see a precipitous cliff with a sheer six-hundred-foot drop. Two men are hanging there, desperate. One of them is Joe DiMaggio, the other is your father. You have time to save only one of them. Which one do you save?" Ruby replied instantly: "Are you kidding! My father never hit over .218 in his life!"[11]

Kalmar and Ruby met when the latter went to work as a song plugger for Kalmar and Puck, a small publishing firm financed by income from Kalmar's vaudeville earnings. Working with his wife, Kalmar drew as much as $1,000 a week. Ruby, a self-taught pianist, had previously worked as a staff pianist with Gus Edwards's publishing company and as a song plugger for Harry Von Tilzer and Jerome H. Remick, where George Gershwin was also employed in the same capacity. When Bert Kalmar hurt his leg in a backstage accident in Washington, D.C.—President Woodrow Wilson, an avid vaudeville fan, reportedly attended the performance—Ruby got him a job as a songwriter at Waterson, Berlin and Snyder, where he was then employed.

One of the first songs Kalmar wrote—it was during a Hawaiian fad—was "Hello, Hawaii, How Are You?" (1915), in collaboration with Edgar Leslie to a melody by Jean Schwartz. With Edgar Leslie, he also wrote "Oh, What a Pal Was Mary" (1919), which reportedly sold over a million copies. Among the first songs Kalmar and Ruby wrote as a team was with Irving Berlin: "I'm a Vamp from East

Broadway," which Fanny Brice turned into a standing-ovation number in the *Ziegfeld Follies of 1920*. Their early collaborations included songs for Belle Baker's vaudeville act. In 1923, the year of
their first big hit, they were also successful in writing their first
Broadway show, *Helen of Troy, New York*, a satire with a book by
Marc Connelly and—writing his *first* musical—George S. Kaufman.
It ran for 191 performances but yielded no hits, as was also the case
with the six musicals that followed, except for *Good Boy*, one of two
shows they wrote in 1928. A feature of *Good Boy* was the pip-squeak
singing by the "boop-a-doop girl," Helen Kane, of "I Wanna Be
Loved by You," which became the show's outstanding song and a
hit. In 1928, too, Kalmar and Ruby scored *Animal Crackers*, a zany
Marx Brothers musical, which yielded "Hooray for Captain Spal-
ding," the role played by Groucho Marx. Groucho adopted the song
as the theme of both his radio and TV shows.

When Tin Pan Alley songwriters trekked West with the advent of
the talkies, Kalmar and Ruby were among the first to join Fox films,
for whom they wrote two of their biggest hits. "Nevertheless" appeared in an inconsequential 1931 film, *I'm So Afraid of You*, but
it became a favorite of both Rudy Vallee and Bing Crosby, who
helped make it a bestseller. Before "Nevertheless," Kalmar and Ruby
wrote "Three Little Words," a mammoth hit and the song that became the title of their biopic when it was made in 1950. "Three Little
Words" was featured in the Amos 'n' Andy film *Check and Double
Check*, sung by Bing Crosby, who was accompanied by Duke Ellington and his Orchestra. It also was popularized by Rudy Vallee. When
Three Little Words was made in 1950 with Fred Astaire and Red
Skelton playing Harry Ruby and Bert Kalmar, Vera Allen and Debbie
Reynolds were the female leads. Vera's songs were dubbed for her
by Anita Ellis, and Helen Kane did her baby-talk version of "I
Wanna Be Loved by You" for Debbie Reynolds. The film brought
a revival of "Nevertheless" in hit recordings by the Mills Bros. and
Paul Weston and his Orchestra. The following year (1951), Kalmar
and Ruby enjoyed their last hit, "A Kiss to Build a Dream On"
(posthumous for Kalmar), from the film *The Strip*.

A proliferation of the blues was audible throughout 1923, with jazz-men, blues singers, and Tin Pan Alley songwriters all contributing. King Oliver made his celebrated disks of "Canal Street Blues" and "Dippermouth," while Fletcher Henderson presented "Dicty Blues," and the New Orleans Rhythm Kings recorded "Farewell Blues" and Jelly Roll Morton's "London Blues." Among blues artists, Ida Cox was represented by "Graveyard Dream Blues," Alberta Hunter by "Down South Blues," Ethel Waters by "Kind Lovin' Blues," Clara Smith by "Every Woman's Blues," and Sara Martin by Clarence Williams's "Sugar Blues," which became a perennial as a result of Clyde McCoy's *wa-wa* trumpet version recorded in 1936.

But with the tremendous popularity enjoyed by "Yes! We Have No Bananas" and "Barney Google," among other nonsense novel-ties, Ira Gershwin's flippant verse seems not inappropriate: "The rhythm is great/the beat immense/so who cares if it doesn't make sense."[12]

✑ 13 ✑

"Rhapsody and Romance in Blue"
(1924)

From the standpoint of popular music, no event of the 1920s, except for the introduction of the talkies, approaches in historic importance and musical significance the "Experiment in Modern Music" presented by Paul Whiteman on February 12, 1924. The story of *Rhapsody in Blue,* the work that stunned the Aeolian Hall audience and shook up the music world—classical as well as pop—has been told in Chapter Four. But the goal of the concert that introduced Gershwin's masterpiece and the overall impact of Whiteman's experiment warrant a fuller examination.

The program was limited neither to popular nor jazz selections. Of the twenty-four pieces, ten, in addition to the *Rhapsody,* fell outside the "popular" range, including the closing selection Elgar's *Pomp and Circumstance,* adaptations of Logan's "Pale Moon," MacDowell's "To a Wild Rose," and Friml's "Chansonette," plus a "Suite of Serenades"—Spanish, Chinese, Cuban and Oriental—by Victor Herbert. This signifies that Whiteman was addressing himself not to pop listeners alone but also to those who would ordinarily attend a concert in what was, after all, a classical hall. Whiteman went

142

so far as to invite music critics to rehearsals and wined and dined them afterward.

The pop material included blues ("Livery Stable Blues" and "Limehouse Blues"); a comedy selection ("Yes! We Have No Bananas"); ragtime piano pieces ("Kitten on the Keys" and "Nickel in the Slot") by Zez Confrey; a group of Irving Berlin songs ("Alexander's Ragtime Band," "A Pretty Girl Is Like a Melody," and "Orange Blossoms in California"); a pop ballad ("Whispering"). "Livery Stable Blues" was presented along with a modernized "Mama Loves Papa" as a demonstration of how jazz had matured. "Yes! We Have No Bananas" was paired with Thomas's *The Carnival of Venice* to suggest that humor was not the sole prerogative of popular music. Berlin's numbers appeared under the heading "Semi-Symphonic Arrangements of Popular Music," and in a turnaround, the compositions of MacDowell, Friml, and Logan were presented under the heading, "Adaptation of Standard Selections to a Dance Rhythm."

Retrospectively, Whiteman appeared to have had a double purpose: to gain respect for jazz (or what was thought of as jazz) among the "longhairs"—audience as well as critics—and also to gain respect for himself and his band, and in turn, for dance band musicians. Eventually his goals were realized, although it is doubtful whether he proved that afternoon that the boisterous female known as jazz was a "lady." Unquestionably, what saved the February 12 enterprise, and gave it historic and musical stature, was the *Rhapsody*. Even though the minions of the classical establishment were reserved, captious, or critical in their reaction, the originality, vitality, fresh sound, and exciting rhythms of the Gershwin work immediately won strong adherents—and eventually captivated the world of music.

Irving Berlin's role in the music scene of 1924 was larger than his representation on the Whiteman program. At his Music Box Theater, he presented the last of his *Music Box Revues,* which included such stars as Fanny Brice, Bobby Clark, Grace Moore, Oscar Shaw, and Clark and McCullough. A featured song was "All Alone," a hit before its interpolation in the show. This sterling ballad, together with

"What'll I Do?"—a hit in the preceding *Music Box Revue*—attained a kind of notoriety that exceeded their appeal as tunes. Whether Berlin or others—most likely the latter—were the source, it became widely known that Berlin was dating and wooing Ellen Mackay, the daughter of the head of Postal Telegraph. She was Catholic and was on the Social Register; he was an immigrant, a Russian Jew from the Lower East Side. It was no secret that Papa thoroughly disapproved of the burgeoning romance. Berlin's two ballads poignantly expressed his distress. Curiously, for the man still known as the "King of Ragtime," both songs were in waltz time. Apparently Berlin found the old-style format and tonality more expressive of the feeling he was trying to communicate than the newer sounds and rhythms. At the height of the vogue for blues, hot jazz, and the Charleston, "All Alone" and "What'll I Do?" were two of the biggest hits of the year, and became two of the biggest standards, recorded and revived, in all of popular music. "What'll I Do?" was interpolated in the *Music Box Revue of 1923–24,* apparently to bolster a weak score.

With his romance still foundering, Berlin again gave expression to his unhappiness in "Always" and "Remember," both hits in 1925 and both again waltzes. (At an Algonquin Round Table luncheon, playwright George S. Kaufman scoffed at "Always," suggesting that the first line be changed to "I'll be loving you, Thursday.") "Remember" became one of Ruth Etting's big request numbers, while "Always" became the property of Ellen Mackay when she and Berlin were married in 1926. That year Berlin wrote "At Peace with the World," bringing the song cycle to a close. Autobiography has become a commonplace with the advent of rock, and it frequently was a facet of the blues. But the Berlin song cycle of 1923–26 may well have been the first if not the only instance of the use of popular song as an instrument for expressing and communicating personal problems and feelings.

1924 was a year of smash operettas—*Rose Marie* and *The Student Prince*—and of giant musicals, *Lady Be Good* and *No, No, Nanette.* It was the year Leo the Lion made his roaring debut in films. It was a year in which the mah-jongg fad gave way to crossword puzzles, a craze that led to the rise of the publishing firm of Simon and Schuster. A music publisher, Jerry Vogel, who later became a specialist in securing copyright renewals, was then involved with Plaza Music Company, an imprint established by Simon and Schuster, presumably to test the market. It was the call for copies at Plaza Music, Vogel told Sigmund Spaeth, that led to a huge printing and a strong ad campaign.

The story of *The Cross-Word Puzzle Book* actually seems to have its beginnings with an aunt of Richard Simon, who wanted to give a relative, an addict of crossword puzzles then appearing regularly in the *New York World*, a gift of a book of such puzzles. Discovering on inquiry that no such book existed, Simon, who was about to launch a publishing firm with M. Lincoln Schuster (the staff would consist of one secretary) suggested they publish one. They turned naturally to the three people who concocted the *World's* puzzles. Despite discouragement from booksellers, they had a book on the market by mid-April 1924. Appearing with a pencil attached, the first crossword puzzle book became an overnight bestseller. Off to a regal start, Simon and Schuster had difficulty keeping up with the demand. The fad rapidly grew to such proportions that the Baltimore and Ohio Railroad placed dictionaries on all its mainline trains.

A certain number of songs throughout the history of popular music have become great standards only after slow starts. One example is "The Man I Love," which began a journey in 1924 that eventually made it one of the most enduring of George Gershwin's elegant show tunes. Yet it was never heard in a Broadway show. Written for the musical, *Lady Be Good*, it was introduced during the pre-Broadway tryout by Adele Astaire. Because it ostensibly slowed the action, it was dropped from the show when it opened on Broadway. It received its premiere in 1925 when Gershwin accompanied Eva Gauthier in a concert. With a revised lyric and retitled "The Girl I Love," it was reintroduced by Morton Downey during out-of-town tryouts of the 1927 version of *Strike Up the Band*, but failed to open in New York. It was next tried by Marilyn Miller in *Rosalie* (1928), and again was dropped. When a new version of *Strike Up the Band* opened in New York in 1930, it was felt that the song was too widely known to be used in the show.

Thus, "The Man I Love" began its life as a separate, printed song. The next stop in its journey was England. Lady Mountbatten, visiting the United States, secured an autographed copy, which led to a presentation by the Berkeley Square Orchestra. British dance bands quickly took it up and it crossed the Channel to become a favorite in Paris, and at last returned to the United States, where it became a standard without ever having been a hit. Among its earliest American exponents was Helen Morgan. In 1946 it became the title of a motion picture in which it was sung by Ida Lupino, hardly an outstanding singer, and used as a recurrent theme on the soundtrack.

But *Lady Be Good* did contain two important Fred Astaire dance numbers. In "The Half Of It Dearie Blues" Astaire, for the first time, performed a dance without his customary partner, sister Adele. More significant was "Fascinating Rhythm," a show-stopper with a tricky rhythm and offbeat accents reminiscent of Zez Confrey's "Stumbling." In his autobiography Fred Astaire explains how Gershwin suddenly became the song's choreographer. Fred and Adele were stuck for "a climax wow step to get us off," until one rehearsal when, after they had been struggling for days to devise a sock finish, Gershwin "stepped from his piano and did a dance step" in which "he wanted us to continue doing the last step, which started stage center, and sustain it as we traveled to the side, continuing until we were out of sight. The step was a complicated precision rhythmic thing in which we kicked out simultaneously as we crossed back and forth in front of each other with arm pulled and heads back. . . ."[1] It proved, as Astaire wrote and the critic of the *Herald-Tribune* confirmed, "a knockout applause getter": "When at 9:15 they sang and danced "Fascinating Rhythm," the callous Broadwayites cheered them as if their favorite halfback had planted the ball behind the goal posts after an 80-yard run. Seldom has it been our pleasure to witness such a heartfelt, spontaneous and so deserved a tribute."[2]

The song became so vital to the show that it served, as Ira Gershwin explained in his *Lyrics on Several Occasions*, "to wind up the plot and relationships." At the time this was done "almost *de rigueur* in the finale" by setting new lyrics to one of the principal songs."[3] In *Lady Be Good*, four couples, each formerly at odds, reunited at 11:00 P.M. each even to *Fascinating Rhythm*, with each couple singing a slightly different set of words to the title "Fascinating Wedding," and the four men joining in unison to sing the last eight bars.

1924 was a most rewarding year for bandleader Isham Jones, who scored a succession of hits with the music he wrote for "It Had to Be You," "I'll See You in My Dreams," and "Spain." The lyrics for all three were written by Gus Kahn (1886–1941), one of the most prolific lyricists of the twenties and thirties. Born in Coblenz, Germany, Kahn was brought to this country by his parents when he was five, and was raised in Chicago. He began writing songs while in high school, collaborated in 1914 on "The Good Ship Mary Ann" with Grace Le Boy, who became his wife. One of his earliest hits was "I'll Say She Does," written for *Sinbad* (1918) with Bud De Sylva, and released by Jerome H. Remick, his publisher for five years. With Richard A. Whiting, he wrote "Ain't We Got Fun" in 1921, and with Walter Donaldson, in 1922, "My Buddy" and "Carolina in the Morning," and in 1925, "Yes Sir, That's My Baby." In time, he collaborated with virtually every top pop composer of the twenties and thirties, producing one of the longest lists of hits of those years.[4]

Of all the hits of 1924, the strangest was a record released October 3 on which "The Prisoner's Song" was backed with "The Wreck of the Old '97." Strange, because it was a hillbilly hit by a singer who was not a hillbilly and because it was the biggest selling record of the pre-electric era, aggregating a whopping six to seven million Victor disks, a figure no pop record of the twenties approached. The disk was the work of a man who called himself Vernon Dalhart, a concoction made from the names of two towns near his childhood home of Jefferson, Texas, where he was born Marion T. Slaughter on April 6, 1883. After receiving a thorough musical education, he went to New York, where he became a member of the Century Opera Company. A tenor who specialized in light opera, he frequently performed in Gilbert and Sullivan productions. He began making records in 1916, but a fantastic change in his career occurred when he heard a recording of "The Wreck of the '97" by its composer Henry Whittier, a Virginia mountain musician who played mouth harp and guitar and sang through his nose. Copying Whittier's words from the old OKeh disk, Slaughter recorded "The Wreck of the Old '97" for Edison Records. Coupled with "The Prisoner's Song (If I Had the Wings of an Angel)" for a Victor disk, it became *the* biggest seller of the year.

Authorship of "The Prisoner's Song" is credited to Guy Massey, a man who presumably did spend time in jail. But Sigmund Spaeth reports the claim that Nathaniel Shilkret, then a Victor musical director, was "largely responsible for the finished product."[5] Spaeth also insists that the tune of "The Wreck of the Old '97" was taken boldly from Henry C. Work's "The Ship That Never Returned." But the lyricist of "The Wreck," which occurred near Danville, Virginia, in 1903, remains a mystery, even though Victor advertised for information regarding the text.

One of the pop hits of the year was "There's Yes, Yes in Your Eyes" by Cliff Friend and Joseph H. Santly, later the co-owner of a very successful publishing company, Santly-Joy Music. The ballad was one of the few songs which led to a successful plagiarism suit. The little-known plaintiffs based their claim on "Without You, the World Doesn't Seem the Same." Plagiarism suits based on similarity of melody seldom are won; through the research of musicologists who serve the industry, publishers are generally able to present even earlier versions of the same set of notes—versions so old they are in the public domain. In the suit on "There's Yes, Yes in Your Eyes," however, it developed that Joseph Santly was not only familiar with the claimant's song but had actually been involved in plugging it. The plaintiffs were thus able to prove access, one of the reasons that music publishers refuse to accept unsolicited manuscripts sent through the mail by unknown songwriters. Unable to deny access, the writers of "There's Yes, Yes in Your Eyes" lost the suit. But, Sigmund Spaeth tells us, through the cleverness of the defendant's lawyers,

Nathan Burkan,"[6] a very able copyright attorney, damages were held down to a minimum of $250.

Two hits of 1924 were the work of Gene Austin, a soft-voiced singer who did not become widely known until four years later. In 1924 he collaborated with Roy Bergere on "How Come You Do Me Like You Do?" and with Jimmy McHugh on "When My Sugar Walks Down the Street, All the Little Birdies Go Tweet Tweet-Tweet." An active vaudevillian and recording artist, he introduced both songs. The latter, first presented at the Cotton Club, eventually was featured by and identified with Phil Harris and his Orchestra. But Austin's identification was with "My Blue Heaven," a ballad introduced in vaudeville in 1924 by the writer of the lyrics, George Whiting, and reintroduced three years later, becoming a smash bestseller with Austin's disk.

One of the best composers of jazz standards, Spencer Williams (1889–1965), scored in 1924 with the memorable (despite its long title) "Everybody Loves My Baby but My Baby Don't Love Nobody but Me," in collaboration with Jack Palmer. The first recording was by Spencer's brother Clarence and his Blue Five, with Louis Armstrong on trumpet. The catchy rhythm ballad quickly became a favorite of Ruth Etting. Spencer left America for Paris the following year to write material for Josephine Baker and returned to Paris again in 1932 with Fats Waller for a long stay. In between visits he accounted for such jazz hits as "I've Found a New Baby" (1926), "Basin Street Blues" (1928), "Royal Garden Blues," "Shim-Me-Sha-Wabble," "Tishomingo Blues," and others. In an effort to avoid *moderato*, the most common tempo marking on sheet music of the twenties, Williams indulged in such inventive directions as "Tempo di weary," "Tempo disappointo," "Tempo di Sadness," and other combinations.

When Paul Whiteman played "Limehouse Blues" on his Aeolian program, it was a rather recent import, having arrived in America with *Andre Charlot's Revue*. Featured in the musical were three stars who thereafter appeared in many American productions: comedienne Beatrice Lillie, dancer and singer Jack Buchanan, and actress and singer Gertrude Lawrence.

On the evening of Whiteman's concert, Louis Armstrong was play- ing at Roseland with the Fletcher Henderson Band. Alternating with Henderson for a time was Vincent Lopez with a standard nine-piece dance band. Within a few days of the Whiteman concert, three Chi- cago musicians made a recording, at the suggestion of bandleader Isham Jones, of "Blue Blues" b/w "Arkansas Blues" that became an enormous hit. Led by Red McKenzie and calling themselves the Mound City Blues Blowers, they played banjo and two unconven- tional instruments: a comb wrapped in tissue paper and a kazoo, the latter a toy horn whose tissue paper "reed" was activated by hum- ming into the mouthpiece. Although they played hot jazz, the record was sold "as a novelty, and high society found them amusing," Mar- shall Stearns reports. He continues: "The Blues Blowers played the Palace, toured Europe and became the darlings of society people who didn't know one tune from another but were thrilled by the freak in- struments."[8] Although more authentic jazz was being played by King Oliver, Fletcher Henderson, Bennie Moten and others, "the Blues Blowers had the distribution and the attention of the public. Their influence accordingly was everywhere. Out in Spokane, 20-year-old Bing Crosby was spellbound and set to work to copy them."[9]

1924 was a "hot" year in jazz and the blues. When Bessie Smith played a theatre on the South Side of Chicago in May, there nearly was a riot. In 1924 Hoagy Carmichael heard the Wolverines with Bix Beiderbecke. "Just four notes . . . but Bix didn't blow them— he hit 'em like a mallet hits a chime—and his tone, the richness . . . I got up from the piano and staggered over and fell on the daven- port. . . ."

Paul Whiteman was not the only bandleader concerned with gain- ing recognition for jazz and with proving that it was an art form. In- deed another symphonic jazz concert took place the same year as the Aeolian Hall program. This concert, which has generally escaped the notice of historians—rightfully, perhaps—occurred on November 23, 1924. It was arranged by William Morris, a top impresario, was given at the Metropolitan Opera House, and featured the band of Vincent Lopez, who prepared by taking conducting lessons at $50 an hour from the Met's famous conductor, Bodansky. "To match Paul Whiteman's coup in signing Gershwin," Lopez wrote in his autobiography, emphasizing both the parallelism and competitive motivation of his concert, "I bought original jazz compositions from the leading jazz composers. W. C. Handy, whose *St. Louis Blues* I helped to introduce, refused to take a cent for his contribution."[10]

Apart from Handy's not being a jazz composer—though the line between jazz and the blues was surely blurred in those days—the work he created, "Evolution of the Blues," with the collaboration of arranger Joseph Nussbaum, had not the originality, the freshness, nor the melodic inventiveness of the *Rhapsody*. Insofar as one can judge from the program notes, it was "a free-form fantasy" or "tone poem," tracing the growth of blues from profane and sacred song, and interweaving material from Handy's famous blues, "St. Louis," "Memphis," "Beale Street," and "Harlem."

There was also another blues on the program, again composed by a respected musician, Fletcher Henderson. "The Meanest Blues," with orchestral development by Lopez and Katzmann, emphasized instrumental comedy effects. "A Jazz Wedding" by arranger J. Bodewalt Lampe also included "a characteristic wealth of humorous detail." (Jazz was associated at that time with funny sounds, animal as well as instrumental, as in the ODJB's "Livery Stable Blues.")

Like Whiteman, Lopez programmed a limited number of popular tunes: "Indian Love Song" from Friml's *Rose-Marie*, Vincent Youmans's "Wildflower," Ray Henderson's "Follow the Swallow," Irving Berlin's "All Alone," and Ted Snyder's "In a Little Rendezvous." The three encores listed on the program were also popular songs: "June Night," "Why Live a Lie," and "Sally Lou." The major portion of the twenty selections exploited exotic tone colors: Russian (Rachmaninoff and Rimsky-Korsakov); Indian ("By the Waters of Minnetonka" and "Indian Love Lyrics"); Chinese ("Pell Street"); Mexican ("Cielito Lindo")—all in orchestral developments by Lopez and Polla.

There were two oddball items on the program. The accomplished harmonica player, Borrah Minnevitch, whom Lopez discovered demonstrating the instrument in the Wurlitzer music store, performed an "Original Jazz Fantasy" by Rubecalle but also "My Heart at Thy Sweet Voice" from the opera *Samson et Dalila*. According to the program notes, these numbers proved "that the mouth harmonica, in the hands of an artist, has a valid claim to be taken seriously as a musical instrument."[11] The other curiosity was a soprano, Yvette Rugel, singing "If Love Were All," a ballad, by Hugo Frey, a good arranger and musician but hardly "a leading exponent of the jazz genre,"[12] as he was described in the program.

The mixed character of the undertaking was underscored most, perhaps, by Lopez's adding Xavier Cugat, soon to become the Rumba King, to his violin section because Cugat pestered him to be included. The highest praise of the concert by a critic was the statement by Olin Downes of the *New York Times:* "It demonstrates the real promise in American music!"[13] It is the only comment that Lopez includes in his autobiography. Nevertheless, Lopez was able to capitalize on the Metropolitan Opera House program that winter with a jazz concert tour through the northeast, booked jointly by William Morris and Sol Hurok. Serious music critics turned out and, according to Lopez, "the inevitable comparisons with Whiteman weren't bad."[14] In fact the reviewer of the *Boston Transcript* wrote, "The crowd was as large and as enthusiastic as that which previously turned out to greet his jazz contemporary, Paul Whiteman. The Lopez orchestra is intrinsically a better orchestra than Mr. Whiteman's, and Mr. Lopez is a firmer, more disciplined conductor than Mr. Whiteman. . . ."[15] Considering the top-notch jazzmen who were in the Whiteman orchestra, this is a strange evaluation indeed.

VINCENT LOPEZ'S "JAZZ" CONCERT, METROPOLITAN OPERA HOUSE
November 23, 1924

Part One

1. RUSSIAN FANTASY   LOPEZ-POLLA*
   This fantasy suite, with the Rachmaninoff C sharp minor "Prelude"

as an introduction presents well-known themes, among them Cui's "Orientale" and "The Volga Boat Song" in quasi-symphonic development. Especially interesting are: the dialogue development of the theme from Rimsky-Korsakow's "Song of India" between soprano saxophone, oboe and bass; and the rhythmic treatment of the brilliant climaxing "March of the Sirdar," by Ippolito-Ivanow.

* The orchestral development of the numbers of this programme has been carried out according to Mr. Lopez's creative indications with regard to instrumentation, dynamics, color and effect.

2. BY THE WATERS OF MINNETONKA   Thurlaw Lieurance
(*Orchestral Development by Lopez-Polla*)
An orchestral version of this "Indian Love Song" by the well-known exploiter of the aboriginal melody of the Yellowstone region, in which the themes of the original have been subjected to special inflections of rhythm and tone color to stress their interesting primitive appeal.

3. BIBLICAL SUITE   Vladimir Heifetz
(*Orchestral Development by Lopez-Nussbaum*)
A suite in three movements—1. Near the Ruined Wall of the Temple; 2. The Mysterious Moment; 3. Hebrew Dance—based on ancient traditional biblical melodies, whose fine themes admit of an especially sonorous orchestral development.

4. INDIAN LOVE SONG   Rudolf Friml
(From "Rose-Marie")
(*Orchestral Development by Lopez-Polla*)
A specific orchestral development by Lopez-Polla, of an outstanding lyric number of one of the most popular of musical comedies now running in New York. There are interesting effects secured in the strings and double-reeds.

5. "THE MELODY THAT MADE YOU MINE"   W. C. Polla
(*Orchestral Development by Lopez-Polla*)
An orchestral version of a popular ballad waltz, in which the trumpet appears in the solo rôle, playing between B flat and G above the staff.

6. PELL STREET   Emerson Whithorne
From "New York Days and Nights." Op. 40
(*Orchestral Development by Lopez-Nussbaum*)
"Pell Street" is the third number of the virile suite for orchestra by this gifted American modernist. The composer has outlined its programme: It is night in Pell Street. An ancient Chinese melody, "The Fifteen Bunches of Blossoms," floats from a fan-tan house, where an old Chinaman, swaying as he rocks his bow, plays the exotic tune on

his single-stringed fiddle. All the clever, colorful exotic possibilities of the composition have been kept in mind in this specific orchestral version.

7. ECCENTRIC   R. Robinson
> (*Orchestral Development by Lopez-Nussbaum*)

"Eccentric" (A Pure "Jazz" Fantasy) is an eloquent exposition of the rhythm and color effects possible in a genuinely imaginative handling of "jazz" values. Its "jazz breaks"—those two measure rests in the melody progression which the accompanying instruments "fill in" with a piquant mosaic of varied rhythm—are especially characteristic.

8. "WILD FLOWER"   Vincent Youmans
> (*Concert Paraphrase for Piano Solo with Accompaniment*
> *by Vincent Lopez*)
> The Transcriber at the Piano

A brilliant and effective concert paraphrase of Vincent Youmans' attractive original, in which the special technique of piano syncopation and tone color is exploited in a series of contrasting variations, with an orchestral background.

9. FANTASY ON THEMES   Arthur Sullivan
> From Gilbert and Sullivan's "H. M. S. 'Pinafore'"
> (*Orchestral Development by Lopez-Lampe*)

A "comedy" fantasy on themes which lend themselves to humorous instrumental effect. In them the principals in the comic opera, supported by an instrumental chorus, appear in solo rôles: the Captain (piano); Sweet Little Buttercup (cornet burlesque); Admiral (trombone); and Dick Dead Eye (baritone).

10. THE EVOLUTION OF THE "BLUES"   W. C. Handy
>   and Joseph Nussbaum
> (*Orchestral Development by Lopez-Nussbaum*)

This "symphonietta in 'jazz' style," as it has been called, presents in a free-form fantasy the evolution of that specifically American negro emotional quality known as "the blues." The composers have been notably successful—after a beginning in which the tribal drums of jungle villages beat—in presenting in a brilliant, stepwise progression the birth of "the blues" out of the profane song (negro tribal dance and occupational melody) and sacred song (the slave-day spirituals). These "blues"—the negro character combinations of a surface melody of carefree happiness on a ground bass of sorrow and melancholy— have been symphonically traced through their evolution in this tone-poem. It is a work rich in effect, and old negro spirituals and the famous "Blues"—Memphis, St. Louis, Beale Street, Harlem—are harmoniously interwoven in its pages to justify the title.

Part Two

11. SCHEHEREZADE   N. RIMSKY-KORSAKOW
     (*Orchestral Development by Lopez-Polla*)
Themes from the different movements of the Russian composer's symphonic poem have been elaborated in free-form style and in a thoroughly symphonic manner, with effects of sonority peculiar to the special orchestral composite presenting the fantasy.

12. CIELITO LINDO (BEAUTIFUL SKY)   MEXICAN FOLK SONG
     (*Orchestral Development by Lopez-Polla*)
A Spanish ballad in tango-rhythm presented in a novel orchestral color-scheme.

13. "FOLLOW THE SWALLOW"   R. HENDERSON
     (*Orchestral Development by Lopez-Polla*)
A popular song of the day in an original orchestral working-out of its rhythm and color possibilities.

14. TWO SOLOS FOR HARMONICA
     a. "My Heart at Thy Sweet Voice" from S. Saint-Saëns' "Samson et Dalila"
     b. Rubealle Original Jazz Fantasy
         Soloist* MR. BORRAH MINEVITCH

    * These numbers are introduced to prove that the mouth-harmonica, in the hands of an artist, has a valid claim to be taken seriously as a musical instrument.

15. "THE MEANEST BLUES"   FLETCHER HENDERSON
     (*Orchestral Development by Lopez-Katsmann*)
This, a typical "jazz" number, is a composition of the genuine negro "jazz" variety, with all the instrumental "comedy" effects (clarinet *glissandi*, melodious wails, crooning, reproaches, insinuations, chuckles, etc., on the part of the other reeds and brasses) which, if spontaneous, as in this instance, are so unquestionably piquant.

16. A STUDY IN SYNCOPATION   HENRY SOUVAINE
     (*Orchestral Development by Lopez-Vodery*)
A brilliant orchestral two-minute-and-a-half "review" of practically all the forms of syncopation in colorful sequence.

17. a. "ALL ALONE   IRVING BERLIN
    b. IF LOVE WERE ALL   HUGO FREY

Ballad YVETTE RUGEL, *Soprano*
A new song by this leading exponent of the "jazz" genre, with an orchestral accompaniment by Lopez.

18. "INDIAN LOVE LYRICS" AMY WOODFORD-FINDEN
    (*Orchestral Development by Lopez-Polla*)
The popular song-cycle by Amy Woodford-Finden in a free orchestral transcription whose instrumentation brings out its exotic color with major effect.

19. "IN A LITTLE RENDEZVOUS" TED SNYDER
    (*Orchestral Development by Lopez-Polla*)
A light, popular number which allows the introduction of characteristic effects in color and rhythm somewhat outside the beaten track.

20. A JAZZ WEDDING J. BODEWALT LAMPE
    (*Orchestral Development by Lopez-Lampe*)
A programmatic tone poem on a miniature scale: the Richard Strauss "Domestica" in a jazz variant. With a characteristic wealth of humorous detail we have note-pictures of bride and groom, their wedding, the departure on the honeymoon (amid the realistic tonal patter of showered rice and old shoes) and—a year later, the introduction of the baby whose cries are convincingly voiced by the trap drummer.

Encores

JUNE NIGHT ABEL BAER
WHY LIVE A LIE WOLFE GILBERT
SALLY LOU HUGO FREY

Chickering Pianos Ampico Recording
Okeh Records Martin Instruments

∽ 14 ∽
"Tea for Two"
(1925)

The same year that Tennessee was the scene of the Scopes trial—in which a teacher was convicted of teaching Evolution—Florida enjoyed a wild real estate boom, Kentucky was in the news because of Floyd Collins who died in the media and in an underground cave, and Manhattan was celebrated in a stunning song by Rodgers and Hart.

The smartly and internally rhymed song made its appearance, as did the pair, in the 1925 *Garrick Gaieties*, a lively, literate revue produced by the "junior members" of the Theatre Guild. Rodgers and Hart quickly followed the *Gaieties* with *Dearest Enemy*, a musical that gave us the rangy ballad, "Here in My Arms" (an octave and a fifth) and the "unique, bittersweet cynicism"[1] of Hart's tart lyrics. The *New York Times* immediately compared the pair to Gilbert and Sullivan.

The cynicism that gave Hart's lyric an individual edge was in the air of the Roaring Twenties, the underside of the gaiety and "Let Yourself Go!" spirit of the decade. Irving Berlin also expressed it: "After You Get What You Want, You Don't Want It" (1920) and "Pack Up Your Sins and Go to the Devil" (1922). Other songwriters explored the feeling in "I'm Gonna Tear Your Playhouse Down" (recorded by Clara Smith in 1924), "I Faw Down an' Go Boom!"

(1928), and "It's Hard to Laugh or Smile" (a theme song of Bennie Moten's Kansas City Orchestra in 1929).

"Thursday, September 16, 1925, began what may have been," Gerald Bordman has said, "the most remarkable seven days in the history of the American Musical Theatre. *No, No, Nanette* opened on that evening, followed by *Dearest Enemy* on September 18, *The Vagabond King* on the 21st, and *Sunny* on the 22nd. If *Rose-Marie* was the biggest musical success of this era, *No, No, Nanette* was the most successful musical comedy."[2] Its run on Broadway (321 performances) was relatively short, but only because it had already spent a year in Chicago and had road companies out in advance of the New York opening.

Of all the shows presented during the twenties, *Nanette* was virtually the only musical which featured the flapper as a central character. The title signified the disapproval of the older generation of Nanette's unconventional lifestyle—unconventional for that era. Apart from its freshness and social relevance, what gave the show its appeal and its amazing success as an out-of-date revival in 1971 was the superb score by Irving Caesar and Vincent Youmans. Out of it came two enormous, long-lived hits, "I Want to Be Happy" and "Tea for Two," the latter the most performed, danced, requested, arranged, recorded, and beloved of all standards.

Irving Caesar, who wrote the sometimes intricately rhymed lyrics—"Day will break and you'll awake and start to bake a sugar cake for me to take"—was born in New York in 1895 and educated at City College. He worked as a stenographer on the Henry Ford Peace Ship that sought to end World War I in 1915 and then as a mechanic on one of Ford's automotive assembly lines. He met his first important collaborator, George Gershwin, at Remick's, a meeting that led to a friendship and the production of his first smash hit, "Swanee" (1920). Throughout the twenties he was active on Broadway, contributing lyrics to several editions of the *Greenwich Village Follies* (1922–25), and collaborating on the book of *Betsy* (1926), on the music of *Yes, Yes, Yvette* (1927), and on the lyrics of *Polly* (1929) and *George White's Scandals* (1929). His biggest hit after the gems in *No, No, Nanette* was "Crazy Rhythm" to music by Joseph Meyer and Roger Wolfe Kahn in *Here's Howe* (1928). It was introduced by Ben Bernie, whose band was featured in the show and who himself attracted notice for his natural ability as a comic.

From the other musicals (and the one operetta) that opened in the same period as *No, No, Nanette* came Rudolf Friml's "Song of the Vagabonds," "Only a Rose," and "Hugette Waltz" (*The Vagabond King*), and "Who?," the runaway hit of Jerome Kern's *Sunny*. "Who?" posed a tough challenge to the lyricist since the opening note of the song was held for nine counts or beats, and held again, after a line or two, for another nine counts. The choice of "Who?" by lyricists Otto Harbach and Oscar Hammerstein II proved ideal.

It was not the only tricky melody of 1925. An imported up-tempo song called "Valencia" became popular despite its use of 8/8 meter, which was not suited for dancing either the fox-trot or the waltz. What saved it was singing the word "Valencia" so that the last syllable was held while the orchestra played the succeeding seven bars under it—the word was then repeated and the final "a" held again until the bridge arrived. Irving Berlin's "Always" was not really tricky, but it was developed on the five notes of the pentatonic scale—the black keys on the piano. (As is widely known, Berlin could play the piano only in the key of F-sharp, the key on the black notes, and had a special piano built with levers that made it possible for him to play in that key but hear the melody in any key he desired.)

There were also tricky titles, like "Who Takes Care of the Caretaker's Daughter? (While the Caretaker's Busy Taking Care)." Then there was the song known as "Then I'll Be Happy" but whose full, registered title was "I Wanna Go Where You Go, Do What You Do, Then I'll Be Happy." Cincinnati-born Cliff Friend (1893–1974), who wrote the music, came from pioneer stock and from one of the first families of Ohio. The family was musical; the father played first violin in the Woods Theatre orchestra. Cliff was educated at Cincinnati College and the Cincinnati Conservatory of Music, and hoped to become a concert pianist until he underwent a three-year struggle with tuberculosis. He teamed with Cincinnati-born Harry Richman, who later became a strutting nightclub singer, and they played Ohio vaudeville theatres, eventually traveling to the West Coast, where they joined Buddy De Sylva, who strummed a ukulele in a pseudo-Hawaiian band, as entertainers at Baron Long's roadhouse.

It was Al Jolson who inspired them to head for Broadway, where Friend and Richman nearly starved for several years, occasionally living on Jolson's bounty. It was Jolson also who helped Friend place songs in *Bombo, The Passing Show,* and in various Winter Garden productions until 1922 brought him his first hit, "You Tell Her—I Stutter," recorded by the country comedy due, Homer and Jethro. He followed with "Mama Loves Papa," a hit for Tony Pastor; "Let It Rain, Let It Pour," a collaboration with Will Donaldson in 1925; and "My Blackbirds Are Bluebirds Now," with a lyric by Irving Caesar in 1928.

Among other show tunes that added to the tunefulness of 1925 were "That Certain Feeling," "Sweet and Low-Down," and "Looking for a Boy," all from *Tip Toes* by George Gershwin; "I Miss My Swiss Miss," written by L. Wolfe Gilbert and Abel Baer for *Chauve-Souris of 1925;* "If You Knew Susie Like I Know Susie," written by B. G. De Sylva and Joseph Meyer, and introduced by Al Jolson in *Big Boy,* but identified with Eddie Cantor, who performed it extensively; and "A Cup of Coffee, a Sandwich and You," which Billy Rose, Al Dubin, and Joseph Meyer contributed to *Charlot's Revue.* The last-mentioned inspired a parody, "An Oyster, a Cloister and You," which did not approach the original in popularity. The *Plantation Revue,* which brought stardom to Ethel Waters when she succeeded Florence Mills at the midtown club, produced "Dinah," an Ethel Waters perennial, which she sang in the revue *Africana* (1927) and in *Blackbirds of 1930.* Early performers of the attractive ballad by Sam M. Lewis and Joe Young (words) and Harry Akst (music) were Eddie Cantor, who interpolated it in *Kid Boots,* and Louis Armstrong, who recorded it on OKeh.

Sam M. Lewis (1885–1959) and Joe Young (1889–1939) were a rare pair in Tin Pan Alley, collaborating on lyrics only. They teamed up for over a dozen years, from 1916 to 1930. In 1925 they wrote not only "Dinah" but also "Five Foot Two, Eyes of Blue" and "I'm Sitting on Top of the World," both with melodies by Ray Henderson.

The latter was given a rousing rendition by Al Jolson in *The Singing Fool* (1928). In 1926, with Mabel Wayne, Lewis and Young wrote "In a Little Spanish Town," popularized by Jimmy Carr, who called himself the "Doctor of Melody." And in 1928, working with band-leader Ted Fiorito, who introduced the pseudo-dramatic ballad, they wrote "Laugh, Clown, Laugh."

For Walter Donaldson (1893–1947), another of the prolific hit songwriters of the twenties, 1925 yielded one of his two biggest sellers, "Yes Sir, That's My Baby," with a lyric by Gus Kahn. ("My Blue Heaven," a solo effort of 1927, was his other great hit.) "Yes Sir, That's My Baby" was introduced and popularized by Eddie Cantor, at whose Great Neck home in Long Island it originated. Legend has it that during a visit lyricist Gus Kahn toyed with a mechanical pig that belonged to one of Cantor's daughters. As he watched the animal hop along, Kahn improvised the opening lines of the song to the toy's movement. When he mentioned them to Donaldson, the well-known tune emerged. After the song had become a hit, Kahn showed one of his royalty checks to Cantor with the comment, "That's a lot of money for a Jewish boy to make out of a pig."

Walter Donaldson was born in Brooklyn, the son of a piano teacher whose prompting led him to write songs for his school shows. But despite his mother's interest in a music career for her son, he did a stint as a Wall Street clerk before he took a $15 a week job as a pianist at a music publishing company. It was at Camp Upton during World War I that he met Irving Berlin, with whose publishing company he was associated for ten years before he became part of Donaldson, Douglas and Gumble. Although he was basically a Tin Pan Alley songsmith, he created two rich standards for *Making Whoopee* (1928), one of two musicals he wrote. In addition to the title song, introduced by Eddie Cantor in the show and thereafter part of his permanent repertoire, there was "Love Me or Leave Me," also with a lyric by Gus Kahn, which was introduced by Ruth Etting and became one of her leading request numbers.

Donaldson's catalogue of hits is one of the longest of any song-writer of the twenties, starting with "My Little Bimbo down on a Bamboo Isle" (1920), with words by Grant Clarke. His bestsellers with Gus Kahn included "My Buddy" (1922) and "Carolina in the Morning" (1922), among other titles. With Sam Lewis and Joe Young, he wrote "My Mammy" (1925), the song that forever froze the image of Al Jolson singing in a half kneeling position with his arms extended wide. Cliff Friend was his cowriter on "Let It Rain, Let It Pour (I'll Be in Virginia in the Morning)" (1925). Bandleader Abe Lyman collaborated on "What Can I Say After I Say I'm Sorry?" (1926), which was introduced, of course, by Lyman and his Orchestra. He also composed "Romance," with words by Edgar Leslie (1926). With George Whiting, who introduced it in vaudeville, he wrote "My Blue Heaven" (1927), reintroduced by Tommy Lyman and interpolated by Eddie Cantor in *Ziegfeld Follies of 1927*. Donaldson was also adept at writing his own lyrics. His words-and-music songs include "At Sundown," introduced by Cliff "Ukulele Ike" Edwards at the Palace Theatre, and "Sam, the Old Accordion Man" (1927), popularized by Ruth Etting and by the Williams Sisters.

In 1925 the college generation heard itself memorialized in a popular hit. "Collegiate . . . collegiate . . . Yes, we are collegiate" was written by Lew Brown, Moe Jaffe and Nat Bonx, and interpolated in *Gay Paree* after being introduced by Waring's Pennsylvanians. Two years later, the college scene was the basis of a hit musical, *Good News*, with a score by De Sylva, Brown and Henderson. F. Scott Fitzgerald, who had addressed himself to the mores and morals of the college world in his first novel, *This Side of Paradise* (1920), now made a mysterious gangster the romantic hero of *The Great Gatsby* (1925).

One late afternoon in the Oyster Bar at Grand Central Station, two strangers struck up a conversation. They quickly discovered they were in the same business. One was Al Dubin, a lyricist, and the other, Harry Warren, a composer. "Al was an excellent conversationalist," Harry Warren has said, "with an extensive vocabulary. I liked him from the first meeting and enjoyed his sense of humor."[4] And so Al was invited for dinner to Warren's Forest Hills home. Separated temporarily and later permanently from his wife, Dubin gladly accepted the invitation to a roast pork dinner. It led to a productive collaboration.

Harry Warren (1893–1981), whose major melodies came in the thirties and later—"That's Amore," "Nakasaki," and three Oscar winners ("Lullaby of Broadway," "You'll Never Know," and "The Atchison, Topeka and the Santa Fe"), among others—came up the hard way. Born in Brooklyn, at fourteen he was a self-taught drummer in a Canarsie band, later sold fruit in the Liberty Theater where Joseph Adler ran a Yiddish stock company, played piano in silent movie houses for $12 a week and for silent actress Corinne Griffith, and after World War I worked for a small music publishing company, Stark and Cowan, for $20 a week. His first published song was "Rose of the Rio Grande" (words by Edgar Leslie and music by saxist Ross Gorman and himself), introduced in 1922 by Paul Whiteman. In the early thirties, he was responsible for such top-notch film musicals as *42nd Street* and *Gold Diggers of 1933*.

Although Warren and Dubin wrote their first song the year they met (1925), it was another Dubin song that became a hit. "A Cup of Coffee, a Sandwich and You" involved Billy Rose on the lyric and Joseph Meyer on the tune. Al's inspiration for the title, according to his daughter, was the classic line, "A loaf of bread, a jug of wine and thou" from Omar Khayyam's famous poem, *The Rubaiyat*. "A Cup of Coffee" . . . started its climb to popularity with a rendition by Gertrude Lawrence and Jack Buchanan in *Charlot's Revue*.

Two years after writing "A Cup of Coffee . . . ," Al penned a lyric on the back of a gas bill envelope, titled "Among My Souvenirs." "He was in debt," his daughter states, "needed quick cash to get a small stake in a poker game and sold that lyric to Edgar Leslie for $25. . . . Al's name never appeared on the lyric. Dubin sold many many lyrics in the same fashion for $5 or $50."[5] It is difficult to judge the veracity of this story. Credits on the published song read: "Words by Edgar Leslie, music by Horatio Nichols," the latter a pseudonym for an English publisher and songwriter. The song was first introduced in England by Jack Hylton and his orchestra, and was first recorded in the United States by Paul Whiteman. But the reference to the possible sales of other lyrics for paltry sums does accord with acts of irresponsibility in which Dubin indulged to satisfy whims and a limitless search for pleasure throughout his life. A heavy drinker and a glutton, he packed as much as three hundred pounds on his five-foot, nine-inch frame. His daughter tells of a dinner at which, completing one hearty meal, Al proceeded to regurgitate it in order to partake of a second.

Al had been a published lyricist for more than fifteen years before he scored with "A Cup of Coffee." Adept at writing and rhyming at an early age, he was inspired to pursue the craft by winning first prize in a poetry contest sponsored by *St. Nicholas Magazine.* His ambition did not win any support at home; his mother was a dedicated science teacher, his father a doctor, and both hoped their son would go into medicine. They had fled Russia to Zurich, where Al was born in 1891, and then settled in Philadelphia.

At fourteen young Dubin was ditching school to see musicals in New York, hanging around 28th Street, then New York's Tin Pan Alley, and trying to sell special material to vaudeville entertainers. Witmark, with whom he remained associated for many years, published his first two inconsequential songs in 1909. To complete high school, he chose a private institution, Perkiomen Seminary, hardly appropriate for a Jew and located forty miles from his home. He excelled in athletics—he was captain of the football team, a winner in track meets, and a basketball star. But alcohol, girls, and nights out resulted in suspensions and in his being expelled days before graduation.

He worked with many composers, but had two steady collaborators. With Joe Burke he produced "Tip Toe Through the Tulips with Me," a hit in 1929 when it was introduced by Nick Lucas in the film *Gold Diggers of Broadway.* (It received a rather sensational revival in 1968–69 when it was recorded by Tiny Tim.) Dubin's most successful collaboration was with Harry Warren. For the film *42nd Street* they created a hit-laden score that included the title tune, "You're Getting to Be a Habit with Me," "We're in the Money," and "Shuffle Off to Buffalo." (When it was revived on Broadway by David Merrick in 1980 for a run of more than five years, the score was enhanced with "Lullaby of Broadway," which Dubin and Warren

wrote for the 1935 *Gold Diggers of Broadway*, and which won the
Academy Award that year for best song.) Between *42nd Street*
(1933) and *Gold Diggers of Broadway*, the pair contributed "I Only
Have Eyes for You" to the film *Dames*, in which it was introduced
by Dick Powell and Ruby Keeler. It remains a standard that has been
recorded by contemporary artists such as Art Garfunkel and groups
like the Flamingos, who had a bestselling disk in 1959. For James
Melton in *Melody for Two*, a 1937 film, they created "September in
the Rain."

The flow of lyrics from Dubin's pen continued until February
1945 when he succumbed to pneumonia and barbiturate poisoning.
On his deathbed, Al Dubin, the Jewish boy from Philadelphia, received the last rites of the Catholic church, for he had converted
when he married Helene McClay, a blonde showgirl.

"Always," one of the songs that Irving Berlin wrote in 1924–26 to
the woman he was wooing and who became his wife, was first heard
by the public in 1925 vaudeville performances by Gladys Clark and
Henry Bergman. For no accountable reason, "Always" attracted a
parody whose authorship was attributed at one point to Larry Hart
of Rodgers and Hart. In 1967, many years after it became known inside the music business, the spoof was printed in *Dramatists Guild
Quarterly*. At that time Berlin admitted his familiarity with the parody and expressed the belief that it was written by Buddy De Sylva,
who first sang it to him. The parody went:

> I'll be loving you
> Always
> Both in very big and
> Small ways.
> With a love as grand
> As Paul Whiteman's band
> And 'twill weigh as much as
> Paul weighs,
> Always.
>
> In saloons and drab
> Hallways

You are what I'll grab
Always.
See how I dispense
Rhymes that are immense,
But do they make sense?
Not always.

In 1925 Paul Robeson, later acclaimed for his role in a revival of *Show Boat* (1932), gave New York City its first hearing of one of the richest basso-baritone voices in all of music. It was a historic concert, for Robeson devoted his entire program to Negro spirituals—the first time such a repertoire was heard on the concert stage. Until then spirituals, or subspecies such as "sorrow songs" or Christian "Jubilees," had been thought of as folk or church songs—and many blacks preferred not to hear them as reminders of a horrible chapter in their history. Robeson's program, repeated through the years in concerts both in the U.S. and abroad, and recorded on several occasions, led to the inclusion of spirituals in concerts by other black artists.

"Deep River" was the spiritual that brought him fame, as "Ol' Man River" from *Show Boat* did later. Published in 1917, "Deep River" was the first of a series (*Jubilee Songs of the United States of America*) in which Henry T. Burleigh arranged spirituals for voice, with piano accompaniment, in the style of art songs. Others in the series included "Go Down Moses," "Nobody Knows de Trouble I've Seen," and "Swing Low, Sweet Chariot," a favorite of Anton Dvorak, for whom Burleigh frequently played it. (Dvorak's *Symphony No. 5*, titled *From the New World*, contained a theme once thought to be a Negro spiritual though actually it was an original melody composed in the style.) In 1925–26, John Rosamond Johnson and his brother, James Weldon Johnson, edited the historic two-volume *Book of American Negro Spirituals*.

Interest in spirituals was spurred, unquestionably, by the concern of the Harlem Renaissance with the history and culture of the Negro. Whatever influence spirituals may have exerted on popular music in terms of depth of feeling, blues tonality, and harmonic freshness, came through the blues, which they antedated.

"Nineteen twenty-five began its climb to the crash," music publisher Edward B. Marks wrote in his autobiography. "Again the theater boomed, and the night club, prohibition's shaky substitute for the wine restaurants of birthdays, flourished like a lone madam in a mining camp. The late Texas Guinan, in the establishment over which she presided, took down $7,000 a week in profits from invited 'suckers' who wanted 'to give the little girl a big hand.' Clayton, Jackson and Durante were at the Dover Club, making them sit up and howl. 'Schnozzole,' of the cellar dives, the one really great low comedian of recent years, had to make them laugh to forget the price of the drinks."[6]

In 1925 sophisticated humor secured representation in a new magazine, *The New Yorker*, founded by Harold Ross as a weekly for "caviar sophisticates." On its initial cover, monocled Eustace Tilley appeared and became the permanent cartoon mascot, reappearing each year in February, the month of the magazine's founding. By contrast, above-the-waist nudity was permitted on Broadway, provided the lady remained absolutely motionless. And in burlesque theatres, girls who were similarly exposed were permitted to move.

As girls began wearing skirts that flapped above their knees, revealing legs enmeshed in provocative flesh-colored stockings, Rudolph Valentino was building a hysterical cult and popularizing a new term, "sheik." "Never before had women fallen so completely," E. B. Marks observed, "under the spell of a screen actor."[7] Anita Loos enhanced the appeal of the flaxen-haired flapper in her novel *Gentlemen Prefer Blondes*. The Loos work was to go through a series of incarnations, from novel to film to musical, as were DuBose Heyward's *Porgy* and Samson Raphaelson's *The Jazz Singer*.

Although vaudeville was on the verge of being phased out of the theatre scene, quite a number of hits were popularized on its boards. Songwriter Benny Davis scored with performances of his songs, "Yearning (Just for You)," "No Other, No One but You," and "Oh

How I Miss You Tonight." In 1925 Sophie Tucker introduced the song that became second in importance in her career to "Some of These Days"—"My Yiddishe Momma." Uneasy at first about the use of the word, "Yiddishe," she elicited an overwhelming response from audiences, singing it just as Jack Yellen had written it. Within three years, her recording of it passed the million mark.

In addition to Paul Whiteman's, the bands that drew crowds in 1925 were led by Paul Specht; Vincent Lopez at the Casa Lopez; George Olsen at the Hotel Pennsylvania; Ben Bernie, who was at the Hotel Roosevelt and played the Palace; and Isham Jones, who was greeted effusively by music business when he came to play the Cafe de la Paix in New York City, having established himself as one of Chicago's favorites. An echo of the early opposition to jazz surfaced when a Spokane professor sued a minor bandleader, Ralph Pollock, for jazzing the classics and thereby "perverting the idea of classical music."

During the year, two completely contrasting performers thrilled audiences. *Variety* used the word "hypnotize" to describe Al Jolson's impact in the musical *Big Boy,* in which he popularized "Keep Smiling at Trouble" and "It All Depends on You," the latter one of the first hits of the sensationally successful team of De Sylva, Brown and Henderson. The other magical performer was John McCormack (1884–1945), an Irish operatic tenor who later sang at the Metropolitan and other American opera houses but occasionally performed select popular songs. He recorded "Moonlight and Roses," later Lanny Ross's theme, and a radio performance of an Irving Berlin ballad sent "All Alone" to the top of the lists.

In the wake of *No, No, Nanette,* a number of lively, up-tempo pop songs dealt with the flapper. "Five Foot Two, Eyes of Blue" exulted over her "turned up nose" and "turned down hose." "O, Katharina," introduced in *Chauve Souris,* stressed the importance of being thin. "If You Knew Susie" by Buddy De Sylva and Joseph Meyer implied the thrills that awaited one on a date with this unconventional lass. The flapper's dance, the Charleston, was now being danced by an older generation, and before long, they would be slapping their backsides and hopping about to the black bottom. Fred Astaire, recalling a visit to the Texas Guinan Club—one flight up in a long, dimly lit room—remembered George Raft, later a film star, as "the fastest Charleston dancer ever. He practically floored me with his footwork."[8]

✎ 15 ✎

"*The Black Bottom*"
(1926)

1926 was the year of Clara Bow's triumph as the "It" Girl, of the maudlin Rudolph Valentino funeral, and of the rise of the suggestive dance, the black bottom, as a competitor to the Charleston. Sex was in the air and made headlines with Daddy Browning and Peaches, his "ward," and evangelist Aimee Semple McPherson. The escapades of the younger generation was embodied in an unexceptional novel by Warner Fabian (the pseudonym for Samuel Hopkins Adams), whose evocative title was taken up by the media to make *Flaming Youth* a sensation.

But the flings, furies, and frustrations of the generation—its disillusionment and denial of standards—were given a piercing and probing portrayal in an extraordinary novel that appeared at the same time. *The Sun Also Rises* rewarded Ernest Hemingway with the overnight eminence that F. Scott Fitzgerald had earlier enjoyed after *This Side of Paradise,* and made him the idol of "the lost generation." The alienated expatriates and mutilated bohemians of the novel, today regarded by many as Hemingway's best, "cried for madder music and stronger wine," welcomed sex without love, and despaired of love without sex. In its superficiality, popular music was closer in outlook to *Flaming Youth* than to *The Sun Also Rises.*

Against this background, the black bottom roared in as a hot new dance. Given an exciting sendoff in *George White's Scandals* of 1926, it was presented in a snappy song by De Sylva, Brown and Henderson, and fetchingly danced by alluring Ann Pennington. Undeniably of black origin, the dance had several people claiming credit or being given credit for conceiving its final form. Producer George White presumably devised the Ann Pennington opening during rehearsals. But black songwriter, publisher, and producer Perry Bradford gave interviews and wrote articles seeking to establish himself as the pioneer of the dance. Blues singer and songwriter Alberta Hunter seems to be recognized as the creator, however, although the dance was not copyrighted until 1926. Regardless of who accounted for it, the black bottom caught on and became as emblematic of the era as the Charleston.

In truth, in 1926 the Charleston was still quite popular, as Louis Armstrong has stated: "The Sunset [Cafe in Chicago] had Charleston contests on Friday night, and you couldn't get into the place unless you were there early. . . . Percy Venable, the producer of the show, staged a finale [one night] with four of us band boys closing the show with the Charleston. That was really something. There was Earl Hines, as tall as he is; Tubby Hall, as fat as he was; litle Joe Walker, as short as he is; and myself, as fat as I was at that time. We would stretch out across that floor doing the Charleston as fast as the music would play it. Boy, oh boy, your talking about four cats picking them up and laying them down—that was us. We stayed there until old boss man got tired of looking at us."[1]

While the Black Bottom may have given the *Scandals* its notoriety, the show also contained a superlative score. Among the outstanding numbers was "Lucky Day," which later became the theme of the celebrated Saturday night network radio show, *Your Hit Parade*, sponsored by Lucky Strike Cigarettes. In the show, Harry Richman and Frances Williams sang the attractive ballad, "The Girl Is You and the Boy Is Me." The song that received the most opulent production and has remained the most performed standard of the score is "The Birth of the Blues." Harry Richman presented the number with its dramatically ascending melody, singing it from the center of a circular staircase on which the show's chorus girls, dressed as angels and stationed on opposite sides, fought a mock battle as adherents of the classics and contemporary blues. An excerpt from *Rhapsody in Blue* served as the climactic reconciliation.

Harry Reichman of Cincinnati (1895–1972), better known as Harry Richman, sang in a florid theatrical style, using a cane and top or straw hat as props, projecting the image of a dapper man about town. Starting as a youngster in blackface, he worked his way as a pianist and singer in small vaudeville houses until he reached New York, where he served as an accompanist to the Dolly Sisters, Nora Bayes, and Mae West. The vaudeville act he developed brought him to the Palace and then to a starring role in George White's *Scandals* of 1926 and 1928. Unbeknown to many in the entertainment field, he was an expert pilot, and in 1925 set the world altitude record for single-motor amphibious planes, flying over 19,000 feet. In addition to "Birth of the Blues," he is remembered for "Singing a Vagabond Song," "Ro-Ro-Rolling Along," "I Love a Parade," and Irving Berlin's "Puttin' on the Ritz," which he introduced in the film of the same name (1930).

It was the *Scandals* of 1925 that brought together the fabulously successful team of De Sylva, Brown and Henderson, first as songwriters and then in a publishing venture. Lew Brown (1893–1958), born Louis Brownstein in Odessa, Russia, and raised in New Haven and New York, began in the music business by working as a song plugger for Albert Von Tilzer. Buddy, or B. G., De Sylva (1895–1950), born George Gard De Sylva in New York City, entered the field through the auspices of Al Jolson while a student at the University of Southern California. Ray Henderson (1896–1970), born Raymond Brost in Buffalo, studied at the Chicago Conservatory of Music, worked as a song plugger for Leo Feist before transferring to Shapiro-Bernstein, where he met Lew Brown through Louis Bernstein. He was the composer of the trio. When they began working together, De Sylva was the most experienced, having collaborated on songs with Victor Herbert, Al Jolson, George Gershwin (*La La Lucille*), and Jerome Kern.

In addition to the *Scandals*, the trio had a hit in "It All Depends on You"—parodied later in "It Holds de Pents on You"—interpolated by Al Jolson in *Big Boy*. On his own, De Sylva wrote the words for the Austrian import, "When Day Is Done," which was introduced to America by Paul Whiteman. Working with Sydney Clare, Lew Brown converted Dvorak's "Humoresque" into "I'd Climb the Highest Mountain," popularized by Lillian Roth and Sophie Tucker. And composer Ray Henderson, collaborating with Mort Dixon, produced "Bye, Bye Blackbird," later George Price's theme and a song whose bird motif was also heard in Harry Woods's "When the Red, Red Robin Comes Bob, Bob Bobbin' Along," introduced by Sophie Tucker and a favorite of Al Jolson and Lillian Roth.

Harry Woods (1896–1970), a very successful denizen of Tin Pan Alley, was born in North Chelmsford, Massachusetts, and educated at Harvard, where he was known for his singing and piano playing. Although he began being published in the early twenties, the "Red Robin" was his first hit, followed in 1927 by "I'm Looking Over a Four Leaf Clover" (words by Mort Dixon)—a bestselling record for the Art Mooney band twenty years later on the strength of Mike Pingatore's banjo solo—and by a song for which Woods wrote both the words and music, "Side by Side." To Rudy Vallee's *The Vagabond Lover* (1929), he contributed "A Little Kiss Each Morning (A Little Kiss Each Night)" as well as "Heigh-Ho Everybody!"

Woods continued to produce hits during the thirties. With Mort Dixon, he wrote "River Stay 'Way from My Door," popularized by Jimmy Savo in a one-man revue. Kate Smith adopted his song, "When the Moon Comes Over the Mountain," written with Howard Johnson, as the theme of her radio broadcasts and turned the ballad into an enormous bestseller. Two years later, in 1933, Woods collaborated with two British songwriters and publishers, Jimmy Campbell and Reg Connelly, on the greatest standard of his career, "Try a Little Tenderness." Its appeal is so broad that it became part of the repertoire of the late Otis Redding, the Georgia soul singer.

A considerable number of pop hits emerged from other big shows of the year. Rodgers and Hart's *The Girl Friend* yielded the title song with its Charleston rhythm and "The Blue Room." The latter ostensibly turned a faltering show into a hit. *Peggy Ann*, also by Fields (book), Rodgers, and Hart, yielded memorable songs in "A Tree in the Park" and "Where's That Rainbow They Talk About?" To his list of growing hits, George Gershwin added "Someone to Watch Over Me," "Do Do Do" and "Clap Yo' Hands" from *Oh, Kay.*

"Do Do Do" in which the tripartite repetition is charmingly maintained throughout the song, was written, according to Ira Gershwin, in half an hour one evening before dinner. "I am certain of the time it took," he writes in *Lyrics on Several Occasions,* "because just as George and I started to work [in George's studio on the top floor of their penthouse on 103rd Street and Riverside Drive], my bride-to-be telephoned that she *could* make it for dinner with us, and when she arrived, taxiing in half an hour—less she says—from 8th Street, we were able to play a complete refrain."[2] As for "Clap Yo' Hands," the title never appears in the body of the song, for the music requires that the words be sung, "Clap-a Yo' Hands." "Someone to Watch Over Me" was fetchingly introduced by Gertrude Lawrence, for whom *Oh, Kay* was her first American musical.

The major singing personality to emerge during the year, but not without travail, was sad-eyed, sad-faced Helen Morgan. *Americana* (1926) was to be her first big role, but during rehearsals the producer decided she wasn't right for the show and was about to fire her. His opinion was fortunately not shared by two of the show's writers, Henry Souvaine and Morrie Ryskind (the latter would eventually be the Pulitzer Prize-winner for *Of Thee I Sing*). Together they wrote a special song for her, "Nobody Wants Me." By the time the song was rehearsed and okayed for the show, there was no time to create a special set. Helen came out in front of the curtain, sat on top of the upright piano in the orchestra pit, and delivered the lachrymose ballad to a show-stopping reception. Whether or not this was Helen's first on-the-piano stint, it gave her a unique identity.

Americana, which closed after a respectable run of 224 performances, included one of Ira Gershwin's earliest uses of syllable-clipping in a lyric, a device that yielded the tantalizing evergreen " 'S Wonderful." To a lively melody by Phil Charig, he wrote "Sunny Disposish," lopping off the last syllable of the title and of other rhyme words. Toward the end of the twenties, it evoked a delightful recording on Columbia by the sultry Frances Williams, a star of several *George White's Scandals*, including the twenty-sixth edition.

1926 produced more "event" songs than most years. Gertrude Ederle's conquest of the English Channel moved Henry Tobias and Al Sherman to write "Trudy." The Daddy Browning–Peaches idyll elicited a comment in "I'm All Alone in a Palace of Stone" by Lou Mooney. Irving Berlin's marriage to Ellen MacKay was celebrated in a song titled "When a Kid from the East Side Found a Sweet Society Rose"; it contained a quote from Berlin's "Remember" and was viewed as "a curiosity of bad taste" by some commentators.[3] The marriage was also the subject of a skit in the *Scandals* titled "A Western Union," a play on papa MacKay's association with Postal Telegraph.

Performed in secret, the wedding ceremony drew headlines when the couple sailed to England for their honeymoon. Front page stories appeared in the British press, anticipating their arrival; and when their ship docked, they were met by a large contingent of reporters. Shortly after this, *Variety* reported in a front page box that Papa Mackey, who refused to be reconciled to the union, had given out an order that no Berlin tune was to be played at any social event in which he was involved.

Two disks broke into Gold Record category during the year, each selling more than a million copies. Both had been recorded earlier, one by George Olsen and his Band ("Who?") and the other by Sophie Tucker ("Some of These Days"). Starting his pre–Swing Era band in 1923, Olsen played the top vaudeville houses, including New York's Palace, Capitol, and Loew's State. In 1923 Fanny Brice persuaded Florence Ziegfeld to retain Olsen for the Eddie Cantor show, *Kid Boots*. Later, Olsen played in the pit of such musicals as Jerome Kern's *Sunny* (1925), Rodgers and Hart's *The Girl Friend* (1926), De Sylva, Brown and Henderson's *Good News* (1927), and Walter Donaldson's *Whoopee* (1928). Olsen's was one of the featured bands at the inaugural of the NBC radio network on November 11, 1926. The following year, as the star of the coast-to-coast on the Canada Dry network radio show he earned $2,500 a week. With his first wife,

Ethel Shutta, as his vocalist, he used "Beyond the Blue Horizon" as his opening theme and "Going Home Blues," with *choo-choo* effects made by members of his band as his closing theme. He fronted his band for nearly thirty years, working in theatres, shows, and hotels. His last hotel date was at the Edgewater Beach Hotel in Chicago in 1950, after which he retired to establish a resturant in Paramus, New Jersey. His bestselling version of "Who?" included a vocal by the trio of Fran Frey, Bob Rice, and soft-voiced Jack Fulton, who became Paul Whiteman's lead tenor vocalist and later a successful bandleader and songwriter ("Wanted").

Sophie Tucker (1884 or 88–1966), the "Last of the Red Hot Mamas," was born of Polish or Russian parents named Kalish, and made her first appearance in 1905 as a singer in her father's restaurant in Hartford. An early marriage to Louis Tuck resulted in a move to New York where in 1906 she sang at the German Village. For the next few years, she appeared in blackface, played cabarets, burlesque, and vaudeville, including Tony Pastor's and Reisenweber's (with her Seven Kings of Syncopation). By 1909 she was in the *Ziegfeld Follies,* where her show-stopping performance quickly earned the ire of stars Nora Bayes and Eva Tanguay.

It was through her maid, a friend of pianist, vaudevillian, and songwriter Shelton Brooks (1886–1975)—a well-known impersonator of the great Bert Williams—that Sophie became acquainted with his song "Some of These Days." (He later wrote "Darktown Strutters Ball," in 1917). Sophie began performing "Some of These Days" around 1910, just before the ragtime fever swept the country in the wake of Irving Berlin's "Alexander's Ragtime Band." Although she recorded "the landmark of popular music"[5]—as Alec Wilder terms "Some of These Days"—several times (on Decca and Victor), it was her Columbia recording with Ted Lewis and his Band that became the million-seller.

Sophie performed in films as early as 1929, singing in her raucous, "coon-shouting" style in *Honky Tonk.* She was a hit in her first appearance in London at the legendary Palladium in 1922. During a sixty-year career in show business, the flamboyant singer conquered every medium of entertainment—cabaret, stage, film, radio, TV and recording, favoring and winning favor with blues- and jazz-oriented songs. Her last engagement was at New York's Latin Quarter in October 1965, accompanied by the Ted Lewis band. She died in February, 1966.

Theodore Leopold Friedman, a clarinetist and vocalist better known as Ted Lewis (1884–1966), was, like Sophie Tucker, a hit in British and American vaudeville during the jazzy twenties. He was famous for appearances in a battered top hat, a lazily paced, half-talking style of delivery, and expressive hand motions punctuated with the question, "Is everybody happy?" It became the title of films that featured him in 1929 and 1943. During his sixty years in show business, he became associated with such songs as "When My Baby Smiles at Me" (his theme) and "Me and My Shadow." He performed the latter with a "shadow," Eddie Chester, working in the dusky background behind him and imitating his gestures simultaneously, a guaranteed show-stopper. Between 1919 and 1933, he recorded extensively for Columbia, cutting many of the blues and jazz numbers performed and recorded by the ODJB, the NORK, and other blues and jazz combos. Although his sidemen included stellar jazzmen like George Brunis (trombone), Muggsy Spanier (trumpet), and Jimmy Dorsey (clarinet), his own standing as a jazz clarinetist was questioned by critics. "Some of These Days," his million-seller with Sophie Tucker, was backed with "Bugle Call Rag." Because of his vocal style, choice of songs, and get-up, he was sometimes known as the "High Hat Tragedian of Song."

"Bugle Call Rag," with music by Billy Morgan, Jack Pettis, and Elmer Schoebel—the latter two members of the famous Friars' Society Orchestra, was introduced by it in 1923. Nineteen twenty-six saw the birth of another jazz classic, "Muskrat Ramble," on a recording by Louis Armstrong and his Hot Five. "Muskrat Ramble" was the work of Edward "Kid" Ory (1886–1973), known as a "tailgate" trombonist but also a multifaceted musician who performed professionally on banjo, string bass, coronet, and alto sax. The term "tailgate" derived from the practice in New Orleans of seating the trombone player at the far edge of the wagon on which the band rode, with the tailgate down, so that when they played, the trombonist could extend his slide for the low notes over the edge without striking other players.

A New Orleans pioneer, Kid Ory began his music career by constructing a banjo out of a cigar box. At ten, he acquired a real banjo and three years later he was leading his own band in Laplace, Louisiana, twenty-nine miles from New Orleans, which he visited on weekends to hear the great players such as Buddy Bolden. After moving to the Crescent City he took up the trombone (valve, then slide), then organized a brass band in which King Oliver played trumpet. When Oliver left for Chicago, young Louis Armstrong took his place.

Ory migrated to the West Coast, partly for health reasons, in 1919, and settled in Chicago three years later, shortly before Satchmo joined the historic King Oliver Band. The Ory Band, with Johnny Dodds on clarinet, Johnny St. Cyr on banjo, and Lil Hardin Armstrong at the piano, played at the Dreamland, but Ory recorded with Armstrong's Hot Five when they made their classic jazz disks for OKeh, including "Heebie Jeebies," a modest hit in 1926 and "Muskrat Ramble." Ory later performed on Orson Welles's celebrated radio series in the forties, and in his own San Francisco club, On the Levee, in the late fifties. In 1966, after playing with many key jazz groups, he settled in Hawaii because of ill health, and died there in 1973.

Male domination of the craft and art of songwriting was an established fact in the twenties, a situation that has prevailed up to the present. In the Tin Pan Alley of the twenties only two women accounted for an impressive number of hits, and one of these, Dorothy Fields, soon became involved with musical shows and films. In the movie capital, two other females contributed significantly as lyricists and scriptwriters. The area in which the ladies made a somewhat better showing statistically was in the blues, many of those singers also functioned as songwriters. Bessie Smith, Alberta Hunter, Lovie Austin, and Ma Rainey are outstanding among a dozen or more black female artists who created some of the songs they sang and recorded.

The first woman to produce a hit song in the twenties was Mabel

Wayne, born in Brooklyn in 1904, who studied singing and the piano in Switzerland as well as at the New York School of Music. Before composing her first moderate seller, "Don't Wake Me Up and Let Me Dream" with Abel Baer (music) and L. Wolfe Gilbert (words), she performed as a concert singer and pianist. Her first big hit came the following year (1926) when Paul Whiteman and his Orchestra produced a bestselling disk of "In a Little Spanish Town ('Twas on a Night Like This)." Wayne further explored the Latin sound in "Chiquita (words by L. Wolfe Gilbert) and "Ramona," both hits in 1928.

By 1930 Mabel Wayne was in Hollywood, where she contributed songs to Paul Whiteman's biopic *King of Jazz*. Once again, Latin flavoring was evident in "It Happened in Monterey" (words by Billy Rose). She continued composing into the late forties, producing "Little Man, You've Had a Busy Day" in 1934 and "A Dreamer's Holiday" in 1949.

The other Tin Pan Alley female hit writer, Dorothy Fields (1905–1974), was the daughter of Lew Fields, of the famous Weber and Fields comedy team, and later a successful producer on his own. Her big break came in 1928 with Lew Leslie's all-black revue, *Blackbirds of 1928* for which she wrote the rhythmic "Diga Diga Do," and the hit ballad "I Can't Give You Anything But Love," both with composer Jimmy McHugh. The latter song, we are told, was originally written for *Delmar's Revels*, from which it was dropped. When Lew Leslie hired Fields-McHugh for *Blackbirds*, they reintroduced the ballad. Critic Gilbert Gabriel panned the show and characterized "I Can't Give You Anything But Love" as "a sickly, puerile song." Other critics were as little impressed. Fields-McHugh waived royalties as the show tottered along until Leslie conceived the idea of presenting it as a midnight show on Thursdays. Then suddenly it caught on, prompted critics to reverse themselves, and it became a hot ticket. The ballad went on to sell over 3 million copies.

Before *Blackbirds*, Dorothy Fields was a schoolteacher and laboratory technician. After a time she wrote some songs with J. Fred Coots, who introduced her to Jimmy McHugh, the professional manager of Mills Music. This contact led to a collaboration on several

Cotton Club floor shows. After *Blackbirds,* she branched out into book writing, her first libretto being a collaboration with brother Lew Fields on *Let's Face It* (1941), with songs by Cole Porter. Between 1930 and 1939, she turned to Hollywood in the heyday of the movie musical, producing such sparklers as "I'm in the Mood for Love" with Jimmy McHugh (*Every Night at 8*), and with Jerome Kern, "Lovely to Look At" and "I Won't Dance" (both for *Roberta*), and for *Swing Time.* "A Fine Romance" and "The Way You Look Tonight," which won the Academy Award as the Best Song of the Year (1936). In the same period, she contributed two perennials, "On the Sunny Side of the Street" and "Exactly Like You," both with music by McHugh, to the *International Revue.* In time, she accounted for the songs and/or librettos for such smash Broadway productions as *Mexican Hayride, Redhead, Sweet Charity* (revived in 1986), and *Annie Get Your Gun.* She wrote the last of eight musicals, *See Saw,* with composer Cy Coleman in 1973.

The two other women who figure in this brief overview of female songwriters are Anne Caldwell (1867–1936) and Dorothy Donnelly (1880–1928). Beginning her career as a lyricist and librettist in 1906 (*Old Man Manhattan*), Anne Caldwell was active in the Broadway theatre into the late twenties. Many of her lyrics adorned songs by Jerome Kern, including *The Night Boat* and *Tip Top,* both produced in 1920, and *The City Chap* and *Crisscross,* both in 1926. But she also collaborated with Vincent Youmans (*Oh, Please,* 1926); Gene Buck and Dave Stamper (*Take the Air,* 1927); and Raymond Hubbell (*Three Cheers,* 1928). She was more successful as a book writer than a lyricist.

Dorothy Donnelly's most frequent collaborator was light-operatic composer Sigmund Romberg. Together they worked on such notable productions as *Blossom Time* (1921), *The Student Prince* (1924), and *My Maryland* (1927). Educated in a convent, she began her career as an actress, performing in Henry Donnelly's Stock Company and in several Broadway plays, including *Madame X* (1909–11). Among the hit songs to which she contributed lyrics, there were "Deep in My Heart, Dear," "Song of Love" and "Your Land and My Land," all with music by Romberg.

1926 brought the opening of the largest dance hall in Harlem. Billing itself as "The World's Most Beautiful Ballroom," the Savoy occupied the second floor of a building that stretched the full block from 140th to 141st streets on Lenox Avenue. Opening night was March 12, but outside Harlem American newspapers were more concerned with the Rudolph Valentino sex cult—so much so that even on the South Side of Chicago Valentino films were billed above the names of the jazz bands playing in the theatre. Savoy owner Moe Gale, later a successful music publisher and manager, booked the Fletcher Henderson Band for opening night, drawing a crowd of five thousand to the Track, as regulars of the Savoy came to type the ballroom.

A feature introduced by Charles Buchanan, the Harlem businessman who managed the ballroom during the 1920s, became known as the "Battle of the Bands," and it was a tremendous crowd-getter. When Fletcher Henderson and Chick Webb, representing New York, were pitted against King Oliver and Fess Williams, representing Chicago, in May 1927, the riot squad had to be called out to control the mass of people that descended on the ballroom. Most bands were aware that, regardless of how good they were, competition brought out a kind of drive and determination from the resident Chick Webb Band so that it could not be beaten. If accounts do not err, the most celebrated Battle of the Bands occurred during the Swing Era when the Benny Goodman Band took on Chick Webb. Twenty thousand patrons felt that the Goodman Band, then at the height of its fame, came out second best.

In 1934 Chick Webb recorded a song before its publication celebrating the ballroom. "Stompin' at the Savoy," according to the best available information, was written by Edgar Sampson and Andy Razaf—although two other names (Benny Goodman and Chick Webb) appear on the credits of the song. Goodman made a cover (a later record based on Webb's original) in 1936, which was a hit. Such dances as the Lindy Hop, Suzy Q, Peckin' and Truckin', among others, are presumed to have originated, and certainly were popularized, at the Savoy. It was torn down in 1958 to make way for a housing project.

Despite the Americanization of the musical comedy and the impact of jazz and the blues, the sounds of European music were still audible in American hits. A big Paul Whiteman seller of 1926 was "When Day Is Done," an Austrian import with words by B. G. De Sylva. The German words and music by Robert Katscher came from an Austrian revue, *Kusse um Mitternacht*. While this work was not presented on the American stage, Emmerich Kalman's *Countess Maritza*, regarded as his masterpiece and imported by the Shuberts in 1926, yielded the hit, "Play Gypsies—Dance Gypsies," with English words by Harry B. Smith. Other Austrian importations included "Gigolette" in *Andre Charlot's Revue* of 1926 (English words by Irving Caesar) and "You Are Mine Evermore" from *The Circus Princess*, another operetta by Emmerich Kalman. Franz Lehar's operetta *Frasquita*, imported also in 1927 under the title *The Love Call*, contributed the hit "My Little Nest of Heavenly Blue," also known as "Frasquita's Serenade" (English words by Sigmund Spaeth).

In March, *Variety* ran a front page story headed "Genius In Music Profitable, 26-year-Olds Make $5,000 a Week." Among the songwriters it mentioned were George Gershwin, Vincent Youmans, Richard Rodgers, and Larry Hart. It noted that there were more composers than lyricists in the golden class and named Harms as the publisher and mentor of the high earners. But Harms was not among the publishers that advertised extensively in *Variety*. Feist was the big money spender when it came to taking full page and double page ads to publicize their plug songs, with Remick as a close competitor. Both of these firms were more involved with Tin Pan Alley rather than with show songs.

In April 1926 Warner Brothers and Western Electric announced a joint venture to produce Vitaphone, a device or machine whereby mechanical recordings would replace live music in movie theatres. Until then silent films had been accompanied by music performed by live orchestras playing scores on cue. These orchestras, fairly large in the bigger houses and cities, also played musical preludes and were frequently emphasized in advertisements. In the smaller film houses and cities, the musical accompaniment was by a lone

pianist on an upright, sometimes abetted by a fiddler. At the time
of the announcement, Warners as well as the movie industry generally considered "talking pictures" impractical.

By August 6, 1926, Warners unveiled the first product of its joint
venture with Western Electric. On that historic evening, it premiered
Don Juan, starring John Barrymore, a film that contained a musical
prelude synchronized to Vitaphone. Two other Vitaphone movies
were released in 1926. On October 7, Warner Brothers offered *The
Better Ole* at New York's Colony Theatre while *Don Juan* was still
running nearby at the Warner Theatre. The appearance of Al Jolson
in the prelude singing popular hits gave vaudeville managements a
sense of uneasiness, not unfounded, as it turned out. They were
worried that the new type of film might make vaudeville obsolete,
which it did, and eliminate the place of live musicians, which it also
largely did. The third Vitaphone presentation came in February
1927 with *When a Man Loves,* and was followed by periodic releases
of other Vitaphone canned-music movies, leading to the storm occasioned in October of the year with the release of *The Jazz Singer*.

∽ 16 ∽

"Talkies"
and Theme Songs
(1927)

1927 was a critical year in the world of motion pictures and equally consequential in the cosmos of popular music. On October 6, at the Strand Theatre on Broadway, Warner Brothers presented Al Jolson in *The Jazz Singer*, "with Vitaphone synchronization." The film was characterized as "the first spectacular demonstration of the potential of the *talkie*,"[1] and Jolson was celebrated as "the man who almost singlehandedly rendered silent films obsolete."[2] On October 6, 1927, "a date enshrined in film history," as a recent commentator observed, "with all the dread decisiveness of Waterloo, Sarajevo and Pearl Harbor . . . the death knell of the 'silent' movie was sounded and the "talkies" were born."[3]

At the first Oscar awards ceremony, held in May 1929, Warner Brothers' contribution was recognized with an honorary award for *The Jazz Singer*, "the pioneer outstanding talking picture which has revolutionized the industry." But the truth is that *The Jazz Singer* was neither the first film to break the sound barrier, as we know, nor was it a "talkie." The picture contained six moments of Jolson singing. Five of them were popular songs: "Dirty Hands, Dirty Face," "Toot, Toot, Tootsie (Goo' Bye)," "Blue Skies," "Mother O'

Mine," "I Still Love You," and "My Mammy." The sixth was *Kol Nidre*, the Hebrew prayer chanted on the day of atonement, and delivered at the close of the film by Jolson in lieu of his rabbinical father, who lay dying—a sentimental scene that contributed greatly to its popularity.

The six sequences each took two to three minutes. The orchestral accompaniment, arranged by the studio's Louis Silvers, was handled through Vitaphone by the projection booth, which switched machines for Jolson's songs, the changeover occurring during intertitles, which appeared as in any silent film. Jolson uttered a single line, the exclamation he used in personal appearances: "Wait a minute! You ain't heard nothin' yet!" In Andrew Sarris's precise characterization, *The Jazz Singer* was less a "talkie" than a "singie."[4]

But it did have sound. Of greater consequence, it did enormously well at the box office, grossing the unprecedented sum of $3 million. This naturally impressed rival film companies, which had been skeptical of the innovation, concerned about the cost of new equipment, and doubtful that the public would welcome the changeover. At showings of *The Jazz Singer*, Warner Brothers also offered a fifteen-minute trailer of a forthcoming attraction, *Tenderloin*, which made its debut on March 20, 1928. It was described in *Variety* as "the first try at character-talking from the screen"—and indeed it was "the first of the talking pictures wherein the characters speak their film roles."[5] Spoken dialogue was heard four or five times, aggregating a total of twelve to fifteen minutes of talk in an eighty-seven minute picture.

So revolutionary and so experimental was the use of spoken dialogue that *Variety* felt impelled to run two reviews, one based on audience reactions on the first night, and another on the third night. The difference in the two groups was that the third-night audience consisted of ordinary moviegoers—the general public—and the first-night group were critics. Partly because the movie was "a very ordinary film crook meller," and partly because of inane dialogue and the limitations in Dolores Costello's voice, the first nighters howled over several of the dialogue scenes, evidencing to *Variety* that "they came into the theater prejudiced against the innovation . . . and some left still prejudiced."[6] By the third night, two of the talking sequences had been removed, leaving only two speaking scenes. But the singing of "Sweet Adeline" by silent movie idol Conrad Nagel and a buddy scored well, as did a talking bit by a former vaudeville song-and-dance man, Georgie Stone.

That the film was an experiment in sound seems clear from the use of captions, as in *The Jazz Singer*. At this juncture, only two film companies were apparently using sound. In addition to Warner Brothers, who were wiring some of their theatres, Fox was issuing newsreels, using Movietone, a competitor to Vitaphone. But *Variety* was not certain that patrons wanted the pantomime of the silent screen disturbed by sound that would destroy the purity of the medium and bring it close to the stage play.

The Musicians Union, moreover, was quite worried in 1928 about the inroads Vitaphone and Movietone machines were making into the domain of live musicians. The central office in Chicago sent out directives urging locals to stop the use of these machines, and active campaigns were waged in Chicago, Baltimore, and St. Louis. By October 1928, about eight hundred theatres were wired for sound and the following month Loew's eliminated orchestras and organists in twenty of its New York City theatres.[7] In August 1928 First National released *Lilac Time,* which included "manufactured back stage sound effects" and the singing of the film's theme song by a vocal trio or quartet "in person." Written by L. Wolfe Gilbert and Nathaniel Shilkret, "Jeannine, I Dream of Lilac Time" was among the earliest instances of a theme song, transformed into a hit through the medium of the screen.

Lilac Time, starring Colleen Moore and Gary Cooper, bore the notation "Sound" in its *Variety* heading. The many different descriptive notations that began to appear on films is indicative of the industry's growing concern with sound as well as its wariness about it. Some like *The Singing Fool* (September 26), just bore the word "Dialog." Then there was "Dialog and Songs" (*Rio Rita*) ; "Musical—Dialog" (*The Desert Song*) ; "5 Percent Dialog," "40 percent Dialog," "Half Dialog," "50 percent Dialog, including Songs" (*Show Boat*) ; "60 percent Dialog," "65 percent Dialog," "100 percent Dialog," "All Dialog," "All Dialog with Songs," and "All Dialog with Songs and Technicolor." Other variants were "All Dialog—with Songs and Dance" (*Hallelujah*); "All Dialog, Songs, Dances, 86 percent Color"; "All Dialog, All Color with Songs" (*Gold Diggers of Broadway*). Occasionally "Silent" appeared as a description. *Single Standard* noted that it was "Silent, with Disc Orchestration," and it further advised in its credits: "Victor records contain musical score with no sound or dialog": its star was appropriately the Great Garbo.

With the introduction of the talkies, theme songs became a sine qua non of motion pictures. The absurd lengths to which producers went is illustrated by the film *Woman Disputed*, which used as its theme, "Woman Disputed, I Love You." The theme song had its beginnings in the year of *The Jazz Singer* with two films that were actually silent. *What Price Glory?*, released in January 1927, was accompanied by a program of Movietone shorts, as was *Seventh Heaven*. Out of the synchronized scores that were later written for and added by Erno Rapee came two schmaltzy waltz hits. Lew Pollack wrote the lyrics to "Charmaine" for *What Price Glory?* and to "Diane" for *Seventh Heaven*. Rapee, it was said, originally wrote the melody for "Charmaine" in Hungary in 1913. Its popularity contributed to the box office success of the film and alerted the music publishing and film industries to the potential of theme songs. (Mantovani's hit recording in 1952 for the remake of *What Price Glory?*, and the use of the melody in the background as a recurrent theme, initiated, it is believed, the vogue of lush, string-dominated recordings.) *Seventh Heaven* brought an Academy Award to Janet Gaynor to which "Diane"'s popularity contributed greatly.

Of the early theme songs, "Ramona," commissioned by the studio to promote the film of the same name, is generally conceded to have been the most successful. Composed by Mabel Wayne to a lyric by L. Wolfe Gilbert, it was given an innovative send-off weeks before the release of the film. The song was presented on a coast-to-coast broadcast, with Paul Whiteman and his Orchestra accompanying a vocal rendition by star Dolores Del Rio. But what made the broadcast newsworthy was that the orchestra and the singer worked three thousand miles apart. Whiteman and his orchestra were playing in a studio in New York, while Dolores Del Rio did her singing in the home of studio executive Joseph M. Schenck in Hollywood. Thereafter, Dolores went on a coast-to-coast tour, performing the song in the country's major film theatres. Of the various recordings, Paul Whiteman's on Victor became a bestseller. But the record that broke all records was Gene Austin's, which reportedly sold over 2 million disks. The sale of sheet music also rose to over 2 million.

"The Passing of Vaudeville" was the theme of an analytical article in the October 1927 *American Mercury*, with talking pictures identified as the cause of its downfall and annihilation. Silent films, which had been the tail on the huge body of the two-a-day bills of ten to twenty variety acts, were now about to turn vaudeville into a telescoped appendage of the no-longer silent silver screen.

The omens of vaudeville's impending demise acquired unanticipated confirmation when September 1927 brought the sudden death of Marcus Loew, the nation's number-one vaudeville and film chain operator. Just fifty-seven years old when he died, Loew owned or controlled three hundred fifty theatres in a chain stretching from New York to California and across the seas to France and Egypt; he was also the head of Metro-Goldwyn-Mayer and of Cosmopolitan Pictures. A dealer in furs into his thirties, he entered the theatre world accidentally through an actor then associated with Weber and Fields who owned an apartment building (which he managed) next to one Loew owned on 111th Street and Seventh Avenue, and who opened with Loew a penny arcade on Union Square. The arcade used a mutoscope, a device that flipped a packet of pictures as a magician flips a pack of cards, giving the images the semblance of motion as a crank was turned. The four partners in the venture included the actor David Warfield, Marcus Loew, and Adolph Zukor, later the head of Famous Players films. Within six months, Loew had forty nickelodeons of his own operating all over New York City. Using a primitive movie machine, he established his first picture house in a dismantled arcade on 23rd Street.

The crude beginning of Loew vaudeville occurred when he experimentally added to one of his nickelodeons an actor who recited "Gunga Din" and "Mandalay." The increase in revenue spurred him to employ another live performer in his homemade circuit, a woman who sang fourteen times a day in his nickelodeons, dressed seven times as a country lass and seven times in blackface. He paid her $20 a week; her name was Sophie Tucker. In 1919 Loew bought the valuable property on 45th Street and Seventh Avenue adjacent to and including the famous Bartholdi Inn, a favorite dining spot of luminaries such as Charlie Chaplin, Mack Sennett, D. W. Griffith, Eva Tanguay, and Pearl White. In place of the inn, Loew erected Loew's State Theatre, which opened its doors in August 1921. While the theatre was being built (in 1920), he displayed an amazing sense of things to come when he raised $3 million and bought Metro-Goldwyn-Mayer. By 1926, when he was paying more for his acts than other bigtime vaudeville operators, he was saying, "It's the film that draws 'em and the vaudeville that fills in."[8]

In 1927 *Variety* was planning a special Marcus Loew issue. With his sudden death, the issue was changed to a Marcus Loew Memorial Number. Dated October 19, 1927, it began on its front page with a lengthy life story written by Alexander Woollcott, the *New York Times* theatre critic, a reprint of a series that had run in *Hearst's International* in September, October, and November 1926.

In addition to *The Jazz Singer*, 1927 was graced by the historic opening of the Jerome Kern-Oscar Hammerstein II musical, *Show Boat*, which had its world premier at the National Theatre in Washington, D.C., on December 16, and opened at the Ziegfeld Theatre on December 27. It proved to be the artistic masterpiece and commercial success of the 1927–28 season, a "musical play" in which dialogue, song, and dance were integrated with character and story. Lavishly mounted with a superb cast that included Helen Morgan, Edna May Oliver, Norma Terris, Howard Marsh, Charles Winninger, and Jules Bledsoe, it had a remarkable array of hits: "Can't Help Lovin' Dat Man," "Make Believe," "Why Do I Love You," "Bill," "You Are Love," and the legendary "Ol' Man River," introduced by Bledsoe and later a perennial for the great basso and actor Paul Robeson.

The Ziegfeld Theatre, at which *Show Boat* was moored, was itself a new addition to the Broadway scene, even though it was located at 54th Street and Sixth Avenue. It was bankrolled by William Randolph Hearst, the newspaper publisher who also owned the Hotel Warwick across the avenue, and its cornerstone was laid by Ziegfeld on December 9, 1926. The premiere of the first show to play the new house was on February 2, 1927.

That evening, Gerald Bordman observes, "not only was the season's biggest musical hit unveiled, but the finest musical playhouse ever constructed in America was revealed to the public."[9] The show was *Rio Rita* (book by Guy Bolton and Fred Thompson, songs by Harry Tierney and Joe McCarthy), and it ran for one week short of the five hundred-performance mark. A tricky song titled "The Kinkajou" as well as the title tune were the hits of the show.

Manhattan also had a new "cathedral of the motion picture" with the opening of the world's largest theatre, the Roxy. Built at an advertised cost of $10 million, it was the brainchild of Samuel L. ("Roxy") Rothafel, reportedly the first manager to bring a symphony orchestra into a movie house to accompany a silent film. Rothafel is credited with this pioneering innovation when he was managing the Regent Theatre on 116th Street and Seventh Avenue in 1913. The Roxy Theatre, a huge Spanish Renaissance structure, was opened to by-invitation, gala, celebrity-attended dedication on March 21, 1927.

There was still another important opening that year. Duke Ellington, who had been performing at the Hollywood (later the Kentucky Club) on Broadway, opened at the Cotton Club in Harlem on December 4. The Duke had just acquired publisher Irving Mills as his manager—also, though he did not know it then, as his ubiquitous "collaborator," with his name appearing on the credits of almost every Ellington composition. The Cotton Club had opened at 644 Lenox Avenue under the ownership of a well-known group of mobsters. Jazz critic Leonard Feather credits Mills not only with booking the Duke at the club—but with selling the management on the Cotton Club Parades, all-black floor shows that were as glamorous and lavish as Broadway musicals.[10]

All these events were dwarfed in significance on May 20 when

Charles A. Lindbergh flew nonstop from New York to Paris in a monoplane, displaying endurance, skill, and courage that stunned the world. When he rode up Broadway on June 13 for a New York reception, over two thousand tons of ticker tape and pages torn from phone books were showered onto the street. Tin Pan Alley struggled mightily to celebrate this event in song with, it is estimated, perhaps as many as one hundred songs written and circulated. Most were swept away with the discarded ticker tape. Three displayed some token of longevity: "When Lindy Comes Home" by legendary songwriter, actor, and entertainer George M. Cohan; "Lindbergh, the Eagle of the U.S.A." by Abel Baer, Howard Johnson, and Al Sherman; and "Lucky Lindy" by L. Wolfe Gilbert and Abel Baer. Although Vernon Dalhart recorded the latter two songs, none was a hit.

A marathon for white dancers had just ended in June 1928 when a nonsegregated dance marathon got under way at the Manhattan Casino. The contestants danced an hour and then rested fifteen minutes. The marathon continued from June 17 until it was shut down by the Board of Health at 4:00 a.m. on July 4. At that time there were just four couples on the floor, including George "Shorty" Snowden, the all-time champion dancer of Harlem's Savoy Ballroom. Earlier in the marathon, Fox Movietone News had sent a camera crew to cover the event. Taking a close-up of Shorty's feet, the interviewer asked what he was doing with his feet. Without stopping, Shorty replied, "the Lindy."[11] Later, they called it the Jitterbug. But Marshall and Jean Stearns claim that the Lindy became a recognized part of the American scene in 1936, stemming from an earlier popular dance, the Texas Tommy. Although the Lindy was a syncopated two-step or box-step accenting the offbeat, it was identical with the Texas Tommy in its breakaway.

When the *Ziegfeld Follies of 1927* opened on August 16, it featured for the first time a single star, Eddie Cantor (in blackface), and most of the songs were by only one composer, Irving Berlin. Mounted for the then-staggering sum of $289,000, it opened on a jungle setting with an expensive, lush curtain by ace designer Joseph Urban, in front of which trotted a live ostrich carrying star Claire Luce. The score, however, was not up to Berlin's standard. But in 1927, hit tunes came bounding out of many shows.

Vincent Youmans's *Hit the Deck* yielded "Hallelujah!" and "Sometimes I'm Happy," neither written specifically for the show. "Hallelujah" had been composed by Youmans when he was in the Navy during World War I. The bandmaster at the Great Lakes Station was so impressed that he encouraged Youmans to compose more and helped make the number a favorite with Navy bands. John Philip Sousa heard it and added it to his repertoire of marches. "Sometimes I'm Happy" likewise used a melody composed earlier, for another song, "Come On and Pet Me," in the musical *Mary Jane McKane* (1923). Eliminated from the show, it was renamed "Sometimes I'm Happy" and tried in *A Night Out*, a musical that failed to reach New York. Scoring in *Hit the Deck*, the song became jazz trumpeter Bunny Berigan's first hit.

"Hallelujah!" met with a bizarre reception when *Hit the Deck* played in London. Glasgow critics attacked the song, which, they claimed, bordered on the sacrilegious. Their argument: the word meaning "Praise Ye the Lord" was being sung and played while sailors engaged in a basic drill. The British producer conceded that, during the show's premiere, two leading critics left the auditorium, imploring him to give it up. Apparently the criticism did not hurt the popularity of the song or the show, for it had an advance sale of over $100,000 for its eleven-week stay at the London Hippodrome.

The De Sylva, Brown and Henderson collegiate musical, *Good News*, gave four hits to the world: the title song, "Just Imagine," "Lucky in Love," and "The Best Things in Life Are Free," which in 1956 became the title of the Twentieth Century-Fox film biography of the trio. The show also gave rise to a new dance, the Varsity Drag, which did not really compete with the Charleston or the Black Bottom but became enormously popular on college campuses.

Two other hit shows—*A Connecticut Yankee* and *Funny Face*— each accounted for three memorable numbers. *A Connecticut Yankee*, continuing the partnership of Herbert Fields (book) with Rodgers and Hart, was based on Mark Twain's *A Connecticut Yankee in King Arthur's Court*. It numbered among its hits "Thou Swell," "I

Feel at Home with You," and "My Heart Stood Still," a song that had its beginnings in another show, Charles B. Cochran's London revue, *One Damn Thing After Another* (1927). It also had its beginnings not in London but in Paris when Rodgers and Hart, riding in a taxi with two girls, were almost in an accident, and one of the girls exclaimed, "My heart stood still." The methodical Rodgers, wrote the title in a notebook, and when they arrived in London to work on the Cochran score, wrote a melody to the title although Hart had forgotten all about it. Enter the Prince of Wales, who became excited about the song when Rodgers taught it to him. Dining and dancing one evening at the Cafe de Paris in London, the prince requested the song, demonstrating it, verse and chorus, for the Teddy Brown band, which quickly picked it up. The incident, written up extensively in the press, helped make "My Heart Stood Still" a hit.

I have heard an entirely different story about its origin. According to this version, Hart got into an argument with another songwriter, who was scoffing at the use of polysyllabic words by show writers and suggesting that writing a song with simple words posed a much greater challenge. Irritated, Hart sat down determined to show what he could do with simple words. A glance at the chorus of "My Heart Stood Still' will reveal that the first eight lines do not contain a single word that is not a monosyllable; the succeeding eight lines are likewise monosyllabic except for five two-syllable words.

Starring the Astaires, the Gershwins' *Funny Face* provided delightful songs in "My One and Only" and " 'S Wonderful," both romantic and both rhythmic, the latter displaying Ira's knack for word distortions. A third ballad, "He Loves and She Loves," more sentimental and less rhythmic, made its appearance when "How Long Has This Been Going On?" was dropped on the road. But Ziegfeld liked the deleted song so much he used it in *Rosalie,* changing it from a duet to a solo number.

Among the less successful shows of the season was *Betsy,* a short-lived musical that opened a few days before New Year's Eve of 1927. Produced by Ziegfeld, starring Belle Baker, and with a score by the new *wunderkinder* of Broadway, Rodgers and Hart, it nevertheless closed after only thirty-nine performances. Yet it launched one of the heartwarming evergreens of the year and decade, a ballad hit that was not written by Rodgers and Hart, even though their contract forbade the interpolation of songs by other composers. How it came to be introduced and written has been recalled by Belle Baker's son, who was six years old at the time. "The night before Belle opened on Broadway [after a so-so tryout in Boston]," he told Max Wilk, "she was brooding because she felt she was missing that one big song. So she picked up the phone and called Irving Berlin."[12] Somehow she persuaded Berlin to come to their apartment, where he worked through the night, nurtured by Maurice Abrahams, an old friend and Belle's husband, accompanist, and rehearsal conductor. Berlin had arrived with the opening strain of what became "Blue Skies," but was stuck for a middle eight. It was not until six in the morning that the young son, whose sleep had been constantly interrupted, heard shouting in the living room and found his father and Berlin playing the middle eight-bar bridge and singing the finished lyric.

When Ziegfeld was told of the song by Belle at 7:00 A.M., along with the threat that she would not go on without it, Ziegfeld said: "Belle, you can do it—but for God's sake, don't tell Rodgers or Hart."[13] "At about eleven [opening night]," Herbert Baker recalled, "my mother came out and sang *Blue Skies* for the first time. The audience went crazy. They really had been starved all night for her to do one like that. Would you believe that the audience made her sing that song over and over twenty-four times? And that on the twenty-third reprise she forgot the lyrics? Berlin stood up—he was sitting down in the front row—and he threw her the words—and they finished the next chorus singing together!

"*Betsy* got fair notices. . . . But *Blue Skies* became a terrific hit . . . and Rodgers and Hart didn't speak to my mother for the next twelve years."[14]

Among the recordings of 1927 voted into the Hall of Fame by the membership of the National Academy of Recording Arts and Sciences were Whiteman's *Rhapsody in Blue* and two jazz-oriented disks: Bix Beiderbecke's piano solo recording of his Debussy-flavored composition, "In a Mist" (OKeh), and Frankie Trumbauer and his Orchestra's "Singin' the Blues."

Although Red Nichols's disk of "Ida, Sweet as Apple Cider" was not named to the Hall of Fame, it had the distinction of selling more than a million copies in 1927. The song dated back to 1903, and was the work of the famous blackface minstrel, Eddie Leonard. It became identified with Eddie Cantor, whose wife's name was Ida.

Ernest Loring Nichols, better known as Red Nichols, was born in Ogden, Utah, in May 1905, the son of a local professor of music, and became one of the chief exponents of white dixieland style. A recording by Isham Jones moved him to leave a three-piece pit band in an Ogden Theatre—after expulsion from Culver Military Academy for smoking—and to head for New York. He made his first recording at the Gennett Studios in Richmond, Indiana, in October 1922, paying for the privilege instead of being paid, and receiving for $25 twenty-five copies of the disk he cut with the Syncopation Five. His well-known combo, the Five Pennies, consisting usually of six musicians, was formed in 1923, and went on to record under various pseudonyms for fourteen different labels. He worked with or employed such outstanding jazzmen as Arthur Schutt (piano), Miff Mole (trombone), Jimmy Dorsey (clarinet), Joe Venuti (violin), Glenn Miller (trombone), Tommy Dorsey, Benny Goodman, Gene Krupa, and Jack Teagarden.

The arrangement of "Ida, Sweet as Apple Cider" was made by Lennie Hayton, pianist, later an MGM musical conductor and the husband of Lena Horne. It was recorded in 1924, by which time Red was leading one of the best-known dixieland groups. But he also organized and conducted pit bands for several Broadway musicals during the twenties. A film, *The Five Pennies*, was made in 1958, with Danny Kaye playing the role of Red Nichols.

Another extremely popular ballad of 1927, whose sales reportedly reached five million records, was Gene Austin's disk of "My Blue Heaven." If the story is true—and stories about the origins of songs should always be viewed with a degree of cynicism—the melody of the song came to hit writer Walter Donaldson one day in 1924 when he was at the Friars Club and was waiting to play a game of billiards. Sometime later, he played the tune for George Whiting, to whom it appealed greatly and who offered to write a lyric. The family song that Whiting devised had little meaning for Donaldson, who was a bachelor, but it found great favor with Eddie Cantor. The ballad was initially introduced by Whiting, a successful vaudevillian, but made no great impression. It fared better when Tommy Lyman, a radio singer, adopted it as his theme in 1927. But it was Cantor who gave the song the send-off it warranted, interpolating it in the *Zeigfeld Follies of 1927* and adding lines to the lyrics about his five daughters as "the crowd" in his own blue heaven.

Gene Austin, who made the enormously successful recording, was born Eugene Lucas in Gainesville, Texas (1900–1972), and grew up in Louisiana. Although he introduced and recorded the two hits he wrote in 1924—"How Come You Do Me Like You Do?" and "When My Sugar Walks Down the Street"—neither approached "My Blue Heaven" in disk sales. It reportedly remained the all-time bestseller until 1942 when it was superseded by Bing Crosby's recording of "White Christmas."

The year also produced an unusual portfolio of standards. "Ukulele Ike" added Walter Donaldson's "At Sundown" to his catalogue of hits. Other songs by Tin Pan Alley songwriters that were being bought, hummed, and whistled by the public included the peppy "Ain't She Sweet," by Milton Ager and Jack Yellen; the nostalgic "Among My Souvenirs," by Edgar Leslie and Horatio Nichols; the scalewise "Just a Memory," by De Sylva, Brown and Henderson; and the Latin-flavored "Ramona," by L. Wolfe Gilbert and Mabel Wayne. Irving Berlin produced "The Song Is Ended," "Russian Lullaby" (a waltz), and the cheerful "Blue Skies"—cheerful despite a minor-keyed melody. A note of optimism was likewise sounded by Irving Kahal and Francis Wheeler in "Let a Smile Be Your Umbrella (On a Rainy Day)." Harry Richman added to his catalogue of hits with "C'est Vous," credited to Al Green, Abner Silver, and Richman.

Ted Lewis's featured number, "Me and My Shadow," which he performed with a live, black "shadow," also had a 1927 copyright. It was composed by Dave Dreyer (1894–1967) with Al Jolson, whom he sometimes accompanied, as a collaborator, and with Billy Rose as the lyricist. A mild-mannered man who came from Brooklyn, Dreyer started as a piano player in several publishing companies—he later accompanied Sophie Tucker as well as Jolson—and scored his first hit with "Cecelia," with words by Herman Ruby, in 1925. It was popularized by Whispering Jack Smith.

In 1928 Dreyer produced "Back in Your Own Backyard" with the same collaborators as "Me and My Shadow," and it became one of Jolson's perennials. In 1928, the trio also accounted for "There's A Rainbow 'Round My Shoulder," introduced by Jolson in the film *The Singing Fool*. "Rainbow 'Round My Shoulder" was included in *Variety's* "Fifty Year Parade," and Dreyer, who functioned as a publisher and manager in his latter days, was elected to the Song-writers' Hall of Fame.

The recording of country music had its beginnings that year during August 1–4 when Ralph Peer, working in a portable, makeshift studio in Bristol, Tennessee, cut a side featuring Jimmie Rodgers, the rail-road brakeman later known as the "Father of Country Music"; he also made disks of the legendary Carter Family. "The Soldier's Sweetheart," Rodger's first record, reportedly sold over a million copies. His initial royalty was a paltry $27.

1927 was also the year that a program on station WSM of Nash-ville, Tennessee, called simply "Barn Dance" became known by a name that is used today. The "Barn Dance" was inaugurated in 1925 by George Dewey Hay, sometimes known as "the solemn old judge," who had previously introduced the "Chicago Barn Dance" on station WLS. Legend has it that one evening when he introduced the WSM "Barn Dance" program after listeners had heard a network symphony or opera broadcast, he spontaneously referred to it by contrast as "Grand Ole Opry." The name became a fixture on December 10, 1927.

Trumpeter Henry Busse (1894–1955), who came from Germany to the United States in 1916, played with Paul Whiteman from 1918 to 1928, when he formed his own orchestra. In 1927, the recording he made with Whiteman of "When Day Is Done" is credited with start-ing the vogue for sweet jazz. He reportedly was the first trumpet player to use a mute and shuffle rhythm as background.

In 1927 the powerhouse publishers that spent large sums to dominate popular music were still M. Witmark, at 1650 Broadway, next to the Winter Garden; Feist, which ran double page ads for Walter Donaldson's "At Sundown" and Whiting and Donaldson's "My Blue Heaven"; Jerome Remick, who plugged Cliff Friend's "Give Me a June Night"; Mills Music, which favored a series of piano novelties—"Dizzy Fingers" and "Flapperette" by Jesse Greer, and "Soliloquy" by Rube Bloom—but also the ballad "I Can't Believe That You're in Love with Me" by Clarence Gaskill and Jimmy McHugh, who was then the firm's professional manager; Waterson, Berlin and Snyder, who advertised "Let a Smile Be Your Umbrella (On a Rainy Day)" by Irving Kahal and Francis Wheeler (words) and Sammy Fain (music); and Shapiro-Bernstein, which promoted "Just Another Day Wasted Away" by Roy Turk and Charles Tobias, the latter a busy Keith-Albee vaudevillian who called himself "The Boy Who Writes the Songs You Sing."

But Broadway boasted a new publishing firm that had come flying into the music scene early in the year with a flock of hits and was now, after six months, parading a bevy of new hits. De Sylva, Brown and Henderson, situated on the top floor of 745 Seventh Avenue, a building with the well-known Brass Rail restaurant on the street floor, started with their own "It All Depends on You" and "So Blue," and had the public singing "Here Am I—Broken Hearted," a torch ballad interpolated by Jack Osterman in the year's *Artists and Models* revue and popularized by Belle Baker. Perhaps the real point of a large two-page ad in *Variety* was the listing of new songs written by established writers who had been associated with the old, established firms, although it did not appear that this first group of outside titles turned into moneymakers.

During the gangster wars that bloodied the twenties, musicians generally escaped violence, though occasionally they had to continue playing while bullets ricocheted around the walls of a club. But in November 1927 a popular Chicago entertainer was the subject of one of the most vicious attacks of the era, never solved or explained but assumed to be the result of a power play between rival cafe owners. Joe E. Lewis, later a celebrated comic, was assaulted in his hotel room at the Commonwealth by several men who slashed him so severely that *Variety's* headline read: "Joe Lewis Survives Cutting/ Minus Voice, Arm and Mind."[15] Lewis "was cut from one end of his body to the other," the story read. "The deepest gash was in his throat; another deprived him of his right arm and hand, while the most serious is the skull fracture. With Lewis's life now seemingly saved, the doctors are concentrating on saving his voice. . . . The several experts called in say it is doubtful if he will recover it."

Lewis did recover it but never to sing again. That's how the bibulous standup comic was born. As for the assailants, Lewis apparently could give the police no help, and *Variety* offered no surmises. It did indicate, however, that Lewis had for two years been head of the show at the Green Mill on Chicago's 23rd Street, building up "one of the staunchest personal followings" in the city and being regarded "as the perfect cafe master of ceremonies." The story continued: "An offer doubling Joe's reputed $650 salary at the Mill was entered recently by the Rendezvous, competitive north side night club, and Joe accepted three weeks ago. . . . Seemingly bewildered at the mysterious, brutal and effective attack on Lewis, police are now predicting a cabaret war to rival the strife of the beer runners. . . ."[16]

The perpetrators of the attack were never apprehended, but the general opinion was that the attack was a reaction to Lewis's decision to leave the Green Mill.

In 1927, as a sign of the times, litterateur Edmund Wilson published a "Lexicon of Prohibition," which contained 104 terms for "intoxicated." Lest that number seem excessive, Wilson noted that Ben Franklin's *Drinker's Dictionary*, compiled more than a century before, listed 228 terms for the condition. Among the synonyms Wilson included: owled, sprung, jagged, buried, jingled, piffed, scrooded, spiflicated, squiffy, sozzled, bloated, corked, corned, polluted, ossified, embalmed, fried to the hat, slopped to the ears, lit up like the Commonwealth.

～ 17 ～

"*The Singing Fool*"
(1928)

Few songs have begun as strangely as "Sonny Boy," a De Sylva, Brown and Henderson opus written for Al Jolson. The songwriting team was then in Atlantic City working on the score of a new show. Jolie (as Jolson was called), shooting a film at Warner Brothers studios in Burbank, California, phoned long distance, citing the need for a new song. Time was of the essence. Working through the night, the trio were on the phone the following morning, demonstrating the song they had written and that became known as "Sonny Boy." If a sequence in the De Sylva, Brown and Henderson biopic, *The Best Things In Life Are Free*, is to be believed, the song was written with tongue in cheek as a satire of tear-jerkers. It surely is an extremely sentimental weeper, and one whose saccharine quality has opened it to humorous takeoffs. It may be some indication of the trio's intent that the manuscript received by Jolson in Burbank did not bear their names but the pseudonym "Elmer Colby." In any case, Jolson's recording of "Sonny Boy," backed by "There's a Rainbow 'Round My Shoulder" by Billy Rose, Dave Dreyer, and Jolson, became the first million seller of the talking film era. It sold over a million in sheet music, too. And *The Singing Fool*, Jolson's follow-up film to *The Jazz Singer*, became the first musical picture to gross over $4 million.

Born Asa Jolson (1886–1950) in Washington, D.C., Jolson was

very much like the character he played in *The Jazz Singer.* He was
the son of an orthodox rabbi, who doubtless hoped to see his son
follow in his footsteps; Jolson did substitute for his father as a singing cantor at the age of thirteen. Nevertheless, by 1909 he was working as a blackface endman with the Lew Dockstader Minstrels. The
Shuberts were so impressed by him that two years later they starred
him in *La Belle Paree,* initiating a relationship that lasted ten years.
Their major Broadway showcase, the Winter Garden on Broadway
and 51st Street, was really Jolson's own playhouse.

During these years and through the twenties, Jolie was among the
most consistent hit maker among singers. His power was such that
most publishers and songwriters were willing to put Jolson's name
on a song if he would record it—thus his name appears as cowriter
on a very large number of songs. Among the tunes he made a permanent part of popular music are "Avalon" and "My Mammy,"
from *Sinbad* (1918); "April Showers," "Toot, Toot, Tootsie (Goo'
Bye)," and "California, Here I Come," all from *Bombo* (1921);
"My Buddy" (1922); "Alabamy Bound" (1925); "If You Knew
Susie Like I Know Susie," from *Big Boy* (1925); "Breezin' Along
with the Breeze" (1926); "I'm Sitting on Top of the World,"
"Sonny Boy," "There's a Rainbow 'Round My Shoulder," and "It
All Depends on You," from *The Singing Fool* (1928); and "Back in
Your Own Backyard" (1928). Jolson's career continued through the
thirties and forties, when the list lengthened immeasurably. Of Jol-
son's rendition of "There's A Rainbow 'Round My Shoulder,"
Charles Chaplin wrote in his *Autobiography:* "He lifted the audience
by an unadulterated compulsion. He personified the feeling of Broadway, its vitality and vulgarity, its aims and dreams."[1]

During World War II, Jolson devoted his time so unstintingly and
so successfully to entertaining the troops that Warner Brothers
mounted a biopic, *The Jolson Story,* that created a new generation of
fans. Larry Parks played Jolie, but the singing was done by Jolson
himself, with Parks lip-synching. The 1945 edition was so great a
success that *Jolson Sings Again* was released as a follow-up in 1946.
Returning in 1950 from an exhausting tour of American troops in
Korea, Jolson died suddenly in San Francisco of a heart attack.

If *The Singing Fool* was the sensation of the musical film scene, *Blackbirds of 1928* was the big news on Broadway. After the all-black, Sissle-Blake revue, *Shuffle Along*, had dazzled theatregoers in 1921, there had been a flock of black musicals. Except for *Runnin' Wild* (1923), none approached *Shuffle Along* until *Blackbirds* ran for over five hundred performances. An inexpensively mounted show, relying mostly on drapes, *Blackbirds* succeeded because of its stellar black cast and its sock score. Dorothy Fields (1905–1974), daughter of legendary comic and producer Lew Fields and brother of Herbert Fields (of Fields, Rodgers and Hart), and Jimmy McHugh (1894–1969) had never written a Broadway show before. But they created a score filled with such hits as "I Can't Give You Anything But Love, Baby," "Diga Diga Do," and the toe-tapping "Doin' the New Low Down," to which Bill Robinson did one of his eye-catching and ear-arresting tap-dance routines. The sterling cast also included singers Adelaide Hall and Aida Ward. The show was a triumph of talent, song, and dance.

The varied musical fare available to theatregoers in 1928 included Sigmund Romberg's last operetta, *The New Moon*, which ran over five hundred performances—after nearly closing during its initial tryout—and boasted an unusual number of pop hits. Among the romantic ballads were "Softly as in a Morning Sunrise," "Wanting You," "One Kiss," and "Lover, Come Back to Me," which became a favorite with jazz combos. A large, rich-voiced male chorus added color to the proceedings, especially during the rousing "Stout-Hearted Men."

Records whose popularity brought a sale of over a million included "Blue Yodel," named to the NARAS Hall of Fame, and "Brakeman's Blues" by Jimmie Rodgers (1897–1933), celebrated as the greatest of the pioneer country artists. Legend has it that Mississippi housewives regularly ordered "the latest Jimmie Rodgers record" along with the foodstuffs they bought. Rodgers was born in Meridian, Mississippi, the son of a railroad section foreman on the Mobile and Ohio Railroad. Growing up he worked as an assistant to his father, functioning as flagman, brakeman, and baggage man for fourteen years. Delicate health prompted him to turn to singing and guitar playing, and led him to audition for Ralph Peer when the Victor producer and publisher came to Tennessee with a field recording unit in August 1927. Rodgers liked to yodel and wrote and recorded thirteen Blue Yodels. In 1933, suffering from tuberculosis and with his finances in a bad state, he went to New York to record. Cutting twelve sides over a period of eight days at the Victor studios on East 24th Street, frequently propped up on a cot, he made his last disk on May 24. He died ten days later in his room at the Hotel Taft on Seventh Avenue. When the Country Music Hall of Fame was established, he became the first member elected by a unanimous vote on November 3, 1961. (Ralph Peer, the father of country recording and publishing—he founded the still-flourishing Southern Music Company—died on January 14, 1960.)

In addition to the "Singing Brakeman," as Rodgers was known, Peer recorded the legendary Carter Family, consisting of A. P. Carter (bass vocalist), his wife Sarah (lead vocalist and autoharpist), and her cousin Maybelle Carter (vocalist and lead guitar). On May 9–10, 1928, they recorded a dozen songs at the Victor studio in Camden, New Jersey, including "Wildwood Flower," a traditional song that became their most requested love song. During their recording years, the Carter Family waxed over two hundred and fifty songs, many of them by Alvin Pleasant Carter (1891–1960), who started out as a carpenter in the Virginia hill country. Maybelle Carter, born in Michellsville, Virginia, sang with her sister over radio stations in Tennessee, including the famous Grand Ole Opry—and later, after the Carter Family dissolved, recorded with her three daughters— Helen, Anita, and June, who later became the wife of Johnny Cash. The Carter Family was elected to the Country Music Hall of Fame in 1970.

Other extremely popular songs that moved up into the million-sales class were "Ramona" and "My Yiddishe Momme." The former, by L. Wolfe Gilbert and Mabel Wayne, was Gene Austin's second million seller. As one of the first of the celebrated film theme songs, it made Tin Pan Alley history, selling worldwide on disk, piano-player rolls, and sheet music. "My Yiddishe Momme," we are told, was originally written in 1925 by Jack Yellen as a personal tribute to his mother,

who recently had died. A few years later, he asked Lew Pollack to
work on the melody with him, and eventually the song credits read
"Jack Yellen (words), Jack Yellen and Lew Pollack (music). "On
an impulse," he told David Ewen, "I called up Sophie Tucker at the
Claridge Hotel in New York. She bawled me out for spoiling her
sleeping pill, but she listened and when I finished singing, she was
weeping. Between gulps, she asked me to send her a copy. She wrote
me that her agents and friends suggested the title be changed to
"Jewish" or "Hebrew Mama," being afraid of the word 'Yiddish.' I
told her that if she sang it, it would be 'Yiddishe Momme' or nothing
at all; and what is more, I insisted that she should sing the chorus
in Yiddish, the way I had written it."[2]

The 1928 disk that sold a million copies was two-sided, with the English version on one side and the Yiddish on the other. The accompaniment was by Ted Shapiro, who worked with Sophie for forty-six
years, up to her death, and wrote much special material for her.
Sophie introduced the song initially at the Palace Theatre in New
York in 1925 to a standing ovation. Requests turned it into one of
her specialties, second in importance only to "Some of These Days."
In her autobiography, she wrote, "I have found whenever I have
sung 'My Yiddishe Momme' in the United States or Europe, Gentiles
have loved the song and have called for it. They didn't need to understand the Yiddish words. They knew by instinct what I was saying. . . . All over the Continent, this is the song which has identified
me, as 'Some of These Days' is recognized as my theme in America."[3]

Two songs that made their first appearance in 1928 had to wait for
years to attain their true popularity. "Together" by De Sylva, Brown
and Henderson was a moderate hit on its introduction, but came into
its own in 1944 when it was interpolated in the film *Since You Went
Away*. Also in 1944 "I'll Get By (As Long As I Have You)," by
Roy Turk (words) and Fred E. Ahlert, (music), enjoyed a robust
revival as a result of the film *A Guy Named Joe*, starring Spencer
Tracy and Irene Dunne, with the latter interpreting the song. Previously, it had been kept in the ears of the public by Ruth Etting.

Other songs also evolved slowly into standards. Introduced in
vaudeville and sung in his first starring role in a talking picture

(*Lucky Boy*), "My Mother's Eyes" by L. Wolfe Gilbert (words) and Abel Baer (music) became George Jessel's theme song—and in time, a Mother's Day perennial. "My Kinda Love" by Jo Trent (words) and Louis Alter (music) introduced in the *Americana* revue, but became popular in 1929 as the result of a Decca recording by Bing Crosby, his first as a solo vocalist. Identified with Sue Carol (Mrs. Alan Ladd), to whom the song is dedicated and whose visage adorns the sheet music, "Sweet Sue—Just You," with words by Will J. Harris and music by the prolific Victor Young, was introduced by Bennie Kreuger and his Orchestra and revived in the forties in the film *Rhythm Parade*, where it was performed by the Mills Brothers. There was also "Sweet Lorraine," by Mitchell Parrish (words) and Cliff Burwell (music) a favorite of Rudy Vallee and also a jazz favorite as the result of a hot version by clarinetist Jimmie Noone.

"Sweet Lorraine" is credited by some people with accounting for the transformation of Nat "King" Cole from a jazz instrumentalist into a pop singer. According to this apocryphal tale, the King Cole Trio was performing in a Los Angeles club in 1937 when a sozzled customer asked Cole to sing "Sweet Lorraine." Since Cole had ostensibly never sung in public before, he balked; but the drunk was so insistent that Cole finally gave in and warbled the ballad. Audience reaction was so strong that Cole thereafter turned his talents from the piano to crooning. The tale does not make sense, however, since as late as 1944 the King Cole Trio appeared in a film, *Here Comes Elmer*, and made a hit of a jazz number titled "Straighten Up and Fly Right," written by Nat. His first solo recording, "Nature Boy," did not come until 1948.

Ralph Watkins, the owner of Kelly's Stable on 52nd Street, offered another story of how Cole came to sing solo. "I didn't know he could sing when I booked him," he told me. "But one day, my sister, who was the bookkeeper at the Stable, phoned me and said, 'My God, you've got to come here. Nat's been rehearsing this one number all day. He has sung it so many times I'm going out of my mind.' I told her she must be mistaken, that Nat didn't sing. That's how we found out and got Nat to sing once or twice."[4]

In my book, *52nd St. The Street of Jazz,* I added in a parenthesis:
"(According to Billy Daniels, Nat did no singing at the time because
he had a speech problem. It was only after he had gotten help from
a speech therapist that he acquired the confidence to sing publicly.)"[5]
And all of this referred to the 1944–1945 period.

A film *The Awakening,* using an unidentified female vocalist off-
screen, introduced Irving Berlin's "Marie," later a signature of the
well-known Tommy Dorsey swing band. A musical, *Whoopee,* brought
popularity to "Love Me or Leave Me" through the vocal artistry of
Ruth Etting. An orchestra, Guy Lombardo and his Royal Canadians,
accounted for the popularity of "Coquette," one of their first Decca
recordings and John W. Green's first published song. All three songs
of 1928 were included in *Variety's* "Golden 100, 1918–35."

"Coquette" was the result of a collaboration of Gus Kahn (words)
and Johnny Green and Carmen Lombardo (music). Carmen was the
lead sax and vocalist for his brother Guy's Royal Canadians, the
saxman whose syrupy alto gave the orchestra one of its distinctive
sounds. Born in London, Ontario, in 1902, Guy Lombardo started a
three-piece band at the age of twelve with Carmen and another
brother, Lebert, who played trumpet. Expanding to nine, and adding
brother Victor on baritone sax, the band gained experience and established itself in Cleveland where it appeared in vaudeville and at
the Lake Road Inn. It then moved to Chicago and New York, beginning its recording activities in 1927. By 1929 it opened at the Roosevelt Grill in New York City, where it became one of the most com-
mercially successful dance bands in America over a thirty-three-year
period. Using "Auld Lang Syne" as its theme, it played what it described as "The Sweetest Music This Side of Heaven." Guy was
regarded by sophisticated musicians as the "King of Corn," but he
always claimed that his corn was golden.

Among the 128 records voted into the Hall of Fame by NARAS
were Gene Austin's disk of "My Blue Heaven," Jimmie Rodgers's
"Blue Yodel (T for Texas)," and Duke Ellington's "Black and Tan
Fantasy." Blues and Boogie were well represented by Bessie Smith's

"Empty Bed Blues," Louis Armstrong's "West End Blues," and Pine Top Smith's "Pine Top's Boogie Woogie."

Ruth Etting, to whom recognition as a Broadway star came in 1928, never had a million-copy disk, though she recorded regularly for Columbia, putting all her request numbers on disks. And yet it was one of her records that moved Irving Berlin to urge her upon Ziegfeld for a role in the *Follies of 1927*. A starring role in *Whoopee* followed in 1928, yielding the Gus Kahn-Walter Donaldson torch ballad "Love Me or Leave Me," which became a perennial and was used as the title of Ruth's biopic in 1955.

Born in David City, Nebraska—sources do not agree whether it was as early as 1896 or as late as 1903—Ruth entered show business at seventeen as a costumer in a Chicago nightclub, the Marigold Gardens, after studying design at that city's Academy of Fine Arts. Before long, she was dancing in the chorus line and began singing after filling in one night for an ailing principal. A turning point in her career came backstage at the Gardens when she met Martin Snyder, better known as Moe the Gimp because of a leg injury that gave him a peculiar gait.

The Gimp, a smalltime politician, worked with some of Chicago's gangsters, who once rewarded him with seventeen bullets, all of which reputedly remained lodged in his body. When the Gimp saw the willowy, honey-haired, blue-eyed Ruth he fell in love, pugnaciously and possessively. Having served at times as a bodyguard for Al Jolson, Eddie Cantor, and others subjected to shake downs by gangsters during appearances in Chicago, he had theatrical connections that proved advantageous to Etting. He became her adviser and manager, and after divorcing his first wife, proposed to Ruth, who, she confessed to friends, "was too frightened to say anything but yes."[6] In 1920, two years after they met, they eloped. It was a stormy, ugly relationship, but one Ruth could not sever: "If I leave him, he'll kill me," she told friends.[7]

After *Whoopee*, Ruth starred in *Simple Simon* (1930), with a score by Rodgers and Hart that gave her "Ten Cents a Dance," another of her great numbers; but she also reprised "Love Me or Leave

Me," even though it was penned by different writers. Between *Whoopee* and *Simple Simon* she appeared in *The 9:15 Revue*, which gave her "Get Happy" by Ted Koehler (words) and Harold Arlen (music). In the *Ziegfeld Follies of 1931*, performing an impersonation of the late Nora Bayes, she stirred a revival of "Shine On Harvest Moon," introduced by Nora Bayes and Jack Norworth in the *Ziegfeld Follies of 1908*.

With her own shows on radio—Oldsmobile in 1934 and Kellogg's College Prom in 1935—nightclub bookings, recordings, and Broadway, Etting's salary soared to $2,500 a week. Her success was partly the result of the Gimp's management, but her life with him was intolerable. Finally, in 1937 she managed, by threatening to give up her career, to secure a Vegas divorce and moved to Hollywood. When the Gimp learned that she was seeing socially Myrl Alderman, her arranger and accompanist, he shot him. Alderman, who had divorced his second wife, lived to marry Ruth two months after the shooting, while the Gimp was on trial. By the time he had completed a one-year prison term, Ruth was in retirement, in part because of damaging publicity resulting from an alienation of affection suit brought by Alderman's ex-wife.

Ruth never took a singing lesson. But from the time she warbled Berlin's "Remember," "Looking at the World through Rose-Colored Glasses," and "Ramona" at the College Inn in Chicago's Hotel Sherman, songwriters clamored for her to introduce their songs. It's impossible to hear such tunes as "Sam, the Old Accordion Man," "Mean to Me," "If I Could Be with You One Hour Tonight," among others, without having Ruth's sound and image crowd one's memory. Ruth Etting was among the three or four outstanding female hit-makers of the 1920s, all of whom were standout torch singers. The feeling of lost, unrequited, or unfulfilled love which they communicated so heartfully, was perhaps the result of the unhappiness in their own lives, for Ruth and Fanny Brice and Helen Morgan were most unfortunate in their choice of mates.

"Payola," a problem in music business from the outset—though public awareness of it has come mostly during the rock era—was the subject of an article in the January 4, 1928 issue of *Variety*. It observed that the older system of weekly payment for plugs to vaudeville and specialty revue performers had been superseded by royalty payments to band directors, masters of ceremony, and stars. "The new racket," *Variety* averred, "runs anywhere from $1,000 to $20,000 a year as salary charged against royalty . . . on the songs supposedly written by them." Concluding, the paper said, "It's the old racket, having the clothes made by a more expensive tailor." Noting further that several unnamed bandleaders were on the payroll of various firms as "collaborators" on songs, the publication named Chicago, the Coast, and New York as the centers of such practices. Curiously, Isham Jones, popular bandleader of the College Inn in Chicago, was singled out as "a shining example." The attack on Jones quickly drew a strong objection from lyricist Gus Kahn, who collaborated with Jones on "It Had to Be You" and "I'll See You in My Dreams," among other hits, and who stated categorically, "I give you my word that he wrote every note of every song I wrote with him."[8]

In January 1928, the Hotel Lincoln opened its doors in the West 40s, and Chez Helen Morgan, a most popular night spot on West 54th Street, was raided and completely demolished by Prohibition agents.

Nora Bayes (born Dora Goldberg), singing star of early editions of the *Ziegfeld Follies* and remembered for "Shine on Harvest Moon," which she cowrote and performed with Jack Norworth, her third husband, died in March 1928, just four days after she had sung "Alabamy Bound," popularized by Cantor and Jolson, at a Bowery Mission House benefit in New York City.

Bandleader Paul Ash was greeted enthusiastically by the Gotham music publishing world when he arrived in New York for a stand at the Paramount Theatre in May.

Donaldson, Douglas and Gumble was added to the roster of New York music publishing firms in June as Walter Donaldson, one of Alley's most consistent hit-writers, scored his first Broadway show, *Whoopee*. With lyrics by Gus Kahn, the show was credited by the *Oxford Dictionary* with introducing the phrase "making whoopee" into the English language, but Broadwayites knew it before the show as an expression frequently found in Walter Winchell's gossip column in the *Daily Mirror*.

By 1928 De Sylva, Brown and Henderson, just a little more than a year in business, was slotted among the big four of popular music publishers, according to *Variety*, with "Among My Souvenirs" rated as the country's number one song.[9]

As the year neared its end, Times Square acquired the illuminated headline sign running around the building at the intersection of 42nd Street and Broadway and Seventh Avenue, with Hoover's defeat of Al Smith for the Presidency as the first headline. The landmark sign operated continuously until 1977. After a hiatus of almost ten years, it came back into operation in 1986.

1928 was a year of marathon dances—that masochistic display of energy misspent before sadistic onlookers—flagpole sitting and other freakish entertainments. An odd-sounding singer, debuting then, became known as the "boop-a-doop girl!" Her name was Helen Kane, and she drew quite a lot of publicity by singing in a squeaky voice, initially attracting attention with a baby-voiced rendition of "I Wanna Be Loved by You (Boop-boop-a-doop)" in the musical *Good Boy*. She was able to command an audience also with "That's My Weakness Now," delivered in the same unique manner. To many observers, 1928 seemed to be reaching heights of humorous absurdity, which, as in a Shakespearian tragedy, betokened the onset of dismal happenings, an omen that the dizzy and unaccountable rise of the stock market was soon to confirm.

Three other new voices were first heard in 1928, each destined to leave a more lasting imprint on popular music than the boop-a-doop lass. Rudy Vallee came from Yale with his Connecticut Yankees— named after the Rodgers and Hart show—to entertain at the Heigh-Ho Club in mid-Manhattan. Although his first recordings "If I Had You," "Honey," and Irving Berlin's "Marie" were limited in appeal, his club performances drew such crowds—"Heigh-Ho, Everybody!"— that the name of the club to which he moved was changed after a short time to Villa Vallee.

Out of the Paul Whiteman Orchestra and its thirty-four pieces came the Rhythm Boys. Al Rinker, Harry Barris and Bing Crosby shook up the record scene in 1928 with "Mississippi Mud," composed by Barris and accompanied by Bix Beiderbecke, Tommy Dorsey, Jimmy Dorsey, and other notables. Bing remained with the Rhythm Boys when they went on to perform with Gus Arnheim at Los Angeles's Cocoanut Grove, embarking on his grandiose solo career in 1931. (In 1928 Johnny Mercer, who was hired by Whiteman to write songs for his Kraft radio show, arrived in New York from Savannah, Georgia.) The third new voice was that of Libby Holman, who caused a sensation in *The Little Show* in 1929, but whose husky-voiced rendition of "I Want a Man" in Vincent Youmans's musical *Rainbow* opened the door to stardom.

Carnegie Hall was the scene in 1928 of the premiere of *Yamekraw (Negro Rhapsody)* in an arrangement for piano and orchestra by William Grant Still. It had appeared in the preceding year as a piano solo by stride king James P. Johnson, composer of "Charleston," who spent his latter years trying to break down the barriers between popular and art music, merging European and Afro-American traditions, and flavoring extended works with the sounds and rhythms of boogie-woogie, blues, and jazz. W. C. Handy, "father of the blues," was the conductor of *Yamekraw* and Fats Waller the piano soloist. In his publisher's preface, Perry Bradford described the piece, written in one movement with four large sections, as "a genuine Negro treatise on spiritual, syncopated and blues melodies, expressing the religious fervor and happy moods of natives of Yamekraw, a Negro settlement on the outskirts of Savannah, Georgia."[10] Four years later, Johnson completed *Harlem Symphony*, performed also at an all-Johnson concert in 1945. All the movements of the work have apparently been lost except "April in Harlem," recorded recently by pianist William Albright.

1928 brought the creativity of two "new" theatre writers to the music scene, and both came to epitomize the world-weariness, and sophisticated gaiety and the *fin de siecle* letdown that marked the end of the decade. Although Cole Porter (1892–1964) had written shows back in 1916 (*See America First*) and 1919 (*Hitchy-Koo of 1919*), and contributed songs to the *Greenwich Village of 1924,* it was the material he wrote for a play with songs that first displayed the true Porter touch and established him as a talent to be reckoned with. The play was *Paris,* starring Irene Bordoni, and to it he contributed the smartly suggestive "Let's Misbehave" and "Let's Do It."

The other "new" theater writer was an Englishman, Noel Coward (1899–1973), a prodigiously productive songwriter, performer, and playwright who was well established in his own country and who had contributed songs to *Andre Charlot's Revue* of 1924 and 1925. In 1928 he arrived on the American stage with *This Year of Grace,* a musical play with book, lyrics, and music by himself. He also starred in the production, whose costars were the great British comedienne, Beatrice Lillie, and G. P. Huntley. The score was rich with such songs as "World Weary," "Mary Make-Believe," the title song, and "A Room with a View," which reputedly was played nine times at London's Ascot Cabaret Ball to satisfy repeated requests by the Prince of Wales.

⤳ 18 ⤳

California Gold Rush
(1929)

Despite its cataclysmic terminus—$18 billion was lost in the October tumble of the stock market—1929 was a rich year in popular music and a bonanza for songwriters. With film enjoying the first full fruits of the new sound technology, songwriters reaped a harvest from the all-talking, all-singing, all-dancing direction that the movies increasingly took. The musical theatre enjoyed an impressive number of smash shows. And Tin Pan Alley, despite the flow of hits from the screen and the stage, produced a number of great standards of its own, including "Star Dust" and, with unintended irony, "Happy Days Are Here Again."

1929 was a year of climaxes. The stock market hit an all-time high just before the crash. Civic corruption peaked in the conviction of former Secretary of the Interior, Albert B. Fall, judged guilty of accepting a $100,000 bribe in the leasing of California naval oil reserves. Chicago gangsterism reached a bloody climax when seven O'Bannion gang members were mowed down by machine guns in the St. Valentine's Day massacre. Textile workers striking in Gastonia, North Carolina, were shot to death, inspiring two impressive novels of the early thirties: Mary Heaton Vorse's *Strike* and Grace Lumpkin's *To Make My Bread*. The novel attained new heights with Hemingway's *A Farewell to Arms*, Thomas Wolfe's *Look Homeward Angel*, William Faulkner's *The Sound and the Fury*, Sinclair Lewis's

Dodsworth. And Charles Lindbergh married Anne Spencer Morrow, daughter of the U.S. Ambassador to Mexico.

1929 was a year of firsts in screen musicals. *Gold Diggers of Broadway* (Warner Brothers) was the first musical to feature color— color sequences in two tones. *The Desert Song* (Warner Brothers) of Sigmund Romberg was the first operetta to make the screen, and the operetta *Rio Rita* (RKO) the first musical to employ the technicolor process. *Hallelujah* (MGM) was the first all-black film musical, featuring, in addition to Negro spirituals, two songs by Irving Berlin. The crowning achievement was *The Broadway Melody* (MGM), acclaimed as the first "100 percent ALL Talking, ALL Singing and ALL Dancing" movie, with the first original score by Nacio Herb Brown and Arthur Freed. It was the first movie in the sound era to win an Academy Award for Best Film.

By 1929 virtually all the studios were producing musicals, and musical numbers were interpolated into as many as one hundred feature films. Even Dorothy Parker was persuaded to try her gifted hand at lyric writing, and came up with "How Am I to Know," music by Jack King, a ballad sung by short-lived Russ Columbo in *Dynamite*. Marion Davies, hardly a singer, introduced "Just You, Just Me" in *Marianne*. And in *The Trespasser* Gloria Swanson warbled "Love, Your Magic Spell Is Everywhere," words by Elsie Janis and music by Director Edmund Golding.

The first singer who became known as a "crooner," Russ Columbo (1908–1934), was believed to be at the beginning of a most exciting career when a fatal accident ended his life at the age of twenty-six. He was at the home of a friend, who kept an antique set of dueling pistols on his desk as paperweights. They were supposed to be unloaded, but when the friend struck a match against one pistol to light a cigarette, the gun fired. A bullet ricocheted off the desk and lodged in Columbo's head, killing him instantly. The news was kept from his mother, who was blind and in delicate health. For years members of the family and actress Carole Lombard, with whom Columbo had been linked romantically, read letters to her from Russ, giving various excuses for his failure to visit her. She died without ever knowing of his sad end.

Among the picture studios that anticipated the increased value of music to films, Warner Brothers sped quickly out in front in a massive move involving more than seven publishing companies. Raising a kitty of $8.5 million, Warners absorbed the catalogues of Harms and Chappell-Harms (Max and Louis Dreyfus), parent companies plus their subsidiaries: De Sylva, Brown and Henderson (Robert Crawford, president); Remick Music Corporation (Jerome Keit, president); Green and Stept (Mack Stark, president); Famous Music Corporation (Paramount-affiliated, theme song publishing subsidiary); T. B. Harms Company, a separate company that handled Jerome Kern publications; and New World Corp, a unit that handled George Gershwin's works. As owners of thousands of copyrights in these companies, Warner Brothers had virtual control of the Executive Board of ASCAP, on which representatives of the various companies sat. Not to be outclassed, MGM purchased the catalogues of Robbins Music Corporation, Leo Feist, Inc., and Miller Music to create the Big Three. It was a shrewd move on the part of the film studios, since they could now largely control the fees paid for the use of songs and could build their own publishing giants by developing new film hits.

With so many publishers becoming adjuncts of the Hollywood studios, Shapiro-Bernstein and Company seized the occasion to boast in a *Variety* advertisement: "We are the foremost Independent Publishers, absolutely unattached. . . ." More than a boast, it was an effort to attract Tin Pan Alley songwriters fed up with firms and whose choice of plug songs was dictated by the film studios and picture commitments. By the end of the year, the consensus of music publishers as to the effectiveness of various media in plugging and popularizing songs yielded the following rartings: 1) talkies and film themes; 2) radio; 3) bands; 4) disks; 5) acts; 6) organists; 7) musicals; 8) nightclubs.

By a wide margin, Warner Brothers' list of musicals was the longest. In addition to *The Desert Song,* it initiated a series of *Gold Diggers* films, the first of which yielded "Tip Toe Through the Tulips" and "Painting the Clouds with Sunshine," both by Al Dubin and Joe Burke. *Honky Tonk* was a vehicle for Sophie Tucker, in which she gave a blues-shouting performance of "I'm the Last of the Red-Hot Mamas" by Jack Yellen and Milton Ager. In *My Man,* Fannie Brice gave outstanding presentations of "Second Hand Rose (with a Yiddish accent), the title song (without the accent), and "If You Want a Rainbow (You Must Have the Rain)." Ted Lewis's signature expression, "Is Everybody Happy?" became the title of a picture starring him and his band, in which they performed "St. Louis Blues" and the ODJB "Tiger Rag."

Other Warner Brothers musicals included *On with the Show,* in which Ethel Waters sang one of her standards, "Am I Blue"; *Time, the Place and the Girl,* which made an appeal to the academic crowd with such songs as "Collegiate" by Moe Jaffee and Nat Bonx, "Collegiana" by Dorothy Fields and Jimmy McHugh, and "Doin' the Raccoon" by Ray Klages (words) and J. Fred Coots (music), a dance-song based on the popular overcoat of the day.

Inevitably a number of motion pictures relied on established hits to carry a film, with "Blue Skies," "Sam, the Old Accordion Man," and "At Sundown" reviving tunes already known to audiences of Paramount's *Glorifying the American Girl;* but the film whose title echoed Ziegfeld's byword also included "Just a Vagabond Lover," a new melody by Rudy Vallee and Leon Zimmerman. RKO Pictures capitalized on Rudy Vallee's soaring popularity, starring him in *The Vagabond Lover,* in which he sang "Piccolo Pete," "A Little Kiss Each Morning," by Harry Woods, and two songs associated with Vallee, the title song and his opening signature, "Heigh-Ho Everybody." "Piccolo Pete," a novelty song by Phil Baxter, an early member of Paul Whiteman's Band during World War I and later a noted arranger, became a million seller for Ted Weems and his Orchestra in 1929. The vocal was by Parker Gibbs, later associated with Chicago's famous *Breakfast Club* program.

In the worldwide publicity attending the riots occasioned by Frank Sinatra's first solo performances at the Paramount Theatre in 1943, sight has been lost of Rudy Vallee's emergence as the first male singing idol whose appearance at a New York theatre provoked a riot. It was in February 1929 that a three-day stand by Vallee and his Connecticut Yankees caused such a commotion that mounted police were called out to restore order. The place was Keith's 81st Street Theater; Vallee's impact was such that his stay was extended an additional four days, and he received a contract to tour the vaudeville circuit that brought him to the top vaudeville house, the Palace, in April 1929.

Born in 1901 in Vermont, Vallee grew up in Maine, attended the state university, and after interruptions to play the saxophone with touring bands, graduated from Yale in 1927. This was before the introduction of the microphone; for amplification, he used a megaphone. It became his trademark, along with his greeting of "Heigh-ho, everybody," which originated during his appearances at the Heigh-Ho Club in Manhattan in 1928. From the Heigh-Ho, he went to the Versailles Club on East 60th Street, renamed the Villa Vallee in 1929, the year he began making records, appeared in his first two films, was put on a weekly retainer by the music publishing firm of Leo Feist, and was signed to his first sponsored network radio show. For the Fleischmann Hour, initiated during the week of the stock market crash, he adopted "My Time Is Your Time," a British import of 1924, as his theme; he had first sung it with the Yale Collegians, then introduced it at the Heigh-Ho Club.

With his thin, nasal voice, Vallee was to the late twenties and thirties the hit-maker that Al Jolson remained through much of the era. In addition to the titles already mentioned, his records and Fleischmann Hour performances made bestsellers of "Deep Night," "Betty Co-Ed," "Life Is Just a Bowl of Cherries," "Stein Song (Maine Stein Song)," the Yale "Whiffenpoof Song," "Sweet Lorraine," "If You Were the Only Girl in the World" (featured in *The Vagabond Lover*), "If I Had You," "S'posin'," and "I Kiss Your Hand Madame," a German import.

Vallee enjoyed a long career on the radio, on Broadway, records, and in films, extending into the 1960s, when he starred in the hit musical *How to Succeed in Business Without Really Trying*. Born Herbert Pryor Vallee, he adopted the name Rudy as a tribute to virtuoso saxophonist Rudy Wiedoeft, and also to Rudolph Valentino. He started his career as a sax player, but was hardly in a class that would have earned him the fame that came to him as a crooner. (He died July 3, 1986 while watching the Statue of Liberty's centennial celebration on TV.)

A number of new musical acting "teams" emerged on the screen via the new medium of sound. The most popular was Janet Gaynor and Charles Farrell for whom De Sylva, Brown and Henderson produced three hits in *Sunny Side Up* (Fox): the spirited title song; "I'm a Dreamer (Aren't We All)"; and, obviously inspired by the possibilities of sound, "If I Had a Talking Picture of You." Another popular team was Nancy Carroll and Buddy Rogers, who appeared in *Illusion* (Paramount) and *Sweetie*. The ground was being laid for the appearance of the masterful pair Fred Astaire and Ginger Rogers, who came to Hollywood in the early thirties.

Two foreign stars made their American film debuts in 1929. Maurice Chevalier briefly left the French music halls to charm American filmgoers with his rendition of "Louise" in Paramount's *Innocents of Paris,* and Gertrude Lawrence made her American talkie premiere in Paramount's *Battle of Paris,* singing Cole Porter's "They All Fall in Love."

One of MGM's most ambitious films was *Hollywood Revue,* with an all-star cast that included a large complement of contract players—Marion Davies, Norma Shearer, Joan Crawford, Conrad Nagel, John Gilbert, Buster Keaton, Lionel Barrymore—and many more. The format was nostalgic minstrel so that many musical numbers could be included. Only two left an imprint. Both were by Arthur Freed (words) and Nacio Herb Brown (music). "You Were Meant for Me" had been introduced by Charles King in *The Broadway Melody;* now it was sung by King again, except that it appeared to be sung by Conrad Nagel. The other song was "Singin' in the Rain," introduced by Cliff "Ukulele Ike" Edwards, the Rounders, and the Brox Sisters. It became the title twenty-three years later of what *The New Yorker* reviewer Pauline Kael has called "the best Hollywood musical of all time,"[1] treasured for Gene Kelly's classic dance interpretation of the tune. (*Broadway Melody* dealt with the difficult transition actors had to make in turning from pantomime to sound, and the trauma some suffered when their voices were out of joint with their appearance.)

Arthur Freed (1894–1973) and Nacio Herb Brown (1896–1964) were the first songwriting team to emerge from the sound screen. Freed, born in Charleston, South Carolina, and raised in Seattle, was involved with vaudeville as writer and performer, collaborating with composer and arranger Louis Silvers also on material for New York cafe revues. He was a theatre manager and show producer before he began writing for movie musicals in 1929, scoring majestically with his first effort (*Broadway Melody*). Other song hits of this and other musical films of 1929 included "Wedding of the Painted Doll," "Chant of the Jungle," and "Pagan Love Song." Later, Freed was a most successful film producer of movie musicals, serving in the sixties as President of the Academy of Motion Picture Arts and Sciences.

Nacio Herb Brown, born in Deming, New Mexico, became a movie composer in a strange way. As the operator of a tailoring business and real estate office in Los Angeles, he became acquainted with members of the movie colony. Although he wrote moderately successful songs before *Broadway Melody*, it was his collaboration with Freed that resulted in hit material. In addition to titles already mentioned, he accounted for "Doll Dance," "You're an Old Smoothie," "Temptation," and "You Are My Lucky Star."

In September 1929, *Photoplay* magazine ran a long article, "Westward the Course of Tin Pan Alley," and announced that "because of the tremendous interest of its readers in theme songs of motion pictures, *Photoplay* . . . will review phonograph and piano records of the music used in screen production."[2] Pictured in the article were a dozen songwriters (with some of their hits) who now frequented the tables of Wilson Mizner's Brown Derby and Eddie Brandstatkis's Montmarte in place of Lindy's and the Paddock in Manhattan. Among the Tin Pan Alley mainstays who had moved to Hollywood were Irving Berlin ("Coquette" and "Marie"), L. Wolfe Gilbert ("Ramona" and "Lilac Time"), Con Conrad ("Breakaway" and "That's You, Baby"), Dave Dreyer ("Rainbow 'Round My Shoulder"), Harry

Akst ("Am I Blue" and "On with the Show"), Fred Fisher ("Strike Up the Band" in *Hollywood Review*), and De Sylva, Brown and Henderson ("Sonny Boy").

In *Photoplay's* estimation, things had never been so easy for song-sters "financially, artistically, comfortably."[3] In the past, the song plugger had to contact and "romance" vaudeville actors, bandleaders, radio entertainers, cabaret performers, and even circus troupers. Now, the screen did the entire job. *Photoplay* posed the question: was the motion picture industry a subsidiary of the music publishing indus-try, or had film producers gone into the business of making songs? No matter how it was viewed, the music business was undergoing vast changes that were trying for the pioneers of music publishing, who felt control of their enterprise slipping out of their hands. It was time to move on—and veteran music publisher Julius Witmark (1870–1929), a founding member of M. Witmark and Sons, died on June 1. He had been a singer whose beginnings went back to the famous min-strel troupe of Thatcher, Primrose, and West, with whom he sang in whiteface though he auditioned in blackface. The amputation of a leg in 1906 terminated his theatrical career.

What was most impressive was some of the prices Hollywood paid for songwriting services. De Sylva, Brown and Henderson, it was re-ported, received $150,000 in advance from Fox for the songs, book, and lyrics of *Sunny Side Up*. The sum was supposed to recompense them for snubbing offers to write Broadway shows. Most songwriters were paid regular checks by the studios, ranging from $250 to $750 a week, half charged against future royalties and half considered salary.

One of the first easterners to go West was songwriter and publisher Fred Fisher, whose hits included "Dardanella," "Peg o' My Heart," and "Chicago." Douglas Gilbert tells the story that on his first day at the MGM studio Fisher passed studio executive Irving Thalberg in the corridor, who was told, "That's Fred Fisher, the symphony writer."

Thalberg reportedly led Fisher back to his office and asked whether he could write a symphony.

"Get me a pencil, boy," Fisher was supposed to have replied. "When you get me, you get Beethoven, Mozart, and Chopin."

"And Thalberg hired him," Gilbert asserts, "to write a symphony. For the next four months, Fisher ambled stealthily about Hollywood, adopted a slouch hat and gait, carrying a large portfolio under his arm, presumably his music score. When anyone addressed him, he responded in Weber and Fields dialect. The act was so perfect that Fisher received $500 a week for sixteen weeks without question."[4]

As 1929 progressed, some consequential songs originated with the freelancers of Tin Pan Alley. "Star Dust," which bore a 1929 copyright and was popularized that year by Isham Jones and his Orchestra, had been recorded the year it was written (1927) by Emil Seidel and his Orchestra with composer Hoagy Carmichael at the piano. An early instrumental version, also in ragtime style, by Don Redman and his Orchestra, failed to capture the song's romanticism.

Carmichael has indicated that he wrote the melody on a visit to Indiana University, his alma mater, when he returned to the so-called "spooning wall." Sitting there, he remembered a girl he had wooed and lost, and the melody came to him. He wrote it down as a piano instrumental in the University Book Nook. It was a former classmate, Stu Gorrell, who called the work "Star Dust" because "it sounded like dust from stars drifting down through the summer sky." Carmichael later wrote in his autobiography, "This melody was bigger than I. It didn't seem a part of me. Maybe I hadn't written it at all. It didn't sound familiar even. . . . To lay my claims, I wanted to shout back at it. 'Maybe I didn't write you, but I found you.' "[5]

Presumably, at the suggestion of Irving Mills, the publisher of both Carmichael and Mitchell Parish, the latter wrote lyrics for the melody, and as a song it was introduced in 1929 at the Cotton Club. The recording made at that time by Isham Jones, employing a Victor Young arrangement, was slower and romantic, trading on the sentiments of the lyric. It was a standard by the time Mary Healy sang it in the film *Star Dust* in 1940 and Artie Shaw made his attractive version. In 1957 it enjoyed a revival in the rock era as the result of a recording by Billy Ward. In 1963, having been translated into forty different languages and recorded over five hundred times, it was se-

lected by ASCAP for its All-Time Hit Parade. It rates among Carmichael's favorite songs, along with "The Nearness of You," "One
Morning in May," and "Rockin' Chair," Mildred Bailey's theme.

Nineteen twenty-nine was a good year for Broadway musicals. January brought a smash hit in *Follow Through* by De Sylva, Brown and
Henderson, "a musical slice of country club life," with two hit ballads, "My Lucky Star" and the freshly romantic "Button Up Your
Overcoat." In a minor role, Eleanor Powell attracted notice with her
tap numbers. In March, Rodgers and Hart presented *Spring Is Here*
with a tuneful score that included the lush ballad, "With a Song in
My Heart."

To many the most important musical of the year was Dwight Deere
Wiman's production of the first *Little Show* in April. The outstanding
cast included singer Libby Holman, comedian Fred Allen, and dancer
Clifton Webb, a trio who scored a triumph the following year in
Three's a Crowd. The lyrics and music were mostly by Howard
Dietz, moonlighting from his job as advertising manager of MGM,
and composer Arthur Schwartz. Their strongest number was "I Guess
I'll Have to Change My Plan," based on a melody Schwartz had writ-
ten as a boy's camp counselor when it was called "I Love to Lie
Awake in Bed," words by Lorenz Hart, then unknown. It was over-
shadowed in the revue by "Can't We Be Friends?," composed by a
George Gershwin disciple, Kay Swift, with words by Paul James,
alias James Warburg, a banker and Kay's husband. But the number
that drew encores was the bluesy "Moanin' Low" by Ralph Rainger
(L. Reichenthal) and Howard Dietz—a song that gave overnight stardom to its performer, Libby Holman.

Hot Chocolates arrived at the Hudson Theatre in June, having
started as a floor show at Connie's Inn. An all-black revue, it launched
Louis Armstrong on his notable career as an entertainer, and not just
a jazzman, for he would nightly rise from the orchestra pit to offer a
stage solo on "Ain't Misbehavin'," the show's smash hit, which also
yielded a classic recording for him on OKeh. The song became Fats
Waller's theme. Andy Razaf, who wrote the lyrics, asserts that the

song was written in record time, a claim that has been made for many hits.

"I remember one day," he has said, "going to Fats' house on 133rd Street to finish up a number based on a little strain he had thought up. The whole show was complete, but they needed an extra number for a theme, and this had to be it. Fats worked on it for about forty-five minutes and there it was—*Ain't Misbehavin'*."[6] If the tale is to be believed about anyone, it would be Fats: his ability to turn out tunes on the spur of the moment was legendary, including his readiness to sell them outright at times in order to meet inconsequential momentary needs. Among other songs, the melody of "I Can't Give You Anything but Love Baby" is attributed to Fats by the producers of *Ain't Misbehavin'*.

Sigmund Spaeth, incidentally, claims that "by a strange coincidence, the melody of *Ain't Misbehavin'* turns up later almost literally in the first movement of Shostakovich's Seventh Symphony."[7] Two other Fats Waller hits of 1929 were "Honeysuckle Rose" and "I've Got a Feeling I'm Falling." The latter involved a collaboration with Billy Rose as lyricist and was introduced in the Paramount musical *Applause*. "Honeysuckle Rose," with a lyric by Andy Razaf, was introduced at Connie's Inn as a dance number in the nightclub revue *Load of Coal*. First broadcast by Paul Whiteman and his Orchestra, it became a specialty of Benny Goodman and also of Lena Horne.

In the Prohibition nightclub era, few acts were as popular as Clayton, Jackson and Durante, formed in 1923 as a performing unit. Whatever Clayton and Jackson contributed as dancers, singers, and comics to the zany destructiveness and violence of the act, it was Jimmy Durante who was the star. The oversized nose—which gave him the cognomen "Schnoz," or "Schnozzola"—the fractured English, the explosive displays of energy, and the comedy songs he wrote—all gave him a staunch and noisy following. The team and Schnoz reached a peak when they were featured in Ziegfeld's *Show Girl*. Like Kern's *Sally*, *Show Girl* told the oft-repeated story of the unknown performer who succeeds in rising to Ziegfeld stardom. Although the Gershwins

were retained to write the score—Gus Kahn gave an assist to help
meet a two-week deadline—Durante used his own material, delivering
songs that were request numbers with speakeasy crowds: "I Ups to
Him," "Jimmy, the Well-Dressed Man," and "Can Broadway Do
Without Me?" among others. Despite the Gershwin score—it yielded
one sterling perennial in "Liza"—a scintillating Albertina Rasch ballet, danced to Gershwin's *An American in Paris,* and the Durante
trio, *Show Girl,* which opened in July 1929, lasted only 111 performances.

In September, Oscar Hammerstein II and Jerome Kern collaborated on a musical romance about the Gay Nineties for Helen Morgan. Out of *Sweet Adeline* came three magnificent melodies: "Why
Was I Born?," "Here Am I," and "Don't Ever Leave Me." They were
tailor-made for Morgan and became permanently identified with her,
although Irene Dunne sang them when the musical was made into a
1935 Warner Brothers film.

Also concerned with a romantic slice of old Americana, specifically
the New Orleans of yesteryear, was Vincent Youmans, who in October produced and composed the score for *Great Day.* A second-rate
book was buttressed by a beautiful score that boasted such classics as
the ballads "More Than You Know" and "Without a Song" and the
rousing title song. Although the show folded after only thirty-six performances, Youmans's songs have lasted, and continue to be sung and
recorded.

November introduced musicals by two sophisticated songwriters
whose outlook epitomized an era now drawing to a close. Ziegfeld
presented Noel Coward's *Bitter Sweet,* whose very title seemed made
for the twenties. It yielded two perennials: the nostalgic ballad "I'll
See You Again" and the gypsy-flavored "Zigeuner." The other November musical was *Fifty Million Frenchmen,* with a playboy (William Gaxton) as its protagonist and a witty score by Cole Porter.
One of the few writers responsible for both words and music in a
show—Irving Berlin and later Harold Rome, Frank Loesser, and Stephen Sondheim joined this select club—Porter, more than any other
contemporary songwriter, sprinkled his lyrics with references to current places, people, and events. The score for *Fifty Million French-*

man provided two memorable tunes in "You Do Something to Me" and "You've Got That Thing." Responding to the twenties' taste for sexual adventures, Porter mastered the art of being naughty but nice, filling his songs with sly and ingenious references to sex.

Only two musicals opened on Broadway in October, the month the stock market crashed: *Great Day* on the seventeenth, seven days before the collapse, and *A Wonderful Night*, the Shuberts' version of *Die Fledermaus*, on the thirty-first, seven days after the debacle. No one could have suspected the ironic appropriateness of the title *Heads Up!*, the Rodgers and Hart show that opened for its Philadelphia try-out on October 25.

"On the day before opening," Rodgers notes in his autobiography, "Alex Aarons came charging down the aisle of the Shubert Theatre with the staggering news. 'Boys, you can forget about the show. You can forget about everything. The bottom's just dropped out of the market!'

"Until that fatal day," Rodgers continues, "everyone had been living through a period of unbelievable affluence. I remember a young elevator boy in my hotel lobby telling me one afternoon, 'Well, Mr. Rodgers, I did pretty well on the market today. I just made a thousand dollars.'

"Despite the blanket of gloom that hung over the country . . . surprisingly, *Heads Up!* didn't do badly and ended its run with 144 performances. . . . It certainly was not the right time to open a large, expensive production. And like every other business, the theatre was going to be in for a long painful period."

Nevertheless, November brought Noel Coward's *Bitter Sweet*, J. Fred Coots's *Sons O' Guns*, and Cole Porter's *Fifty Million Frenchmen*, while December 1929 saw the lights go up on *Top Speed*, produced and written by Guy Bolton, Bert Kalmar, and Harry Ruby, and *Wake Up and Dream*, an English revue that included Porter's outstanding hit "What Is This Thing Called Love?" January 1930 opened with a bang—the innovative *Strike Up the Band* by the Gershwins, George S. Kaufman, and Morrie Ryskind, the creative combination that soon produced the first Pulitzer Prize–winning musical, *Of Thee I Sing*.

With the onset of the Depression, the Harlem Renaissance came to an untimely end. "We were no longer in vogue, anyway, we Negroes," Langston Hughes wrote in his autobiography. "Sophisticated New Yorkers turned to Noel Coward. Colored actors began to go hungry; publishers politely rejected new manuscripts; and patrons found others uses for their money. The cycle that had Charlestoned into being on the dancing heels of *Shuffle Along* now ended in *Green Pastures* with De Lawd. The generous 1920s were over."[8]

Amidst the havoc wrought by the Great Depression, little attention was paid to the destruction of a grand New York architectural landmark. At the time, the Waldorf-Astoria Hotel, located between 33rd and 34th streets on Fifth Avenue, now the site of the Empire State Building, was the tallest and largest hotel in the world with 2,200 beds, and was renowned for its physical grandeur and its dominance of the city's social life. For the so-called 400, New York's wealthy upper crust, it was the home away from their homes farther north on Fifth Avenue, the choicest place for dining, dancing, and celebrating. But the Waldorf was only thirty-six years old when it was reduced to a heap of rubble in 1929—a symbol, perhaps, of a time that was no more.

The collapse of the stock market on October 24, 1929—"Black Thursday"—brought the celebrated *Variety* headline, "Wall St. Lays an Egg."[9] Succeeding front-page banner heads read: "Amusements Off 262 Pts." and "Broadway Takes the Slap." In the issues that followed, *Variety* charted the financial devastation wrought by the crash in "Box Scores of the Havoc" and in numerous stories, most tragic, a few humorous:

> Without an exception, every night club, speak, hideaway, dive and joint in the rialto took the stock market's lacing, many knocked out cold and the rest so groggy they'll lick up rosin before the end of the season. . . .
> The Club Lido, Embassy, Montmartre and Trocadero had a biz tailspin of 65 to 90 percent during the blackest days. . . .

One young chap drew up to Reuben's at 2 a.m. in a Du-
senberg car that stood him $12,000 six months ago. He
offered it for $1,500 cash. No takers! . . .

The openings of the Casanova and Richman clubs saw
fewer ermines, sables and jewels as a result of 150 can-
cellations for coats at one store alone. . . .

Two song publishers are reported to have cancelled
night club reservations, and the captains maintained the
boys were crying on the phone. . . .

Bookmakers who haunt the night clubs were cast in the
deepest sorrow because Irving Beatie, one of the most
popular Broadway bookmakers and Wall Street plungers,
had dropped dead at Empire City, due to tremendous ill
luck on the track and the street. He and Leo Donnelly had
been boxing playfully on the 48th Street corner only a
few days before. . . .

A vaudeville producer, elderly, was found weeping like
a child by his son, who returned to his office at seven
that night by chance. The old boy had lost all his cash,
$75,000. . . .

Viewed generally, the situation as it concerns Broadway made history, catapulting the Street into the darkest
despair it has ever experienced.[9]

Curiously, "Happy Days Are Here Again" (words by Jack Yellen;
music by Milton Ager) was introduced to the public by chance on
the very day known as Black Thursday. The song's history actually
antedated the financial catastrophe. It was written for the film *Chasing Rainbows*, to be sung by Charles King. For unaccountable reasons, its release was delayed. But the publishers of the song—Ager,
Yellen and Bornstein—were obligated by contract with the picture
company, MGM, to maintain a twenty-nine release date. Accordingly,
they arranged for George Olsen to introduce it at the Hotel Pennsylvania, where the band was playing.

"In the big dining room of the hotel," Jack Yellen later recalled,
"a handful of gloom-stricken diners was feasting on gall and worm-
wood. Olsen looked at the title on the orchestration and passed out
the parts. 'Sing it for the corpses,' he said to the soloist. After a cou-

ple of choruses, the corpses joined in sardonically, hysterically, like doomed prisoners on their way to the firing squad. Before the night was over, the hotel lobby resounded with what had become the theme song of ruined stock-market speculators as they leaped from hotel windows."[10]

Legend has it that some weeks later, when Olsen and his Orchestra were playing at the Hotel Roosevelt in Hollywood, Irving Thalberg heard the song. Bessie Love and Charles King, stars of *Chasing Rainbows*, were hurriedly summoned, and the scene was re-shot with the song. Apparently it did not help the picture very much. But in 1932 Franklin Delano Roosevelt adopted "Happy Days Are Here Again" as his presidential campaign song, giving it such status that eventually it became the unofficial anthem of the Democratic party. Both Harry Truman and John F. Kennedy entered the White House to its strains, heard extensively at nominating conventions. In 1963, the year Barbra Streisand made a highly personal recording of the song, it was named by ASCAP as one of sixteen songs on its *All-Time Hit Parade*.

"Happy Days Are Here Again" and Black Thursday—they are an expressive if contradictory combination to cap an era that was a strange mixture of unconventional, high-spirited living and subliminal despair and disillusionment.

IV

The Musical Theatre

19

The Musical Revue

"Out of the vulgar leg-show," wrote critic George Jean Nathan, "Ziegfeld has fashioned a thing of grace and beauty, of loveliness and charm; he knows quality and mood. He has lifted, with sensitive skill, a thing that was mere food for smirking baldheads and downy college boys out of its low estate and into a thing of symmetry and bloom."[1]

Along with the flock of revues that flourished in the 1920s, the *Ziegfeld Follies* traded on girls, girls, girls, naughtiness and nudity (actually the illusion of nudity), and the delicate stimulation of erotic desires, while the ladies in the audience were stunned by the priceless furs, gems, and laces adorning the seductive figures on-stage.[2] But the revues—Ziegfeld's, Shuberts', George White's, and others—not only made stars of dozens of beautiful females and bright comedians; they served as incubators of the great show composers of the golden age of the musical theatre and accounted for a substantial number of popular song hits.

There were many reasons why revues enjoyed their golden age during the twenties. As a form, the revue had flexibility: without being tied to a story line or book, the producer was free to introduce performers, songs, and songwriters according to his taste or judgment and stirred a response in audiences. "In a musical," producer Lew Fields, formerly of Weber and Fields, said, "give them gags, blackouts, belly laughs, great performers and great performances;

that's what they come for. They don't come to a musical comedy for a story."[3] Apart from offering girls, costumes, eye-arresting sets, and songs, the revues tended to be extremely topical and to trade on burlesque, wit, and satire. In this respect, they were the medium par excellence of a time when a breakdown in traditional values and established conventions prompted performers and people to poke fun at things. Consider such items as sportswriter Damon Runyon's stories that kidded mobsters and gamblers, Ring Lardner's mockery of the baseball clan, not to mention the witty luncheon sessions of the celebrated Algonquin Round Table crowd. Was there another period in American life when writers, critics, editors, columnists, and other cultural icons regularly met to exchange bon mots, and were quoted in newspapers and magazines for their wit? When someone like Dorothy Parker, who wrote excellent short stories and superb verse, was best known to the general public for her wisecracks?

The revues captured the spirit of the times in another way. Just as frequenting a speakeasy and drinking forbidden liquor (especially from a teacup) represented a sly nose-thumbing at the Establishment, so the revue was another expression of daring, urbanity, and sophistication. Nudity was the essence of the form. Elegant sets, luxurious costumes, and opulent secenery, naked girls were what tired businessmen came to see. And the producer's problem was to present beauties onstage, as undressed as he could make them without getting into trouble with the law. Earl Carroll, who most aggressively tested the limits of legality, put a lovely nude on a swinging pendulum (*Vanities* of 1924) in order to evade the requirement that nudes must not move on stage. The vogue of the annual revue died as the era's underlying moral and economic bankruptcy began to surface, though revues of a different style continued through the thirties and forties.

The man who set the pace and was the undisputed king of the revue scene was, of course, Florenz Ziegfeld, who presented his first *Follies* in 1907 (he first added his name to the title with the 1911 edition), at the height of the craze for Viennese operetta, a craze generated by the inordinate popularity of Franz Lehar's *Merry Widow*.[4] Although his approach was "American," Ziegfeld gave his revue a Continental—more specifically a French—flavor. He did so, reportedly, at the urging of Anna Held, the European soubrette who was his wife (though there are doubts that they were legally married). The use of the word "Follies" was designed to suggest the famous *Folies Bergere*, and lest the association be missed, Ziegfeld renamed the New York Theatre Roof "Jardin de Paris."

Librettist and lyricist Harry B. Smith, who wrote the book and lyrics for the first *Follies*—and also for four of the succeeding five editions—offers a different version of how the series acquired its name. In his autobiography, he notes that when he worked as a newspaperman he wrote a column titled "Follies of the Day." When he sat down to write the book of the new revue he recalled the columnist, which seemed appropriate because the revue was a scan of the season's foibles. He titled the libretto *Follies of the Year*, altered to *Follies of 1907* by Ziegfeld, who superstitiously preferred using thirteen letters. A number appeared above each letter and digit in the title, from 1 to 13. (Throughout his life, Ziegfeld carried and fondled miniature ivory carved elephants for good luck.)

Born on March 21, 1869, Ziegfeld was the son of the director of the Chicago Musical College, which helped account for Florenz's aversion to classical music. His interest in show business was sparked in his teens, when he viewed the Buffalo Bill-Annie Oakley exhibitions. He himself staged a show called *The Dancing Ducks of Denmark*, which was closed down by the American Society for the Prevention of Cruelty to Animals. But he had demonstrated his resourcefulness: he got his ducks to dance by heating the bottoms of their feet. His real move into the show world came when his father was made musical director of the 1893 Columbian Exposition in Chicago, and hired his son to secure performers. Among the jugglers, acrobats, and circus people he engaged—much to his father's disgust—was a strong man named Sandow, whom he personally signed. The ingenuity and imagination he later displayed in publicizing his shows, himself, and his stars were evident in his handling and promotion of Sandow. It led to his entering in a partnership with a comic and producer to stage a Broadway show. During their search for talent in Europe,

Ziegfeld met and fell in love with Anna Held, the Parisian music-hall singer whom he turned into a star.

The *Follies* that is of special interest is the edition of 1919, hailed by reviewers as *the* outstanding Ziegfeld production. "Thirteenth Ziegfeld Follies Eclipses Predecessors in Beauty, Color and Action" was the headline in the *Herald*. "Ziegfeld outziegfelds Ziegfeld," exclaimed the *Evening Sun*. As the revue scene unfolded, 1919 seemed also to signal a gush of productions, for, in addition to the *Follies*, George White launched his *Scandals* and John Murray Anderson presented the first *Greenwich Village Follies*.

Out of the 1919 score by Irving Berlin came the lilting song that became the theme of all *Ziegfeld Follies*—"A Pretty Girl Is Like a Melody"—and that has served as the traditional walk-on music for models exhibiting new styles in fashion shows all over the world. Eddie Cantor introduced "You'd Be Surprised," a song that caught on so fast that within a matter of weeks it was being interpolated in two other shows: *Shubert Gaieties of 1919* and *Oh, What a Girl!* Working with the illustrious black comic Bert Williams—appearing in his last *Follies*—Eddie Cantor presented the nostalgic "I Want to See a Minstrel Show." Viennese-born Joseph Urban, long associated with Ziegfeld, created the eye-arresting sets; John Steel, "the greatest of all revue tenors," according to Gerald Bordman,[5] sang the major ballads, none the equal of "A Pretty Girl"; and petite, Indiana-born Marilyn Miller, whom Ziegfeld wooed unsuccessfully and for whom this was her last *Follies,* starred. Two songs, not written by Berlin, are mentioned as enjoying a brief vogue: "My Baby's Arms" by Joseph McCarthy and Harry Tierney, the team later responsible for the giant hit of 1927, *Rio Rita;* and "Tulip Time" by Gene Buck and Dave Stamper, the former a longtime Ziegfeld factotum, prolific librettist, and for years a top ASCAP executive.

Fannie Brice sang the show-stoppers of the *Ziegfeld Follies* of 1920 and 1921, creating standards with "Second Hand Rose," revived in recent years by Barbra Streisand, and with the poignant ballad, "Mon Homme," a French import that became a worldwide winner as "My Man," the quintessential female expression of undying love.

Paul Whiteman's polished band was in the pit of the *Follies of*

1923, from which a background piece, "Chansonette" by Rudolf Friml, emerged as an instrumental hit a dozen years later retitled, "The Donkey Serenade." George Olsen's solid band occupied the pit of *The Follies of 1924–25*, the longest-running of the annuals (401 performances), in which Ethel Shutta, Olsen's wife, sang "Eddie Be Good" to twenty-four Ziegfeld beauties, all made up to resemble Eddie Cantor. Although the score by Harry Tierney and others yielded no hits, the cover of the sheet music by Albert Vargas was apparently a hit. "Many aficionados remember [the 1924 Follies] best," according to Gerald Bordman, "for the beautiful cover . . . a single smiling brunette invitingly fingering a necklace."[6]

Advertised as "The Sweetheart of Columbia Records," Ruth Etting was featured in the *Follies of 1927*, which starred Eddie Cantor. Appearing in blackface and white gloves after his success as *Kid Boots*, Cantor sing three Irving Berlin songs but scored with the interpolated "My Blue Heaven" by Tin Pan Alley hit writer, Walter Donaldson. Although Etting made a memorable hit of Berlin's "Shaking the Blues Away," Ziegfeld was compelled to close the show after 167 performances when Cantor walked out of the show to protest his salary.

Ziegfeld's last *Follies*—he died in July 1932 in Hollywood—was the 1931 edition, designed by Joseph Urban and presented not at the New Amsterdam Theatre on 42nd Street, where the revue generally played, but at the new Ziegfeld Theatre on Sixth Avenue at 54th Street.

There were more *Ziegfeld Follies* after its creator was gone—in 1934, 1936–37, 1943 (553 performances), 1945 (an MGM film *Follies*), 1956, and 1957. All strove to capture the magic that was Ziegfeld's and that came from gimmicks and devices that were sometimes elegant, sometimes corny, sometimes garish—live show curtains composed of scores of Ziegfeld beauties; "glorified beauty contest winners, elaborate Gene Buck song stories, jungle numbers with elephants . . . "[7] "a live ostrich with a bejewelled collar carrying Claire Luce across a jungle setting."[8] And there was always the scintillating staircase down which descended the most glorified of pretty showgirls, attired in mink, satin, chinchilla, lace, and petticoats of Irish linen. Backers of Ziegfeld shows who objected to the cost of linens that nobody would see were told by him, "But it does something to their walk!"[9]

Before he became a producer, George White (born George Weitz on the Lower East Side of Manhattan) was a messenger boy, Bowery-style hoofer dancing on the street for handouts, burlesque performer, turkey-trotter in a Shubert *Passing Show*, and a dancer in the *Ziegfeld Follies of 1915*. When White began producing his *Scandals*, Ziegfeld regarded the move like an outraged father witnessing the treachery of a son. White's shows were among the most musically rewarding of all the revues, yielding more hits[10] than the *Follies*, and their prime asset, apart from developing several superlative songwriting talents, was their dancing.

For his first *Scandals*, mounted the year of Ziegfeld's greatest revue (1919), White employed Richard Whiting and Arthur Jackson to write the undistinguished score. (By 1920 Whiting had a hit in "Japanese Sandman" and became an outstanding Hollywood songwriter in the 1930s.) The show's power lay in the dancing of White and Ann Pennington, a *Ziegfeld Follies* regular (1913–1918), with whom White had danced in the *Follies*.

For the 1920 edition of *Scandals*, White turned to George Gershwin, whom he had met when George served as rehearsal pianist for a *Miss 1917* flop. By then Gershwin, who had done his first revue chore for the Shuberts' *Passing Show of 1916* in a partial collaboration with Sigmund Romberg, had had a hit in "Swanee" (1918), and had written his first complete score ("the incarnation of jazz," according to the *Times*),[11] in *La, La, Lucille* (1919). Gershwin wrote the scores for five *Scandals*, with the 1922 edition proving the blockbuster. Winnie Lightner (b. Winifred Hanson, 1901–1971) gave George his first show-stopper with her rendition of "I'll Build a Stairway to Paradise" (lyrics by B. De Sylva). Paul Whiteman led the pit band, and his "slick playing of the electric Gershwin music during intermission gave the show special sparkle."[12]

For the show, George composed a twenty-five-minute jazz opera, *Blue Monday Blues*, set in Harlem, which opened Act II and which unfortunately lasted just one performance. Although George White himself performed a key role as the dancer, the work was judged too lugubrious and was yanked after opening night. It was later re-orchestrated by Ferde Grofe, renamed *135th Street*, and performed at Carnegie Hall.

Winnie Lightner accounted for another Gershwin perennial when she soloed "Somebody Loves Me" in the 1924 *Scandals*, with the last score Gershwin wrote for White. During his tenure with the *Scandals*, Gershwin had raised himself from $50 a week (1919 edition) to $125 a week plus royalties (1924 edition). White refused to raise this figure, and Gershwin left.

With his 1925 *Scandals*, White took up with De Sylva, Brown and Henderson, Tin Pan Alley songwriters who had had limited contact with the musical theatre but who proceeded to produce substantial scores for four editions, scores with a surprising number of smash hits. There were three blockbusters in the 1926 edition alone. "Birth of the Blues," still an evergreen, was presented as a battle between the blues and the classics. As Harry Richman delivered the song, the McCarthy Sisters appeared on one flange of the revue staircase in gowns suggesting "The Memphis Blues" and "St. Louis Blues," while the Fairbanks Twins appeared on the opposing side, costumed to suggest Schubert and Schuman; the contest was harmoniously resolved with the climactic interpolation of a portion of Gershwin's *Rhapsody in Blue*. "*Black Bottom*," a variation on the very popular Charleston dance, was sped on its worldwide conquest by the wild, seductive dancing of Ann Pennington. Although a number of artists, including Alberta Hunter and Perry Bradford, have claimed credit for devising the dance, it was Pennington's dancing and the De Sylva, Brown and Henderson song that made the "Black Bottom" a fad in 1926). The third smash in the 1926 score was "Lucky Day," a rousing, up-tempo number presented by Harry Richman, who also gave stature to "The Girl Is You and the Boy Is Me," which he sang with Frances Williams. The show was one of the longest-run revues of the era—424 performances.

Although the 1931 edition of the *Scandals* is outside the chronology of this book, it deserves mention, not only because of the quality of the De Sylva, Brown and Henderson score but because of its relevance to the temper of the 1920s. Among its many hits—"This Is the Missus" (Rudy Vallee), "Ladies and Gentlemen, That's Love" (Ethel Merman), "That's Why Darkies Were Born" (Everett Marshall), and "My Song" (Ethel Merman)—were two songs whose titles were emblematic of the Roaring Twenties: "Life Is Just a Bowl of Cherries" (Ethel Merman) and "The Thrill Is Gone" (Everett Marshall).

Emerging from the literary, creative, and bohemian community of Greenwich Village—low rents then made it an oasis for struggling poets, writers, painters, and actors, but its mystique attracted recognized figures as well—the *Greenwich Village Follies* early achieved an identity as the most sophisticated and intellectual of the revues. And well it should have. There were curtains by Reginald Marsh; James Reynolds designed a fiesta number in the style of a Velasquez painting; producer John Murray Anderson introduced a unique form he called "Ballet Ballade" in which literary works such as Poe's "The Raven" or Oscar Wilde's poem "The Nightingale and the Rose" were conveyed through a mixed presentation of poetry, music, and dance. That Broadway audiences were not exclusively lowbrow or middlebrow became clear when the *Greenwich Village Follies*, presented originally in the intimate quarters of the Greenwich Village Theatre, moved after its first two editions to the uptown Schubert Theatre and even into the cavernous Winter Garden.

John Murray Anderson, who eventually numbered 143 productions to his credit and wrote the lyrics for 64 songs, launched the series in that annus mirabilis, 1919. It was the curtain for the 1922 edition that epitomized its character and spirit. In a huge montage which embodied many of the Village locales (MacDougal Alley, the Hotel Brevoort, the Washington Square Book Shop, Harry Kemp's Playhouse, and so on), artist Reginald Marsh caricatured almost one hundred denizens of the Village, including Zelda Fitzgerald making her notorious dive into the Washington Square fountain. A truck tearing through Seventh Avenue carried Stephen Vincent Benet, John Peale Bishop, John Dos Passos, John Farrar, F. Scott Fitzgerald, Ben Hecht, Burton Rascoe, Gilbert Seldes, Donald Ogden Stewart and Edmund Wilson—all celebrated intellectuals of the day.[13]

According to Robert Baral, "the curtain went up at the Greenwich Village Theatre, and 'I Want a Daddy Who Will Rock Me to Sleep' [A. Baldwin Sloane] emerged as a sock Tin Pan Alley hit."[11] Bandleader Ted Lewis interpolated "When My Baby Smiles at Me" (Andrew B. Sterling, Ted Lewis and Bill Munro), an immediate hit that thereafter served as his theme song. After six weeks in the Village, the *Greenwich Village Follies* moved uptown to Broadway, and being non-Equity during the Actor's Equity strike, ran for 212 performances before it went on tour.

The 1920 edition, "a smash," says Baral, likewise moved from its theatre in the Village to the Shubert in Times Square. Sexier, "but with the Village brand, not Broadway"[14] and funnier, it introduced comic-strip characters set to music—*As Thousands Cheer* later did it in "The Funnies"—invited audience participation through the use of miniature tambourines (instead of hand applause), and presented Frank Crummitt playing the ukulele, then a big fad.

Out of the 1921 edition came one of the biggest hits to emanate from a twenties revue. "Three O'Clock in the Morning," with a lyric by Dorothy Terriss to a melody written in 1919 in New Orleans by Julian Robledo, closed the show, with two ballet dancers serving as chime ringers for the waltz's triple-bell effect. (The full history of the song appears in Chapter Eleven.) Venetian blinds were used to sparate the inner and outer stages, providing opportunities for unusual lighting effects.

In the 1922 edition, with the "bibliographical" curtain by Reginald Marsh, which also employed an intermission curtain by Cleon Throckmorton, another well-known artist, Anderson presented the first of his series of "ballet ballads." In the same edition, the *Greenwich Village Follies* further demonstrated its urbanity by having a Parisian diseuse, Yvonne George, sing "Mon Homme" in the original French at the same time that Fanny Brice was delivering the lachrymose ballad in English.

The 1924 edition remains memorable for the use of music by Cole Porter, which was quickly dropped and supplanted by a score, equally unimpressive, by Jay Gorney and Owen Murphy. The Porter score did contain a memorable ballad, "I'm in Love Again," but it apparently made no impression as done by the Dolly Sisters; it became a hit in 1951 when it was recorded by April Stevens. The lackluster score was still a problem when the show went on tour, and it is said that Rodgers and Hart's "Manhattan" and "Sentimental Me" were interpolated,[15] although these two songs are unequivocally identified with the *Garrick Gaieties* of 1925.

The 1925 edition of the *Greenwich Village Follies* was the last and, perhaps, the least of the series. An attempt was made to resurrect the show in 1928, yielding the first hearing of a West Indian sound known as calypso. It was clear that "the day of the annual like the day of the operetta was ending.[16] In Robert Baral's view, John Murray Anderson contributed "intellectual beauty" to the revue form.[17]

Mention should be made of a series that emanated from a theatre closer to Greenwich Village than to Broadway, the Neighborhood Playhouse at 466 Grand Street. The Playhouse housed the oldest experimental theatre groups in the country, having been founded in 1915 to perform classical plays and popular dramas. In 1922, bright young members of the group, perhaps inspired by the *Greenwich Village Follies,* put together a *Grand Street Follies* for their subscribers, advertising the event tongue in cheek as "a low brow show for high grade morons."

Two years later, in 1924, the first *Grand Street Follies* was unveiled to the general public. Although there were six editions between 1924 and 1929, nothing of musical consequence came from them, even though the young Arthur Schwartz was involved with the later editions. The emphasis of the series, with Albert Carroll and Dorothy Sands taking the lead, was on impersonations, spoofing, and lampooning current plays and players. Most of the series managed to last through the summer.

In a comparison with most of his contemporaries, Irving Berlin, like Cole Porter, has a double distinction: he wrote both words and music. He was also one of the very few songsmiths who functioned successfully both as a pop songwriter and as a theatre writer, scoring enormous hits in both media. In addition he early became his own publisher and up to the present[18] has retained publisher as well as writer ownership of his copyrights. No wonder Alec Wilder has said of him: "I can speak of only one composer as the master of the entire range of popular song—Irving Berlin."[19]

In 1921 Irving Berlin became a producer. With Sam Harris, a former partner of George M. Cohan, he built the Music Box Theatre on West 45th Street, regarded by many as an exquisitely beautiful house. There were four *Music Box Revues*, all with music by Berlin. Bordman sees them as a "bridge between the lavishness of the 20s revues and the thoughtful intimacy of the 30s revues."[20] But even though audiences left each production with a tune in their memory, the *Music Boxes* as a whole did not invite superlatives.

The 1921–22 edition included "Say It with Music," the lovely ballad that became the theme of the series: also "Everybody Step," a rousing rhythm number delivered by the bouncy Brox Sisters. Berlin himself appeared onstage in a song, "Eight Notes," in which eight lovelies representing the notes of the scale accompanied him. The score of the 1923–24 edition apparently lacked a haymaker, so that Berlin's sad ballad, "What'll I Do," already a hit, was interpolated. It was sung by Grace Moore and John Steel. Another Berlin hit was interpolated into the 1924–25 edition, "All Alone," which used the vocal talents of Grace Moore and Oscar Shaw, who effectively employed lighted telephones set on opposite sides of a darkened stage.

Perhaps the most important song to emerge from the series appeared in the 1922–23 edition. For many years, Berlin said that "Lady of the Evening," sung by John Steel against a simple setting of moonlit rooftops, was his favorite song. The same edition contained a special piece, "Pack Up Your Sins (And Go to the Devil)," which proved a hilarious high point as delivered by Charlotte Greenwood. Appearing in a hoop skirt that spread out eventually to engulf the entire stage, operatic prima donna Grace La Rue sang "Crinoline Days," it was reprised by Steel, then the ever-present golden-voiced tenor of musicals but now hardly remembered. "Yes! We Have No Bananas," wildly popular on the air and off, was treated to a pseudo-operatic takeoff. Untarnished by the limitations of the *Music Box Revues*, Berlin returned to the Broadway scene in the early thirties with two top-notch scores in the Moss Hart revues *Face the Music* and *As Thousands Cheer*.

The revue producer who sought to challenge Ziegfeld's preeminence as the glorifier of ladies was Earl Carroll, a former songwriter from Pittsburgh who put a sign over the stagedoor of his theatre: "Through these Portals Pass the Most Beautiful Girls in the World." Carroll made a fetish of the "living curtain" of lovelies, posing floods of girls, draped and mostly undraped, against every conceivable type of colorful and scincillating background. When Billy Rose produced *Jumbo* at the Hippodrome, he put up a sign that read: "Through these Portals Pass the Most Beautiful Elephants in the World." The competition between Ziegfeld and Carroll involved star stealing. For his *Sketch Book* in 1929, Carroll drew comics Leon Erroll and Fanny Brice away from Ziegfeld. He also boasted that he had Eddie Cantor, another Ziegfeld stalwart. In fact he had only a film showing Carroll negotiating with Cantor, and some sketches that Cantor wrote for the show. When Ziegfeld gave Cantor a gold watch to demonstrate his affection for the comic, Carroll gave him a grandfather's clock.

Carroll's competitive spirit stirred him to lock horns as a publicist with Ziegfeld, who had a formidable talent for grabbing space in the media. Carroll's publicity ploys reached a climax on February 22, 1926, when the birthday of one of his backers, a Texas oil tycoon, coincided with that of George Washington. Under a portrait of the Father of Our Country, Carroll arranged for one of his attractive chorines, Joyce Hawley, to take a champagne bath onstage. A select audience viewed the event. Newspaper reporters who attended bypassed the story except for a *Daily Mirror* writer whose article brought the federal law authorities into the situation. They charged Carroll with violating the Prohibition law. Although it was clear that the liquid in Miss Hawley's bathtub was mostly ginger ale and not champagne, Carroll was convicted of perjury for denying he had violated the dry law. Sentenced to one year and a day in a federal penitentiary, he remained there only four months and eleven days.

Launching his series in 1923, Earl Carroll produced five editions during the 1920s, three in the 1930s, one in 1940, and two *Earl Car-*

roll Sketch Books in 1929 and 1935. "No real music of import figures with the *Vanities*," writes Robert Baral, "and few stars came
out of the series."[21] Carroll's "finds" were apparently limited to
Patsy Kelly and Lillian ("I'll Cry Tomorrow") Roth. Vincente Min-
nelli pioneered in production with Carroll. Although Carroll availed
himself of the talents of E. Y. Harburg, Harold Arlen, Burton Lane,
and others he drew frequently on Tin Pan Alley writers such as Billy
Rose, Harry and Charles Tobias, Benny Davis, and Ted Snyder.

Lacking Ziegfeld's elegant taste, Carroll's extravaganzas, with their
scantily clad lovelies, attracted a coarser audience than the *Follies*,
and his sketches occasionally drew warnings from the police. He built
a handsome theatre, named after himself, at 50th Street and Seventh Avenue, and in the 1931 edition of the *Vanities* that broke in
the theatre he became the first to use Ravel's famous *Bolero* to ac-
company a dance number. The *Bolero* has since been used widely on
stage and in films.

The *Passing Show* was well named, for its twelve editions, from 1912
to 1924, left a limited legacy of material. Produced by the Shuberts,
who once owned so many Broadway theatres that Shubert Alley could
have been the name of the entire theatrical district, and not just the
thoroughfare between 44th and 45th streets, the *Passing Show*s were
housed at the Winter Garden. They were "basically designed to liven
up the summer doldrums," Robert Baral tells us.[22] Originally a Dutch
farmhouse, the site of the theatre became the American Horse Exchange at the turn of the century, a horse ring that was a magnet for
Manhattan's fast set. Bought by the Shuberts, it became the Winter
Garden, with a seating capacity of over 1,700 when it opened as a
music hall in 1911. The horsey origin of the theatre was revived on
occasion when a redolent epithet was needed to characterize one of
the less impressive *Passing Shows*.

Sigmund Romberg, responsible for such blockbusters as *The Student Prince* and *The Desert Song*, and Jean Schwartz, writer of "Au
Revoir, Pleasant Dreams," Ben Bernie's theme song, wrote most of
the scores. But the hits were generally Tin Pan Alley interpolations.
In 1919 when Schwartz wrote the score, the interpolated hit was

"I'm Forever Blowing Bubbles," a ballad that sold over 2 million copies, by Jean Kenbrovin (pen name for James Kendis, James Brockman, and Nat Vincent), with music by John William Kellette. In 1922, it was "Carolina in the Morning," a song by Gus Kahn and Walter Donaldson, harmonized by Willie and Eugene Howard.

The *Passing Shows* "never equalled Ziegfeld, John Murray Anderson, Earl Carroll, George White or Irving Berlin for style, taste, or imagination. Lots of potential stars were groomed along the way, but the Shuberts couldn't hold them," Baral has observed.[23] The Shuberts were obviously fine and sharp realtors. Their numerous theatres did not earn money unless they were occupied, and the *Passing Shows* helped fill the seats of their flagship.

So did a series they produced called *Artists and Models*, of which there were editions in 1923, 1924, 1925, 1927, and 1930. The prolific Sigmund Romberg and J. Fred Coots, a Tin Pan Alley writer, supplied the scores for several without producing any memorable songs. The unabashed emphasis of *Artists and Models* was nudity, and not all the girls measured up to the Ziegfeld standard. The series was designed to compete with *Earl Carroll's Vanities*, just as the more opulently mounted *Passing Show* aimed at competing, though not too successfully, with the *Ziegfeld Follies*.

All though the 1920s and 30s, revues popped up to challenge the big six annuals—*Ziegfeld Follies*, the Shuberts' *Passing Shows*, John Murray Anderson's *Greenwich Village Follies*, *George White's Scandals*, *Earl Carroll's Vanities*, and Irving Berlin's *Music Box Revues*—all of which were gone by the early thirties. Some of these competitive entertainments were imports from England or France; others were based on the marquee power of star performers like Ed Wynn. The most potent of the star singers was Al Jolson (1886–1950) for whom the Shuberts mounted revues every two or three years, usually at the Winter Garden. When *Whirl of Society* was presented in 1912, *Variety* wrote, "The Shuberts may run the Winter Garden, but Al Jolson owns it."[24] Starting with *Sinbad* (1918–19), during whose run and tour Jolson made a smash of "Swanee" and drew attention to George Gershwin, Jolie appeared in blackface to sing an unbelievable number of songs into the permanent repertoire of American popular music. As with *Sinbad,* whose score was by Sigmund Romberg, it was Jolson's interpolations that produced the hits: in addition to "Swanee," "Rock-A-Bye Your Baby to a Dixie Melody" (Joe Young, Sam Lewis, and Jean Schwartz) and "My Mammy" (Irving Caesar and Walter Donaldson).[25]

The three performers of the first *Little Show* (1929) were so well received (331 performances) that a series seemed in the making. There was a second *Little Show,* not too consequential, but an audience-rousing *Three's A Crowd.* Clifton Webb added comedy to his talents as a suave dancer. Fred Allen's sandpaper voice and dry delivery heightened the impact of George S. Kaufman's classic skits. The show-stopper was Libby Holman's low throat rendition of the bluesy "Moanin' Low" (Howard Dietz and Ralph Rainger), interpreted after her initial rendition in an erotic dance by Webb and Holman. The score was by Arthur Schwartz and Howard Dietz, who did not reach their peak as songwriters until the legendary *Band Wagon* revue of 1931. However, "I Guess I'll Have to Change My Plan," delivered by Clifton Webb, which made little impression in the show, developed into a hit in the 1950s as a result of its use in a number of films.

The charismatic trio—Webb, Allen, and Holman—repeated their hit performances in *Three's A Crowd* (1930), with another torch song giving the opus the same erotic electricity that "Moanin' Low" had. The new torcher was "Body and Soul" (Edward Heyman, Robert Sour, Frank Eyton, and John Green), a hit in England for Gertrude Lawrence (Green wrote it for her when he was her accompanist) before it was sung by Libby Holman. In Act II of the revue, it was used in a stunning, show-stopping dance sequence on a darkened stage by Clifton Webb and Tamara Geva. The show also produced another hit in "Something to Remember You By" (Dietz and Schwartz), sung by Libby Holman to a sailor—an unknown named Fred MacMurray—whose back alone was visible to the audience.

In the latter twenties, the personality revue built around a charismatic figure found a new exponent in Noel Coward. *The Year of Grace* (1928) was a smash import with book and songs by Coward: "It had pace," writes Robert Baral, "a steady flow of barbed black-

outs to pinpoint Coward's rapier brand of wit and an overall polish,"
plus sets that "radiated provocative beauty."[26] Moreover, it added
at least three standout songs to the popular repertoire: "World
Weary," sung by the inimitable Beatrice Lillie, whose comedic talents shone in "Britannia Rules the Waves"; "Dance Little Lady,"
delivered by Coward himself; and "A Room with a View," another
Coward presentation and a song that became widely known for being detested by the eminent critic for the New York *World*, Alexander Woollcott. *This Year of Grace* gave Coward the stature of
"the George M. Cohan of the International set."[27]

Two other importations that enchanted American theatregoers
were *Chauve Souris* (1922) and *Andre Charlot's Revue* of 1924. Of
Russian origin, with music by composers like Glinka and Gretchani-
noff, *Chauve Souris* was a triumph for its master of ceremonies, Nikita Balieff, whose handling of English was a major comedic attraction of the show, out of which came one of the big instrumental hits
of the twenties, "Parade of the Wooden Soldiers." The *Charlot*
revue traded on three scintillating performers: Beatrice Lillie, Gertrude Lawrence, and Jack Buchanan. There were many high points—
Lillie's side-splitting performance of "March with Me" and Gertrude
Lawrence doing Noel Coward's "Parisian Pierrot." But the show-
stopper was Lawrence's rendition of "Limehouse Blues" (Douglas
Furber and Philip Brahan).

Although Rodgers and Hart were represented on Broadway before
1924, their careers really took off with the *Garrick Gaieties* of 1925.
It is an oft-repeated story that the Theatre Guild needed drapes for
their newly built 52nd Street Theatre and that junior members under-
took to raise funds by producing a weekend review. Apart from accomplished young performers like Sterling Holloway, June Cochran,
and Philip Loeb, and a winning combination of wit and charm, the
Gaieties boasted two songs that became overnight hits—the irresistible song-tour of "Manhattan" and the lovely ballad, "Sentimental
Me." What was intended as a weekend jaunt became a success and
invited a follow-up in the *Gaieties* of 1926, which produced another
Rodgers and Hart perennial, "Mountain Greenery."

Of the opening of the first *Gaieties*, Richard Rodgers has written in his autobiography: "After the finale—a full-company reprise of *Gilding the Guild* with new lyrics—the theater was in an uproar. . . . Everyone was standing. Not standing to leave, just standing. Not just standing either. Standing and clapping, cheering, yelling, stomping, waving and whistling. I turned back to the orchestra [Rodgers was conducting] and had the boys strike up 'Manhattan.' The cast sang it. The musicians sang it. Even the audience sang it. After about ten curtain calls, the houselights went on, but still no one wanted to go."[28]

The next morning's reviews were so laudatory that Rodgers felt confident in asking the Guild to give them added performances and to make the theatre available for matinees the following week, except for the two afternoons that *The Guardsman* was playing. Despite summer heat in a theatre without air conditioning, the matinees were sell-outs, stirring Rodgers to request a regular run. It meant closing *The Guardsman*, which had been running successfully with Lunt and Fontane since the preceding October. But that's what the Guild did, and *The Garrick Gaieties* reopened on a regular basis on June 8, 1925, and continued until late in November for twenty-five capacity weeks.

After they scored with "Manhattan" and their follow-up show, *Dearest Enemy*, Rodgers received a call from Max Dreyfus, the venerable publisher of Kern, Gershwin, and Youmans, among other star show composers. Offered the opportunity to become part of this distinguished group, Rodgers accepted. But before he left the office, Dreyfus inquired why he had not been given an opportunity to publish the songs in *The Garrick Gaieties*. "Attempting to keep calm," Rodgers writes in *Musical Stages*, "I told him that we had tried desperately to get someone from his firm to attend one of the special matinees but that Harms hadn't even bothered to send an office boy. Then feeling a bit more secure, I told him that 'Manhattan' . . . was one of the songs I had played when Larry Schwab had brought me to see him a few years before and I couldn't help reminding him that he had said there was nothing of value in what he had heard."[29] (Thus "Manhattan" and "Sentimental Me" were published by Edward B. Marks Music.)

In 1930 Florenz Ziegfeld, reacting to the success of a C. B. Cochran import based on the story of a dream, put together *Simple Simon* for Ed Wynn, the "Perfect Fool." At first the show faltered, so Ruth Etting was brought in. Rodgers and Hart supplied her with what became one of her all-time hits, "Ten Cents a Dance," a touching ballad about a dance hall hostess. What made Ziegfeld drop from the score another Rodgers and Hart song, "Dancing on the Ceiling," is difficult to surmise, since it became a smash when it was used by C. B. Cochran in the London Rodgers and Hart production, *Evergreen.*

It was Cochran who brought into the United States one of two scores written by Cole Porter in 1930. *Wake Up and Dream* was a hit in England and drew superlatives from all the New York critics. June Mathews won plaudits with her rendition of the title song, while Tilly Losch deeply moved audiences with her singing of one of Porter's best ballads, "What Is This Thing Called Love?" In 1930, too, Porter composed "Love for Sale," the minor-keyed song whose lyrics were judged too raw for radio audiences: the melody was strong enough for the piece to make it as an instrumental. But in *The New Yorkers* (1930), it was heard, lyrics and all, as sung by a female quartet. (It remained one of Porter's favorite songs, together with "Begin the Beguine.") Featuring the violent buffoonery of Clayton, Jackson, and Durante, the warbling of Frances Williams, the music of Fred Waring's Pennsylvanians, and the striking sets by Peter Arno of *The New Yorker* magazine, the show proved a triumph for the destructive antics of Jimmy Durante.

At the same time foreign revues and operettas were being imported into the United States, the songs of American tunesmiths were being exported, especially to England. Irving Berlin, Jerome Kern, George Gershwin, Cole Porter, Eubie Blake, Rodgers and Hart—all had songs or shows performed on the British stage, some of them flopping, others generating enthusiasm.

One Damn Thing After Another, produced in 1927 by C. B. Cochran, exemplified the value of international exchange. This was the production for which a near taxi accident generated one of the finest Rodgers and Hart ballads, "My Heart Stood Still." Introduced by Jessie Matthews and Richard Dohnen, it was reprised by Edythe

Baker on her white baby-grand piano. Florenz Ziegfeld was so taken with the song that he tried to buy it for his *Follies;* but the composers persuaded Cochran to sell the American rights to them for use in *A Connecticut Yankee* (1927). Edythe Baker's piano figured in Rodger and Hart's "I Need Some Cooling Off," "Play Us a Tune" by Cole Porter, and the De Sylva, Brown and Henderson hit, "Birth of the Blues," her biggest request number. Rodgers and Hart contributed a third gem to the score, "My Lucky Star," beautifully sung by Mimi Crawford and Sonnie Hale.

"During the mid-20s," Rodgers explains in his autobiography, "the vigor and originality of the American musical stage were much admired and were envied by British producers, who began importing Broadway musicals in ever-increasing numbers.[30]

∾ 20 ∾

The Golden Coterie

Although the 1920s were a peak period for the Revue, they also saw the creation of the early works—and on occasion, the masterpieces—of the golden coterie of theatre writers: Jerome Kern, Rodgers and Hart, Vincent Youmans, George Gershwin, Sigmund Romberg, and Rudolf Friml, and, toward the end of the era, Cole Porter and Noel Coward.

Jerome Kern (1885–1945) was not only the pioneer figure in the modernization of the musical theatre but a composer held in almost universal esteem by his contemporaries and successors. "Without exception," Alec Wilder states, "all the prominent American composers of modern theater music, consider his songs as greater inspiration than those of any other composer, and his music to be the first truly American in the theater."[1] His admirers and followers included, among others, Richard Rodgers, Irving Berlin, and George Gershwin, who wrote, in a letter to Isaac Goldberg, "Kern was the first composer who made me conscious that popular music was of inferior quality and that the musical-comedy music was made of better material. I followed Kern's work and studied each song that he composed. I paid him the tribute of frank imitation."[2] Add to the list of Kern admirers the surprising name of Milton Babbitt, the classical composer and theorist, who annotated an album of Kern songs, sung by Joan Morris with William Bolcom as accompanist.[3]

Born into a well-to-do New York City family—his father owned the concession that watered the city streets—Kern studied piano first with his mother, then at the New York College of Music, and, when his father yielded to his son's interest in music, with private teachers in Europe. In London, Kern worked for a pittance for producer Charles K. Frohman and composed songs and pieces for the opening numbers of musicals—material almost never heard by the habitually late theatregoers. The first complete score he wrote was for *The King of Caledonia* (1910), and his first hit was "They Didn't Believe Me" an interpolation in *The Girl from Utah* (1914). When Victor Herbert heard the song, he said, "This man will inherit my mantle."

But while American audiences were rushing to hear the operettas by Herbert and other European or European-derived composers, and with revues rising in popularity, Kern and two English friends, Guy Bolton and P. G. Wodehouse, created a series of musicals between 1915 and 1919 known as the Princess Theatre Shows. The theatre, on the south side of West 39th Street, was small—299 seats—and the sets were few, two to a production. But the stories were contemporary and made for intimate musicals that pointed a new realistic and indigenous direction for the American musical. As Gerald Bordman has observed, "They brought American musical comedy into the twentieth century."

By 1920 Kern had completed an apprenticeship that involved not only the Princess Theatre shows but also extremely busy years in which he functioned as the leading composer of interpolated songs. Alec Wilder indicates that between 1904 and 1917 Kern composed interpolated songs for at least 43 musicals and plays, or an average of four different shows a year. In preparing his analysis of Kern, Wilder played over and examined 652 songs from 117 shows, plays, and films. During the twenties Kern wrote at least ten complete musicals, including several that were among the biggest of the decade, Partial to the letter "S" as a positive force—"sun," "smiling," "success," and so on—Kern scored hits with *Sally, Sunny, Show Boat,* and *Sweet Adeline.*

Sally was the biggest musical of 1921, accumulating 570 performances, at a time when few musicals reached the 500 mark. Produced by Ziegfeld, it was characterized as "the idealized musical comedy" in the *World,* and petite Marilyn Miller danced forth as the reigning queen of the Broadway musical. Among other tunes, Marilyn sang the evergreen hit of the show, "Look for the Silver Lining"—originally written by Kern for an unproduced musical—which later became the title of her screen biography. In the 1921 edition of the *Ziegfeld Follies,* Van and Schenck introduced a tribute to Marilyn: "Sally, Won't You Come Back to Me?" written by Ziegfeld's factotum, Gene Buck (words), and Dave Stamper (music). To "Look for the Silver Lining," Alec Wilder adds two other songs, which he characterizes as "phenomenal,"—"Wild Rose" and "Whip-Poor-Will," and praises as "a leap forward in invention, style and experimentation," reflecting the influence of the "1919–1920 revolution in dance band arranging."[4]

Late in 1921, Kern wrote the score for *Good Morning, Dearie,* not a rousing success despite the drawing power of Louise Groody. The only song that attracted notice, apart from the fetchingly harmonized "Blue Danube Blues," was a Hawaiian number, "Ka-lu-a." It was the song that brought a plagiarism suit from the publisher of "Dardanella," a suit which Kern lost when the judge ruled that "the bass materially qualified if it did not dominate the melody."[5]

Like *Sally, Good Morning, Dearie* was a Cinderella story, produced in the period when the theme of rags-to-riches dominated musicals. (They were unquestionably a reflection of the get-rich-quick, two-cars-in-every-garage mania of the 1920s.) The Cinderella trend persisted for three theatrical seasons, initiated by the record run of *Irene* (670 performances) in her "Alice Blue Gown," book by James Montgomery, lyrics by Joseph McCarthy and music by Harry Tierney. Irene was a shopgirl out of the Ninth Avenue slums of Manhattan who succeeds in marrying into the wealthy Long Island set. In *Mary* (1920), Otto Harbach and Frank Mandel (book and lyrics) combined the Cinderella and get-rich-quick themes. Jack Keene sets out to build low-cost homes ("love nests") in Kansas and flounders until oil is suddenly discovered; he becomes wealthy overnight and marries his mother's simple secretary, Mary. Louis Hirsch, who supplied the music, created a bestseller in "The Love Nest," which advertised the domestic joys of the portable home.

Sally starts out as an orphan, earning her livelihood as a dish-washer, but ends by becoming a Ziegfeld star and the bride of Blair Farquar of the "Long Island Farquars." All three of these musicals possessed a kind of homely domesticity, devoid of high jinks, that hardly gave a clue to what was happening in the Roaring Twenties. By 1922 the Shuberts tried to capitalize on the Cinderella theme with a show titled *Sally, Irene and Mary,* wherein three girls living in a tenement succeeded in becoming Ziegfeld stars. In a turnabout, Mary, now rich, goes back to her old hometown boyfriend.

Sunny of 1925–26, starring Marilyn Miller and featuring George Olsen's "jazz" band on stage, was the first musical in which Kern teamed with librettist and lyricist Oscar Hammerstein II. It yielded only one hit, "Who?," that quickly became a standard. It was a blockbuster, but also a song that posed almost insuperable problems for the lyric writer. The opening note of the melody was held for two and a quarter bars, or nine counts, and was repeated five times in the course of the refrain. The choice of the word "who" by Otto Harbach and Oscar Hammerstein was clearly an inspiration, since it stimulated listener interest conceptually through the long, sustained melody note.

The best known of Kern's scores and the high point of his distin-guished career came in 1927 with the production of *Show Boat,* re-garded by historians as not just a musical comedy, but, as David Ewen has said, "an artistic entity [with] dramatic truth, authentic characterization, effective atmosphere and a logical story line. This was a musical in which music, dance and comedy were basic to the stage action."[6]

Based on the sprawling Edna Ferber novel of the same name, *Show Boat* told the story of a group of people involved with riverboat en-tertainment, faced with serious problems, domestic and professional, and not the hokey situations exploited in most musicals of the period. The captain had his headaches with a shrewish wife. His daughter Magnolia married a boozing gambler, who deserted her with child. Julie, played by sad-eyed Helen Morgan, was attacked for being part-Negro by a local sheriff and accused of miscegenation because she was married to a white man. As the author of the book and lyrics,

Oscar Hammerstein II boldly confronted the black-white problem in a period when lynching still scarred the South.

Kern's score was one of the richest ever created for a musical, with scarcely a song that did not immediately or eventually become part of the permanent repertoire of American popular music. The mention of the titles brings the glowing melodies flooding into the mind: "Make Believe," "Can't Help Lovin' Dat Man," "You Are Love," "Why Do I Love You?," "Ol' Man River," and "Bill."

Of her first hearing of the river ballad, Edna Ferber, on whose hit novel *Show Boat* was based, wrote, "Jerome Kern appeared at my apartment late one afternoon with a strange look of quiet exaltation in his eyes. Then he sat down and played and sang *Ol' Man River*. The music mounted, mounted, and I give you my word my hair stood on end, the tears came to my eyes, and I breathed like a heroine in a melodrama. This was great music. It was music that would outlast Kern's day and mine."[7]

The song "Bill" was an unusual interpolation in *Show Boat*, since its lyric was not written by Oscar Hammerstein II, who was the show's lyricist. It was the work of P. G. Wodehouse, written nine years earlier for Vivienne Segal in the Jerome Kern/Princess Theatre mini-musical *Oh, Lady, Lady!* Dropped from the show, it was tried by Wodehouse and Kern in the musical *Sally* (1920), but Marilyn Miller could not muster the pensive sweetness the song demanded. It was, of course, perfectly suited for Helen Morgan, even though all the other songs in the musical were by Hammerstein. A scrupulously fair man, Hammerstein, who was frequently credited with the song, had a special note inserted in the program of the 1946 revival of *Show Boat:* "I am particularly anxious," it read, "to point out that the lyric for the song *Bill* was written by P. G. Wodehouse. Although he has always been given credit in the program, it has frequently been assumed that since I wrote all the other lyrics for *Show Boat*, I also wrote this one, and I have had praise for it which belonged to another man."[8]

A success at the box office as well as an artistic triumph, *Show Boat* played to sellout audiences in New York for almost two years, enjoyed an extended road tour, and has since been revived more frequently than perhaps any other musical.

Oscar Hammerstein II (1895–1960) was thirty-two years old when he wrote *Show Boat*. He came to it with a rich theatrical background. His grandfather was an opera impresario, an uncle was a Broadway producer, and his father was the manager of the Victoria Music Hall. Although he graduated from Columbia University, where he was actively involved in the musical Varsity shows—he met and worked with the young Rodgers and with Hart at the time and went on to study law and to work in a law office—he turned early to the theatre. His desire to get married and the refusal of the law firm where he labored as an apprentice to grant him a small raise, led to his taking a job as assistant manager of a theatre.

When his first effort at playwriting failed, he interested himself in the musical theatre, writing his first show, *Always You* (book and lyrics) in 1919–20. His talent soon brought him collaborations with such top composers as Kern, Friml, Romberg, and Youmans as well as with veteran librettist and lyricist Otto Harbach (1873–1963). With Harbach he collaborated on book and lyrics for Youmans's *Wildflower* (1923—477 performances), Friml's *Rose-Marie* (1924—577 performances), Kern's *Sunny* (1925—517 performances,) and Romberg's *The Desert Song* (1926—471 performances). Following *Show Boat,* and working with other librettists and lyricists, or by himself, he wrote book and lyrics for Romberg's *The New Moon* (1928—509 performances), Youmans's *Rainbow* (1928—29 performances), and Kern's *Sweet Adeline* (1929—234 performances). Hammerstein began his golden partnership with Richard Rodgers and their record-breaking hit, *Oklahoma!*, in 1943. At the end of that year, when he was also enjoying the success of *Carmen Jones,* his adaptation of Bizet's opera in a black version, he ran a famous advertisement in *Variety*. Listing the flops he had had and the small number of weeks they ran, he closed the ad with the line: "I've Done It Before and I Can Do It Again."

Such self-deprecation was indicative of the man's humility and humanity, qualities admired by all who knew him, including the au-

thor of this book, whose application to ASCAP he cosigned with
Peter De Rose and who worked with him as a member of the Music
War Committee, which Hammerstein chaired during World War II.
The committee was composed of songwriters dedicated to writing for
the war effort. As indicated by the book and lyrics of *Show Boat,*
Hammerstein was a man of liberal sentiments; and during the Mc-
Carthy era he was one of the theatre people who did not run scared.

The last show Kern scored during the 1920s was *Sweet Adeline,*
which he and Hammerstein concocted specifically for the charismatic
Helen Morgan. A series of songs written for her all played on a
similar note of poignancy, embodying the hope and despair visible in
her face and audible in her voice. Of these—"Don't Ever Leave Me,"
"Here Am I," " 'Twas Not So Long Ago"—the undisputed hit was
"Why Was I Born?," a favorite with female singers to the present.
An interesting and novel departure in the show was the use in the
overture of a medley of tunes from the 1890s instead of Kern's own
songs. The show opened on October 3, 1929, just before the stock
market crash. Ticket sales tumbled with the stocks, but *Sweet Adeline*
managed to remain at the Hammerstein Theatre until April 30, a run
of seven months.

Alec Wilder divides Kern's career into four phases: 1903 to 1915,
the year of the experimental Princess Theatre Shows; 1915 to 1927,
the year of *Show Boat,* another departure from the conventional;
1927 to 1935, the year of his first film score; and 1935 to his death,
his years in Hollywood.

Kern died quite suddenly when he came to New York in 1945 to
compose the score for *Annie Get Your Gun* being produced by
Rodgers and Hammerstein. He collapsed as he was walking on East
57th Street. It is reported that, as Kern lay dying, Oscar Hammerstein II sang into his oxygen tent, "I've Told Every Little Star,"
which they wrote in 1932 for *Music in the Air* and which was revived later in 1961 with a bestselling record by Linda Scott. After
Rodgers and Hammerstein recovered from the shock, they turned to
one of Kern's friends and admirers as a substitute, and Irving Berlin
turned out one of the greatest scores of his distinguished career in
Annie Get Your Gun.

Of all the songwriters whose work Alec Wilder analyzed in his impressive book, *American Popular Song: The Great Innovators, 1900–1950*, Richard Rodgers's songs, he concluded, "show the highest degree of consistent excellence, inventiveness and sophistication. As well, they bear the mark of the American song."[9] Between 1925 and 1930, he wrote fifteen scores for Broadway and London, with 1926 registering as the banner year with six shows. It was never Rodgers alone, except for two scores he wrote by himself (*No Strings* in 1962 and *Androcles and the Lion* in 1967) after Oscar Hammerstein's death. It was always Rodgers and Hart, or, after Hart's death in 1943, Rodgers and Hammerstein. That he was extremely fortunate in having these two gifted lyricists as steady collaborators is unquestioned—and both richly rewarding collaborations had their inception, so to speak, at Columbia University, which all three attended at different times and where they were involved in the Columbia Varsity show.

Richard Rodgers was born in Long Island on June 28, 1902, seven years after Larry Hart. His father was a physician and his mother an amateur pianist. Although he began taking piano lessons from an aunt and then a private teacher before he started school, he early abandoned formal lessons for self-study and improvisation. The first musical he attended at the age of six attracted him to the music of Victor Herbert, some of whose songs he had heard his father sing. But when he saw one of the Princess Theatre shows, he became a Kern devotee, sometimes returning to see the same show half a dozen times. He was fifteen when, through his brother Mortimer, he wrote a show for a boy's club; it was presented at the Plaza Hotel. He was sixteen and Larry Hart was twenty-three when they met at Hart's home through a mutual friend. "It was a case of love at first sight," Rodgers always said. "I acquired in one afternoon a partner, a best friend—and a source of permanent irritation."[10] The irritation stemmed from Hart's inability to adhere to schedules (as Rodgers was wont to do), his aversion to work, and a tendency to go off on binges. Regardless of the problems that his lack of discipline posed for the duo, Hart's brilliance and originality as a lyricist made for one of the great show-song collaborations.

Lorenz Hart, born in New York City on May 2, 1895, was privately educated, and entered Columbia University after a European holiday. An inveterate theatregoer from his school days, like Rodgers, he appeared as a female impersonator in a Columbia Varsity show in 1915–16. Although he left the university without a degree, he was extremely well read and developed a rich cultural background. For a time, he translated German operettas into English for the Shuberts. While at Columbia—Rodgers entered in the fall of 1919—he and Rodgers wrote the Varsity show, *Fly with Me,* with Rodgers becoming the first freshman ever to write and conduct a Varsity show. Lew Fields, formerly part of the famous duo Weber and Fields and then a theatrical producer, was so impressed by the songs in *Fly with Me* that he offered to use them in his forthcoming musical, *Poor Little Ritz Girl.* Fields had already used one of their songs, "Any Old Place with You," in a 1919 production, and this tune not only marked their entry into the theatre but became their first published song. When *Poor Little Ritz Girl* opened on July 28, 1920, at the Central Theatre, Rodgers and Hart were stunned to find that eight of their songs had been dropped from the score and replaced with songs by Sigmund Romberg and Alex Gerber.[9]

Unbelievable as it may seem, five years elapsed before they really made Broadway. During those troubled years, they acquired a collaborator in Herbert Fields, son of Lew Fields and brother of Dorothy Fields, with whom they wrote *The Melody Man*—a Tin Pan Alley comedy with two songs by Rodgers and Hart—a flop. Rodgers left Columbia to study music at the Institute of Musical Art, now known as the Juilliard School of Music. Between 1920 and 1924, Larry and he wrote scores for eleven amateur productions, including two during the two years he was at the Institute. But "the winter of 1924–25," he noted in his autobiography, "was the most miserable period of my life. No matter what I did or where I turned, I was getting nowhere. I would get up each morning, take my songs to a producer or publisher . . . audition them—or more likely, be told to come back some other time—and go home. This happened day after day. After the drubbing he had taken with *The Melody Man,* Lew Fields turned us down. Larry Schwab never returned my call.

Russell Janney was busy with . . . *The Vagabond King.* I couldn't
get past the reception desks at the Shubert and Dillingham offices.
And I certainly wasn't about to approach Max Dreyfus. . . ."[11]

During this period he developed severe insomnia. He reached a
point of such despondency and desperation that he decided to forget
about music and considered accepting a position as a manager and
salesman in the babies' underwear business. Then lightning struck.
Through a lawyer friend of the family, Rodgers was brought into
contact with the group of Theatre Guild youngsters about to produce
what became known as *The Garrick Gaities.* As we know, what
started as a two-performance show on May 17, 1925, turned into a
twenty-five-week run, established Rodgers and Hart as a hot song
team, and led to a second edition, with "Manhattan," "Sentimental
Me," and "Mountain Greenery" becoming a permanent part of the
American song repertoire.

In the period of the two Theatre Guild revues, 1925–26, Rodgers
and Hart had four other shows open on Broadway. With *Dearest
Enemy,* which bowed on September 18, 1925, and yielded the hits
"Here in My Arms" and "Bye and Bye," Herbert Fields joined
Rodgers and Hart as the librettist, and from then until 1931 most
of their shows were by Fields, Rodgers and Hart. Two hits came also
out of *The Girl Friend,* which opened on March 17, 1926: the zippy
title tune effectively exploited the Charleston rhythm, while "The Blue
Room"—"the first wholly distinctive Rodgers song," according to
Alec Wilder[12]—is sometimes credited with saving the show for a run
of over 300 performances.

Opening on December 27, 1926, *Peggy-Ann* was based on a Marie
Dressler musical vehicle, *Tillie's Nightmare.* The tale of a smalltown
girl who escapes from her humdrum existence and her fiancé in fantasies and wild dreams, it was developed with strong Freudian overtones, one of the first instances of such usage. This was not the only
respect in which *Peggy-Ann* departed from conventional musical
comedy lines. For the first fifteen minutes of the show, there was no
singing or dancing, and the end came on a dark stage with a slow
comedy dance. The effort to integrate the music with the story development led Rodgers to write material that captured the surrealistic

character of some of Peggy-Ann's fantasies. But there were a number of hit songs, specifically, "A Tree in the Park" and "Where's That Rainbow," which I recall playing with a small dance combo that helped me earn my way through college. *Peggy-Ann* foreshadowed the unconventional themes and procedures that Rodgers and Hart essayed in the shows they wrote during the thirties and forties.

Perhaps the biggest show they produced in the 1920s was *A Connecticut Yankee*, a delightful adaptation of the Mark Twain novel that opened on November 3, 1927, and occupied the Vanderbilt Theatre for 418 performances. It included the classic tunes "Thou Swell" and "My Heart Stood Still," the latter written originally for a London revue. There were also such memorable melodies as "On a Desert Island with Thee" and "I Feel at Home with You." *A Connecticut Yankee*, revived in 1943, was the last show that Larry Hart worked on before his untimely death; to it he added "To Keep My Love Alive," one of the funniest and most cynical songs he ever wrote. Who can forget the lady that kept her love alive by killing off each husband: one with arsenic, another with a poisoned drink, a third by stabbing, with Hart indulging in triple rhymes like "fratricide," "patricide," and "mattress side"; also, "wreck to me," "horse's neck to me," and "appendectomy."

In 1928 Rodgers and Hart were represented by *Present Arms*, in which dance director Busby Berkeley sang the show's only hit, "You Took Advantage of Me," and by *Chee-Chee*, described as a "sassy, cynical jazz musical."[13] Based on Charles Petit's novel *The Son of the Grand Eunuch*, it dealt with the man who wanted to be the Grand Eunuch without paying the price. It had only six complete songs, and lasted only four weeks, but it emphasized Rodgers and Hart's determination to write musical plays and not just musicals. *Chee-Chee*'s playbill contained a program note that read, "The musical numbers, some of them very short, are so interwoven with the story that it would be confusing for the audience to peruse a complete list."[14]

Rodgers and Hart had two shows in 1929, neither of which lasted much beyond one hundred performances. A major problem with *Spring Is Here* (March 11, 1929) was Glenn Hunter's lack of a voice, with the result that the demanding love ballad, "With a Song in My Heart," had to be sung by a character who was not the romantic lead. *Heads Up,* also based on an Owen Davis libretto, moved into the Alvin not too long after *Spring Is Here* left. Neither "A Ship without a Sail" nor "Why Do You Suppose" quite made it. But by the time *Heads Up opened,* the country was plunging into the Depression. The thirties turned out to be a great decade for Rodgers and Hart whose sterling scores and shows included *On Your Toes, Babes in Arms, Jumbo,* and *The Boys from Syracuse.*

While theatre composers like Kern, Berlin, and Rodgers were writing music that was American-flavored, Vincent Youmans caught the upbeat, rhythmic pulse, the frenetic tempo of the times. In this respect, he was close to Gershwin, with whose brother, Ira, Youmans wrote his first complete musical, *Two Girls in Blue* (1921). And yet he acknowledged Victor Herbert, whose songs he rehearsed as a staff pianist at Harms, as one from whom he "got something in less than a year that money couldn't buy."[15]

Youmans's career was neatly encompassed by the 1920s. His first musical came in 1921, and only two of the twelve shows he wrote went into the early 30s. Just three of his musicals were really box-office successes, but all of them contributed imperishable melodies to the permanent repertoire of popular music. Among these is, of course, the most widely recorded and performed of show songs, a favorite even today, more than fifty years after it was first heard in *No, No, Nanette:* "Tea for Two." No song of the twentieth century approaches it for universal acceptance, popularity, and use.

Vincent Youmans (1898–1946) "wrote only 93 published songs," theatre historian Stanley Green has observed. "His Broadway output consisted of 12 scores, and his Hollywood contribution comprised two original film scores. He became a professional composer at 22, an internationally acclaimed success at 27, and an incurable invalid at 35."[16] And, as Max Wilk has noted, "From 1932 until his death in 1946, Youmans was absent from the Broadway scene. . . . His health was bad and progressively worsened [because of tuberculosis and alcoholism]. Unable to write for Broadway, he kept very busy studying. In New Orleans he studied composition and counterpoint with Ferdinand Dunkley at the Loyola School of Music. . . ."[17] A young writer who worked at the Hotel Roosevelt in New Orleans remembered Youmans as "a tired, thin little man, very nervous, who somewhat resembled Fred Astaire or Hoagy Carmichael. He had been sweated out for his alcoholism and was only drinking ale. . . . One night I arranged with the band that was appearing in the Blue Room at the Roosevelt to do an evening of Youmans tunes. It was advertised in the papers, and people crowded in to hear all those songs, and it was a big success. Youmans sat in a corner drinking ale, occasionally smiling at what he heard. But he wouldn't be introduced to the crowd. He stayed off in the shadows and listened."[18]

Born a day after George Gershwin (September 27, 1898) in New York City, Youmans came from a well-to-do family of hat store owners. He was educated at private schools and began taking piano lessons in his boyhood. He had no interest in the engineering career planned for him by his father and settled for a job on Wall Street, which left him free to spend his evenings on music. Stationed at the Great Lakes Naval Station during World War I, he wrote a rousing march featured by John Philip Sousa. It surfaced later as "Hallelujah" in *Hit the Deck*.

Youmans's first Broadway musical, *Two Little Girls in Blue* (May 3, 1921), possessed also the first complete libretto written by Ira Gershwin who used the name Arthur Francis, concocted from the first names of a brother and sister. The most popular tune in the show, "Oh Me, Oh My, Oh You," not quite a hit, retained the title that had been proposed as a dummy by Ira when they were working on the score. The two succeeding shows, *Mary Jane McKane* (December 25, 1923) and *Lollipop* (January 21, 1924) incorporated melodies that later showed up in *No, No, Nanette*. *Wildflower* (February 7, 1923), on which he collaborated with Herbert Stothart, with book and lyrics by Otto Harbach and Oscar Hammerstein II, was the show that "established him as a major figure."[19] "Bambalina" is the only tune that caught on with audiences. But it was the songs that made the show; the *Times* critic, who lost his head over the music, attributed it to Rudolf Friml.[20] *Wildflower* racked up an impressive run of 377 performances.

The pinnacle of Youmans's career was, of course, *No, No, Nanette,* not only "the most successful musical comedy of the era,"[21] but the show that epitomized the jazzy world of the flapper. It captured the gaiety, kookiness, daring, and innocence of that world, and embodied it so well that when the show was revived in 1971, it was a smash all over again. Despite being presented to a new audience and to a generation drastically different from that of the twenties, it bodied forth its era with such verity that it worked both as spine-tingling nostalgia for the oldtimer and revelation for the newcomer.

Before its first arrival in New York, *No, No, Nanette* thrived for fifty weeks in Chicago. (Its tryout in Detroit was so dismal that the show might have died without recasting and the new songs that were added, including "Tea for Two" and "I Want to Be Happy.") The New York run accumulated 321 performances, and in London it lasted for 665. At one time there were as many as seventeen companies performing the show in Europe, South America, New Zealand, the Philippines, and China. Even the songs that did not turn into evergreens were tuneful. One need only glance at their titles to have the melodies instantly pop into the ear: "Too Many Rings Around Rosie," "You Can Dance with Any Girl at All," both with lyrics by Irving Caesar, who also accounted for the two blockbusters, and the title tune, whose lyric was the work of Otto Harbach.

Two years later, Youmans enjoyed the feeling of having a new hit on Broadway. *Hit the Deck* (April 25, 1927), based on a play, *Shore Leave,* by Hubert Osborne, with a book by Herbert Fields and produced by Lew Fields, inhabited the Belasco Theatre for 352 performances. Louise Groody, the original Nanette, starred and introduced "Sometimes I'm Happy" in a duet with her sailor boyfriend. "If *Sometimes I'm Happy* isn't sung all over the world," wrote drama critic Alan Dale, "until sometimes you'll be unhappy, I'll eat my own chapeau." As for the rest of the score, Dale wrote, "The melodies will be radioed and gramophoned and whistled and pianoed and pianoled and even jazzed until you'll cry for mercy."[22] ("Sometimes I'm Happy" was one of a number of songs in theatrical history that started out with another title in another show, failed to make it, and then became smashes. It was originally called "Come on and Pet

Me" and was written for the musical *Mary Jane McKane* in 1923.) "Hallelujah" was also not written specifically for *Hit the Deck*. But sung by a rip-roaring sailor's chorus, it brought the audience to its feet. It was effervescent, as was the entire show, with an emphasis on dancing—the black bottom, Charleston, and others. The song itself embodied offbeat syncopation, a mark of some of Youmans's up-tempo numbers. One heard it in "I Know That You Know,"[23] a rouser that survived from the 1926 flop *Oh, Please* and in "I Want to Be Happy" from *No, No, Nanette*.

Youmans worked on four shows after *Hit the Deck*, all failures. But each had its gem-like melodies. The romantic musical play *Rainbow* (1928), with a book by Laurence Stallings and Oscar Hammerstein II, brought Libby Holman to notice as a torch singer with "I Want a Man." *Smiles* (1930), based on a story by Noel Coward, with a cast that included Marilyn Miller and Fred and Adele Astaire, closed after ninety-two performances—and the gorgeous ballad, "Time on My Hands," forced out of the production by Miss Miller, did not become a hit until later. *Through the Years* (1932), whose title song was Youmans's own favorite, included the throbbing "Drums in My Heart."

The heartbreak show for Youmans was unquestionably *Great Day*, which he himself produced in 1929. It went through four grueling months of tryouts, during which every effort was made to save the show, and then, opening twelve days after the stock market crash, it folded after just thirty-six performances at the Cosmopolitan Theatre on Columbus Circle.[24] Harold Arlen, then a singer, was to have sung "Doo Dah Dey," which was dropped before the opening; but reports have it that young Arlen happily served as the messenger boy carrying Youmans's leadsheets to lyricists Billy Rose and Edward Eliscu. Despite its failure, *Great Day* gave three great standards to popular music. The title song was a rousing choral number, and two ballads remain oft-recorded and oft-sung: "Without a Song," employing a repeated rhythmic figure deriving from the title, worked as a baritone solo and group number: "More Than You Know," which became a Jane Froman favorite, was rated by Alec Wilder as Youmans's "best ballad . . . and among the best of popular songs."[25]

Jazz and the blues really made their imprint on the American musical with the emergence of George Gershwin (1898–1937)—not ethnic jazz or Delta blues but a white adaptation. Gershwin's friend Vincent Youmans had initiated the process, reflecting his contact with the sounds of the dance bands of World War I and the Jazz Age. With Gershwin, syncopation, blue notes, and the harmonic colors of jazz became an integral part of his music, not only of his songs but in longer works like *Concerto in F*, *An American in Paris* and, of course, *Rhapsody in Blue*. With Gershwin the Jazz Age—its cut-time tempo, its frenzy, its anxieties, its fun-and-gamesmanship, and its zaniness—found stirring and infectious expression.

Born in Brooklyn, Gershwin began taking piano lessons at twelve and studied with a number of teachers; Charles Hambitzer, who introduced him to the classics and the French impressionists, was impressed by his pupil's interest in jazz, and regarded him as a genius; Edward Kilenyi tutored him in theory, harmony, and instrumentation; and, much later, after Gershwin was a recognized composer, he worked with Joseph Schillinger, approaching music through mathematics. At fifteen Gershwin became active in Tin Pan Alley as a song plugger and rehearsal pianist for Remick publishing and began composing popular songs. His first published tune, "When You Want 'em, You Can't Get 'em," was released by the Harry Von Tilzer firm, and his first theatre song, "The Making of a Girl," was heard in *The Passing Show* at the Winter Garden. The most fruitful association of this period, came when Max Dreyfus of Harms publishing put him on staff at $35 a week just to write songs and submit what he wrote to him. Harms was the "home" of Jerome Kern and in time of virtually all the top theatre composers of the 1920s, 30s, and 40s.

Through Dreyfus, theatre assignments came to Gershwin. Nora Bayes sang two of his early songs in *Ladies First* (1918). But his first break occurred when he and lyricist Irving Caesar wrote "Swanee," a song born during a lunch at Dinty Moore's in the theatre district and developed as they rode atop a Fifth Avenue bus to Gershwin's apartment in Washington Heights. When the Capitol Theatre, a new motion picture palace, opened at 51st Street and Broadway in October 1919, "Swanee" was featured in the lavish stage show—prepared by Ned Wayburn—preceding the film. Sixty chorus girls, with electric lights glowing on their slippers, danced to "Swanee" on a darkened stage, after which the Arthur Pryor Band, performing in the theatre, presented a band arrangement. Despite the full-blown treatment given the song, the audience sat on its hands.

Fortunately for Gershwin and Caesar, singer Al Jolson had an entirely different reaction and introduced it on one of his Sunday night concerts at the Winter Garden. The audience response was so tremendous that Jolson interpolated "Swanee" in his musical extrava-ganza, *Sinbad,* turning the song into an overnight hit, and its com-poser into an overnight sensation. Within a year, "Swanee" report-edly sold over 2 million records and over 1 million copies of sheet music. And before the year was out, Gershwin had his first show on Broadway in *La La Lucille,* which opened on May 26, 1919.

Even in Gershwin's first outing as a theatre composer, the *Times* sensed a freshness of approach, a rhythmic vitality in him that led it to type *La La Lucille* "the incarnation of jazz."[26] In actuality, Gershwin was then still under the spell of Jerome Kern. But the ap-pearance of a new voice and new sounds was also sensed by a young producer, Alex A. Aarons, who chose Gershwin over more experi-enced composers, and who later, with his partner Vinton Freedley, produced most of the Gershwin brothers' shows. *La La Lucille* did not add any standards to the Gershwin catalog, and its run was shortened by the Actors Equity strike. But it doubtless led to his being chosen by George White to score the *Scandals.*

The five years between 1920 and 1924, when Gershwin was scor-ing the *George White Scandals,* yielded some hits—"Drifting Along with the Tide" (1920), "I'll Build a Stairway to Paradise" (1922), and, especially, "Somebody Loves Me" (1924), characterized by Gerald Bordman as "demonstrating the grammar of the [Gershwin jazz] style."[27] But more importantly they were vital years in which Gershwin was able to experiment (as in the writing of the short opera, *Blue Monday Blues*) and to develop and perfect his unique style.

The fruit of those years was apparent in the first complete show

Gershwin did after the *Scandals—Lady Be Good*. "With this show," Bordman observes, "the rhythm, tensions and color of stage jazz were defined; the gutsy Negro creation was given a cerebral white reinterpretation." *Lady Be Good* was produced in December 1924 by Aarons and Freedley, who picked Gershwin despite Fred Astaire's reservations regarding his ability to write hit songs. The *World* typed the show, "the best musical in town." The *Sun* hailed the score as "brash, inventive, gay, nervous." To match his brother's fresh sound, Ira Gershwin wrote lyrics that were "fresh, colloquial and frequently sassy."[28]

In addition to the haunting title song, whose melody had the contours of an improvised tenor sax solo, *Lady Be Good* included hits in "So Am I" and the catchily syncopated "Fascinating Rhythm." "When at 9:15, the Astaires and Ukulele Ike sang and danced "Fascinating Rhythm," wrote the *Herald Tribune*, "the callous Broadwayites cheered them as if their favorite halfback had planted the ball behind the goal posts after an eighty-yard run. Seldom has it been the pleasure to witness such heartfelt, spontaneous and so deserved a tribute."[29] In his autobiography, Fred Astaire credits Gershwin with suggesting and demonstrating "the wow step" that climaxed their dance and proved "a knockout applause getter."[30]

Tip Toes of December 1925 was the first of three blockbuster shows, all produced by Aarons and Freedley. From the score of *Tip Toes*, mounted in art deco style, came "That Certain Feeling," "Looking for a Boy," and a swingy, bluesy "Sweet and Low Down." The last-mentioned, Ira Gershwin noted, was "sung, kazooed, tromboned and danced" by a quartet of the leads aided and abetted by the ensemble. The phrase, coined by Ira for a discarded song "Little Jazz Bird," was accorded recognition in *The American Thesaurus of Slang*. Applauding the music as the muscle and marrow of the show, critic Alexander Woollcott wrote, "*Tip Toes* was a Gershwin evening, so sweet and sassy are the melodies he has poured out . . . so fresh and unstinted the gay, young blood of his invention."[31]

Guy Bolton collaborated on the book of *Oh, Kay!*, as on *Tip Toes*, and was joined this time by his old Princess Theatre crony, P. G. Wodehouse. Concerned with a contemporary situation, bootlegging

and rum-running, *Oh Kay* (November 1926) was Gertrude Lawrence's first American musical, and also starred comic Victor Moore
of the sad face and cracked voice. Lawrence introduced three songs
that became standards: the lilting ballad "Someone to Watch Over
Me," "Maybe," and the snappy "Do Do Do." In addition to the
lively title song, there were jazzy numbers in "Fidgety Feet" and
"Clap Yo' Hands."

Writing about "Clap Yo' Hands" in his *Lyrics on Several Occasions*, Ira Gershwin points out that when the title occurs in the song,
it is sung as "clap-a yo' hands." He also notes that the refrain's first
segment is repeated verbatim in the last segment to maintain the
momentum of the song as a dance number.[32] The line, "On the sands
of time, you are a pebble," elicited criticism from Irving Caesar's
brother until a trip to the beach with a group of Gershwin friends
convinced him that a pebble could be found on the sand.[33]

Funny Face (1927), the third of the Aarons and Freedley hit
presentations, opened at the newly built Alvin Theatre (*Alex* + *Vinton*) on 52nd Street. Almost a flop with a Robert Benchley book in
its out-of-town tryout, it was turned into a catchy vehicle for the
Astaires and Victor Moore by Paul Gerard Smith and Fred Thompson. The score overflowed with memorable tunes, three of which
remain unforgettable standards: " 'S Wonderful," the lovely ballad
with Ira's sly verbal contractions, "He Loves and She Loves," and
"My One and Only," sung and tap-danced by the inimitable Fred
Astaire. There was also the melodious "Let's Kiss and Make Up" and
"High Hat," with Astaire in tuxedo and hands in pocket, doing a
tap dance as a male chorus aped his footwork. In 1983 *My One and
Only* became the title of a new posthumous Gershwin show, made up
of his tunes plus a new book. About the same time, the Minskoff
Theatre was renamed the Gershwin.

A most unusual number in *Funny Face*, whose lyric was potent
enough to win a place in an *Anthology of Light Verse*, was "The
Babbitt and the Bromide." The word "Babbitt" had been introduced
into the language by Sinclair Lewis's 1922 bestselling novel of that
title. It had come to define a philistine, adhering to accepted conventions of conduct and satisfied with the standardized gadgetry of

American life. Ira's satiric lyric provided a humorous interlude, enhanced as it was by a runaround dance routine by the Astaires.

Gershwin's last show of the 1920s, *Show Girl*, which opened in
July 1929, was a mixed bag of pickles—and a flop. It had Clayton,
Jackson, and Durante, the last of whom did a brace of his own spe-
cialities like "I Ups to Him" and "I Can Do Without Broadway." It
had Harriet Hoctor and the Albertina Rasch Girls, who performed
a stirring ballet to Gershwin's *An American in Paris*, recently introduced at Carnegie Hall by Walter Damrosch and the New York
Philharmonic Symphony. It had Duke Ellington and his orchestra
accompanying Ruby Keeler on "Liza." It had Al Jolson, recently
married to Ruby Keeler, running up and down the aisles of the
Ziegfeld Theatre opening night and singing "Liza" with her. A swinging, sophisticated, up-tempo ballad, "Liza" was Gershwin's favorite
song—and it was the solid hit that came out of the show. Ruby
Keeler, incidentally, left the production before it reached its 111th
performance, when it closed. Those who try to explain its failure
attribute it to the way the massive Ziegfeld production numbers
slowed down and overwhelmed the action. Reports have it that Gershwin had to threaten a lawsuit before he could collect the money owed
him by Ziegfeld, who suffered reverses in the stock market along with
other losses, not to mention those on the production of *Show Girl.*

The innovative character of Gershwin as a composer found match-
ing books and themes in several shows with which he was associated
in the 1930s. Although they are outside the scope of this book, mention must be made of *Strike Up the Band,* which opened on January
14, 1930, and took a swipe at American big business, secret diplo-
macy, and Babbitry. Also of *Of Thee I Sing,* which opened on
December 26, 1931, satirized American politics, and won the first
Pulitzer Prize ever awarded to a musical. (There was a 1927 version
of *Strike Up the Band,* in which the title song, a rousing march, was
first heard, but the show closed out of town. With a rewritten book,
the musical did open on Broadway, and the song was introduced by
Jim Townsend, Jerry Goff, and the chorus to the accompaniment of
the Red Nichols Orchestra in the pit.)

In discussing George Gershwin, I have disregarded two shows with which he was involved during the twenties. "Involved" because in each instance he was not the sole composer. Part of the score of *Song of the Flame* was written by Herbert Stothart and more than half the score of *Rosalie* was composed by Sigmund Romberg. The mention of Stothart and Romberg will indicate that both works were operettas, one produced in 1925 and the other in 1928. Clearly, there was still an audience for the type of arioso music that became the rage of the American musical theater during the 1910s as a result of Franz Lehar's stunning hit *The Merry Widow*. Gershwin was added to update the sound.

᧢ 21 ᧢

The Operetta Revival

"The date when jazz became an established and even welcome idiom (on Broadway)," Gerald Bordman has written, "can be pinpointed to December 1, 1924. On that night *Lady, Be Good* opened. Musical comedy was never quite the same."[1] An even earlier candidate for the jazzy transformation of the musical would be the all-black revue of 1921, *Shuffle Along*. Regardless of which composer or date is accepted, the 1920s introduced a new style of musical that employed excited tempi, modern melodic lines, bluesy harmonies, and whirlwind dancing.

Curiously, however, even as this transformation was occurring, the European-styled operetta, modernized to a degree, returned to bring audiences into the Broadway theatre. Beginning the same year as *Lady, Be Good* and *No, No, Nanette*, a series of operettas became huge box-office attractions over a four-year period from 1924 to 1928. Naturally, the major creators had European backgrounds, the two most important, Sigmund Romberg and Rudolf Friml, coming from Hungary and Czechoslovakia. In considering the vogue for operetta in this period, one must assume that the primary audience was the older generation, some of whom may even have enjoyed "the most successful musical ever written,"[2] Franz Lehar's *The Merry Widow*, which played at the magnificent New Amsterdam Theatre in 1907 and whose "gorgeous free-flowing well of unforgettable melody"[3] was doubtless familiar to that generation. But since a number of these new operettas racked up substantial runs of over five hundred performances, the romanticism of remote times and exotic lands must not have been lost on the younger generation.

Sigmund Romberg (1887–1951) came from Hungary, and, while studying to be an engineer, became assistant manager of Vienna's largest operetta house. Work as a pianist in London and then in New York led to his becoming the leader of the orchestra at Bustanoby's, one of New York's most elegant restaurants. Songs published by Jos. W. Stern and Company later known as Edward B. Marks Music, led to a longtime association with the Shuberts. During his prolific career, he wrote about fifty operetta-styled Broadway shows. In the twenties, Romberg produced four enormous operetta hits: *The Student Prince* (1924), *The Desert Song* (1926), *My Maryland* (1927), and *The New Moon* (1928). The biggest box-offce smash was *The Student Prince,* which had 608 performances and 9 touring companies. To get it produced, Romberg had to break down Shubert resistance to the bravura music, to the unhappy ending (the student prince had to give up his waitress love), and Romberg's demand for a large male chorus in place of a bevy of beauties. The male chorus turned out to be such a rousing success that it was adopted by other producers and almost became a Shubert trademark.

The Desert Song (1926), based on the real life of a heroic Berber renegade, ran for 471 performances, just short of the season's biggest hit, *Rio Rita.* Apart from the stirring title tune, the score included the martial "Song of the Riffs" and the arioso ballad "One Alone." It became the first Broadway operetta to be filmed with sound. *My Maryland* (1927), a romantic treatment of the Barbara Frietchie legend, produced the perennial, "Your Land and My Land." Musically, the most potent was *The New Moon* (1928), the only show of the season to break the 500-performance mark after being rewritten, recast, rescored, and finally reopened. Set in Louisiana in the eighteenth century, it yielded "Softly as in a Morning Sunrise," "One Kiss," "Wanting You," and the imperishable "Lover Come Back to Me." All these made their appearance during the revisionary process, with only the stirring "Stout-Hearted Men" remaining from the original version.

Rudolf Friml (1879–1972) settled in the United States in 1906, having been born in Prague, where he attended the Conservatory headed by Antonin Dvorák. A child prodigy, his first composition, a barcarolle, was published when he was ten. Eventually, he became the accompanist of violinist Jan Kubelik, touring the United States with him, and then alone, as a concert pianist in 1901 and 1906. Having achieved publication of some light concert pieces after settling here, he found supporters in two important publishers, Rudolph Schirmer and Max Dreyfus. Through them he made contact with Oscar Hammerstein II and collaborated on *The Firefly*. Completely European in sound, *The Firefly* opened at the Lyric Theatre in December 1912 to become "the season's most endearing and most enduring musical."[4]

Friml's work during these years included *Rose-Marie* (1924), *The Vagabond King* (1925), and *The Three Musketeers*, a modest hit in 1928. An attempt to revive the *Musketeers* in 1985 was a dismal flop, despite the entrance of the three musketeers on live nags thumping up from the rear of the auditorium. Both *Rose-Marie* and *The Vagabond King* aggregated over 500 performances each; the former was not only the biggest hit of the season but the top grosser of the decade. The title song proved a viable ballad, and the operatic "Indian Love Call" was popular enough to invite parodies. Oscar Hammerstein II, intent on moving the musical in the direction of the integrated musical play, wrote in a program note, "The musical numbers of this play are such an integral part of the action that we do not think we should list them as separate episodes"; it was more a perspective than an achievement.

The Vagabond King (1925), based on Justin Huntly McCarthy's *If I Were King*, presented an irresistibly romantic and heroic figure in the fifteenth-century poet François Villon, stirring Friml to compose his most exciting score. Villon's "Song of the Vagabonds" was an audience rouser, balanced by tender ballads like "Only a Rose" and "Some Day" and the passionate duet "Love Me Tonight." The prostitute who kills herself for love of Villon won over the audience with her heartbreak rendition of "Love for Sale."

Operettas by these prolific Europeans—including six flops for Romberg and two for Friml, in addition to their numerous successes—

hardly exhausted the flow of operetta fare on the musical stage in 1924–28. 1926 brought Emmerich Kalman's masterpiece, *Countess Maritza*, "the unsurpassed example of the poignant Hungarian side of Austro-Hungarian" operetta,[5] its hauteur projected majestically in "Play Gypsies—Dance Gypsies." The following year *Rio Rita* had the good fortune to open in the city's newest and most elegant theatre, the Ziegfeld, a magnificent art deco creation by Joseph Urban. The show lived up to the promise of the house. Though billed as a musical comedy, it had the trappings of an operetta—Texas Rangers hunting a Mexican bandit with the odd name of the Kinkajou—but most of all it had a ravishing score that earned comparisons with *Naughty Marietta* (1910) and *Rose-Marie* (1924). Memorable melodies included the rhythmic title tune, "When You're in Love, You Waltz," the raggy "Kinkajou," and the roaring male choral number, "The Rangers' Song." For Harry Tierney and his partner Joe McCarthy, who had produced *Irene* (1919) and *Kid Boots* (1924), *Rio Rita* was an exciting culmination. *Rio Rita* arrived in the season before Romberg's last great hit, *The New Moon*, which brought an end to the renewed vogue of the Viennese-American operetta. As Bordman notes: "Its incredibly melodious heyday encompassed a mere five seasons 1924–28. They were the same seasons that saw the coming of the sassy, cynical, jazz musical comedy."[6]

❦ 22 ❦

Song Laureate of the Roaring Twenties

Close to Christmas of 1934, when theatregoers were hurrying to view a musical since regarded as "the quintessence of the lavish, bawdy, swift-paced, uninhibited Music Comedy of the mid-thirties,"[1] a young stagewriter named Moss Hart journeyed to Europe to see the man responsible for the slick words and satin melodies of *Anything Goes*. They met, appropriately enough, in the fashionable bar of the Ritz in Paris—appropriate, because Cole Porter had unfurled the unbuttoned lyrics of "You're the Top" and "I Get a Kick Out of You," performed by a brass section known as Ethel Merman, while cruising in high fashion down the Rhine. (Hart and Porter were to write *Jubilee*, the show with "Just One of Those Things" and the sultry 108-bar ditty "Begin the Beguine," on a trip around the world.)

Armed with a letter of introduction from Irving Berlin, young Hart carried a small gift package sent by a friend of Porter's. When the red-leather Cartier box was opened, it disclosed two long strips of gold inscribed with the letters C.P. Hart was amazed to discover that these were garters and quite overwhelmed when Porter immediately rolled up his trouser legs, removed the gold pair he wore and, after donning the new set, blithely presented the old gold to the bartender. "It's the way Christmas is supposed to start, isn't it?" Porter asked in his surprisingly high-pitched voice.

To Moss Hart, who came from an impecunious Brooklyn background, this was incredible, although afterward he felt that the scene
embodied "some of the gaiety, the impishness, the audacity and the
wonderful insouciance of his songs. Also of his pocketbook, Hart
might have added. For Cole Porter was born to wealth in Peru (Indiana), married wealth in Paris, and inherited part of a $7-million-
estate left by his maternal grandfather. Giving away gold garters was
as inconsequential as hiring the entire company of the Monte Carlo
Ballet for a private party, which Porter also did in the dizzy days
just after World War I.

Like many gifted veterans of that war, Porter spent most of the
succeeding decade as a rootless expatriate in Europe. He went to the
bull fights at Pamplona (à la Hemingway's *The Sun Also Rises*). He
spent summers on the Riviera or at the Lido in Venice. He attended
the endless round of parties given by wealthy Americans for gifted
Americans—or, rather, he gave them. He lived in Paris, as did a host
of American writers and artists, though not on the Left Bank. (In
fact, he had a Paris apartment during the war that became famous
for its luxurious accoutrements: platinum-textured wallpaper, zebra-
covered chairs, that well anticipated those of El Morocco.) And yet,
except for his wealth, Porter was as much a member of the Lost Generation as F. Scott Fitzgerald, John Dos Passos, Kay Boyle, and
Hemingway himself.

In truth, though it is not customary to view songwriters and novelists from the same perspective, Porter's journey from his beginnings
in Indiana parallels that of his literary contemporaries. Like Fitzgerald of St. Paul, Minnesota, and Hemingway of Oak Park, Illinois, he
came from a nineties background in the Midwest—and worked dili-
gently at eradicating his Hoosier roots. He began the process by attending an exclusive Eastern university. Just as Fitzgerald went to
Princeton, Porter attended both Yale and Harvard, contributing two
famous football songs "Bingo Eli Yale" and "Yale Bulldog Song" to
the former. The parallels continued with the war. Before Hemingway
was eighteen, he joined the Norton-Harjes Ambulance Corps in France,
as did Louis Bromfield, e.e. cummings, Sidney Howard, and John
Dos Passos; and when the American army moved in, he moved on to

the Italian ambulance section (as described in *A Farewell to Arms*). So with Porter, who, having written a flop musical, *See America First*, while he was still at the Harvard School of Music, enlisted in the French Foreign Legion, at the prompting, it is said, of a suggestion that he needed experience if he were to become a fine writer. He spent part of his time in the Legion entertaining the troops on a portable piano he carried strapped to his back; and on America's entry into the war he became an artillery instructor as well as a parttime party-giver in his swank Paris apartment.

When the news of the Armistice came in 1918, most American writers in Europe got drunk, according to Malcolm Cowley, who chronicled their bizarre escapades in *Exile's Return*. With Porter, as with some of the others, this was a binge, emotional as well as liquid, that was to last for the better part of a decade—until the worldwide Depression struck and sobered almost everybody. By the end of the twenties, many of the expatriate refugees of the Left Bank came drifting back to our shores. Not Porter, who had added the fortune of Linda Lee Thomas—a Social Registerite—to his own and was now spending his summers at the Palazzo Rezzonico in Venice (where Robert Browning had died) at $4,000 a month. E. Ray Goetz, who wanted the man who was to write the cannily suggestive song "Let's Do It" for *Paris*, starring his wife Irene Bordoni, had to seek Porter out on the Lido.

Gershwin, Kern, and Vincent Youmans, three other theatre composers of the golden age of musical comedy, began their songwriting careers as rehearsal pianists, song pluggers, and so on, in Tin Pan Alley. Porter entered both this and Shubert Alley through his wealthy social connections. Elizabeth Marbury, who produced his first full-length Broadway musical while he was studying at Harvard, encountered young Porter at fashionable weekend parties at Southampton on Long Island. And Raymond Hitchcock, the actor and producer who sponsored a series of *Hitchy-Koos*, signed Porter to write the 1919 edition as the result of a shipboard meeting on a trip from Europe.

In short, Porter's personal situation made it easy for him to become an exponent of the sophisticated, cynical, and nonconformist outlook considered "in" during the Roaring Twenties. Inevitably, he came to be to the American musical theatre what Fitzgerald, H. L. Mencken, and Hemingway were to the lost-generation world of the hip flask and the hijacker, the 52nd Street "speaks" and easy sex, the wisecrack and *vo-do-de-o-do*. His work had the romantic glitter and despairing sophistication of Fitzgerald. He was as irreverent and as loftily satirical toward the "booboisie" as Mencken. Like Hemingway's prose, his lyrics were tough and lean. And his outlook, an ever-deepening sense of world-weariness, was not imperfectly characterized by Hemingway's famous parody of the Lord's Prayer—"Our nada who art in nade, Nada be thy name . . ."

But something did matter to Porter through the years. Whether on a world cruise, at an Elsa Maxwell party, beside a Hollywood swimming pool, or sunning himself on the Lido, Porter could shut out the world and people—and he did so whenever he was preoccupied with song. Since he could write music without the aid of an instrument, this singlemindedness could occur without notice. That is why friends often commented on his "distracted" air. When he was at work on a show, his absorption and immersion became so complete, according to Abe Burrows and other collaborators, that you could fire a howitzer next to him without his being aware. A man of wealth, he felt no pressure to work other than the inner yearning to create something great. And this pressure did not let up until his right leg was amputated in 1958. But by then he had written words and music for more than forty stage and screen productions, was responsible for more hits than any other songwriter, except possibly Berlin and Rodgers, and had achieved the enviable position, along with Berlin, of being the most performed member of ASCAP, which meant being the most performed songwriter of his time.

As the Roaring Twenties modulated into the Troubled Thirties, composers who had blossomed during the opulent years of the musical theatre began to add sociology to sex and, under the impact of the Depression, manifested "twinges of liberal conscience." The Gershwins turned from the scanties of the *Scandals* and *Oh, Kay* to *Strike Up the Band*, an assault on Babbitry and warmongers, and, in *Of Thee I Sing*, to mordant political satire. Rodgers and Hart swung from the flaming youthfulness of *The Girl Friend* and *The Garrick Gaieties* to political commentary in *I'd Rather Be Right* (with George M. Cohan playing Franklin D. Roosevelt). Even Irving Berlin became involved in the sociology of the era: *Face the Music* was a travesty of police corruption then under federal scrutiny, and *As Thousands Cheer* a journalistic exposé of contemporary issues, including lynching. (Who can forget Ethel Waters singing "Supper Time," a blues for women waiting with the evening meal for men who will never come to eat it?)

At the same time, there was a movement, experimental and groping, toward a type of musical whose songs and dances would be an integral part of the book. As early as 1927 Oscar Hammerstein II and Jerome Kern demonstrated that it was feasible in *Show Boat*. By using a saga of ballet life, Rodgers and Hart created in *On Your Toes* a show whose dances, including the first ballet sequence in a Broadway musical, were inseparable from the story. Ranging far and wide in their search for new subjects, Rodgers and Hart finally achieved in *Pal Joey* a story *with* music, whose characters, including a heel as hero, were acclaimed for being three-dimensional people.

From these developments in form, content, and outlook Cole Porter remained aloof. Working within the traditional confines of Rockette dancing, brassy singing, gaudy costumes, and zany comics like Jimmy Durante and Bert Lahr, he nevertheless created a body of material so unique that, while the songs of other show writers have been mistaken for his, his have seldom been attributed to anyone else. "Give him a choice between sacrificing the integrity of a character . . . and a rhyme," wrote a historian of the musical theatre, "and he would unhesitatingly sacrifice the character."[2] But the Porter touch is unmistakable: the lean lyrics, urbane, suggestive, trickily rhymed, set like sparkling stones in minor-keyed melodies that are long-lined and throb-rhythmed.

Porter was not part of the wisecracking Algonquin Round Table, but his kinship with them is inescapable. The motive power of Porter's songs is, of course, in his words, the jeweled product of a creator not merely of song lyrics but of light verse. The difference is that the former always need to be clothed in music, while the latter are attractive in their nudity. (Along with Oscar Hammerstein II, he is one of the few songwriters whose lyrics have in fact been printed as a volume of light verse.) Who else but Porter would rhyme "Padua" with "cad-you-ah" and "mad-you-ah," "Ponte Vecchio" with "Becky-wecky-o," "puberty" and "Shuberty," "lymphatics" with "ecstatics," and "heinous" and "Coriolanus" (with the double entendre on the Roman's ultimate and penultimate syllables)?

Other lyric writers of the musical theatre of the 1920s–40s had a way with the topical patter song. But few cultivated this genre as assiduously as Porter, and no one raised it to such a level of literate and allusive perfection. The time signature is to be found constantly in the very rhymes: "Waldorf salad" and "Berlin ballad," "Inferno's Dante" and "the nose of Durante," "Shakespeare sonnet" and "Bendel bonnet," "Nathan panning" and "Bishop Manning," "sweet suburban ideas" and "Deanna Durbin ideas," "Whistler's mama" and "O'Neill drama," "sweet Snow White, Ambrose Light" and "Eleanor, wrong or right."

Porter's wit was actually Elizabethan. In a song like "You're the Top," which he rewrote in "Cherry Pies Ought to Be You" and in reverse in "You Irritate Me So," he felt constrained to demonstrate the endless variety, almost to the point of exhaustion, of the tropes he could invent, listing, for instance, every conceivable annoyance from "the fall in my arches" and "the shark in the sea," piling them to the telegraphed rhyme of "the rust in my gear" and "the pain in my . . ." In "The Physician" from *Nymph Errant*, produced in England, no facet of human anatomy is disregarded: "he thought a lotta / my medulla oblongata, for my spleen / [he] was keen as could be." In the ever-popular "Let's Do It," no organism is omitted as an argument for falling in love: "In shallow shoals, English soles do it . . . Goldfish in the privacy of bowls do it . . . Why ask if shad do it / Waiter bring me shad roe!" Porter had the most fun with this type of song in *Kiss Me Kate*, where the titles of Shakespeare's plays permitted him to play havoc with language: "Troilus and Cressida" rhymes with "the British embessida"; "A Midsummer Night's Dream," with "Washington Heights dream"; "just cite *The Merchant of Ven-*

ice" if her "sweet pound of flesh you would menace" and "When you would flatter her / Tell her what Tony told Cleopatterer." All this leads to the charming couplet about "mussing" her clothes and the play on the Shakespearean title, *"Much Ado about Nussing."* Porter's inventive distortion of language ran riot, of course, in the tongue-twisting song in *Red, Hot and Blue!,* "It's De-Lovely." Here he piles line upon line, extending and embellishing words like "de-reverie," "de-rhapsody," and "de-regal" to climax in the title phrase, "It's De-Lovely."

Apart from his skill as a rhymester and his variety as a wit, Porter displayed versatility in expressing the basic theme of all musicals. He was arrogant enough to write a song called "I Love You" in *Mexican Hayride,* obviously determined to demonstrate that he could devise a hit even with this mundane and much-abused title. In "I Concentrate on You," "So In Love" and "Ev'ry Time We Say Goodbye, I Die a Little," he created some of the theatre's most touching and tender love ballads. It was the negative side of love, however, the agony rather than the ecstasy, the frustration rather than the fulfillment, that yielded some of Porter's most memorable songs: "What Is This Thing Called Love?," "In the Still of the Night," "I Get a Kick Out of You" (though you obviously don't adore me), "All Through the Night," and the ineluctable "Begin the Beguine" (with its shifting moods, all of them twisted by nagging doubts). But what is unique in the Porter catalogue is his approach to the physical side of love. In songs like "Let's Misbehave," "I've Got You Under My Skin" and "Night and Day" ("there's oh such a hungry yearning burning inside of me"), he achieves a degree of sexual heat rare in song literature.

Porter participated not only in the Lost Generation's attack on sexual taboos but also in its exposé of the distorting and destructive power of money. Free from the striving for social position and from the wealth-envy that complicated Fitzgerald's outlook, he was the cynic par excellence on the subject of money. So blunt is his exposé of the life of the prostitute that, despite the popularity of the tune, the moving words of "Love for Sale" have never been heard either on radio or TV. In "Two Little Babes in the Wood," "Always

True to You in My Fashion," and "I've Come to Wive It Wealthily in Padua," Porter runs the gamut from the playful to the sadonic in deriding the price label on respectable love.

> If my wife have a bag of gold,
> What care I if the bag be old

The high point of Porter's remarkable career was, of course, the production that included this song. *Kiss Me Kate*, produced in 1948 after Broadway wiseacres were whispering that he was finished, enjoyed the longest run of all Porter shows, winding up in the golden circle of musicals with more than 1,000 performances. Viewed solely from the standpoint of song this is not surprising since, as with *Oklahoma!*, *Annie Get Your Gun*, *My Fair Lady*, and a handful of other musicals, there is not a weak number in the score. It's all "top-drawer," to use a word that Porter detested. It's also pure Porter, embodying a volatile mixture of Shakespearean cynicism, contemporary sophistication, and the world-weariness of Ernest Dowson's "I've been faithful to thee, Cynara, in my fashion."

Song laureate of the Lost Generation, man of high society, "litterateur and genteel pornographer," as Cecil Smith dubbed him—they add up to only one side of Cole Porter. Another is quite evident from the other crucial element of his songs, their brooding music. Had either Gershwin or Harold Arlen delved as deeply into the domain of minor-keyed, Slavic melodies, one would see nothing except the normal, perhaps, inevitable response to melodic material they had absorbed at home or in a synagogue in their childhood and youth. But for Cole Porter, a Midwestern, farm-bred, Protestant lad, the preference for the minor mode (which he employed more extensively than any show composer before or after him) represents a response to deep feelings seldom put into the concrete form of words. In Porter's melodies, we encounter the man whose legs were so badly crushed in 1937 when a horse he was riding fell on him that he was seldom without discomfort or pain—the nerve tissue was badly mangled; who suffered through more than thirty operations in a vain effort to escape the amputation which, finally, occurred in 1958. In his music we come close to the troubled man who married a woman older than himself, whom he loved deeply and whose death in 1954 turned the gay party-giver into a recluse, but with whom he shared an unresolved relationship that included separate apartments (albeit both were in the Waldorf Towers).

In his autobiography, Richard Rodgers tells of a dinner date in Venice in the summer of 1926. Porter was then sojourning at the Palazzo Rezzonico, where he, Noel Coward, and Cole played some of their songs for each other. (If only that musical feast had been recorded or videotaped for posterity!) When Rodgers heard for the first time "Let's Do It," "Let's Misbehave," and "Two Little Babes in the Wood," he demanded to know why Porter wasn't writing for Broadway. "To my embarrassment," Rodgers observes, "Porter told me he had already written four musical comedy scores, three of which had even made it to Broadway. But little had come of them, and he simply preferred living in Europe and performing his songs for the entertainment of his friends."[3] Later, Porter told Rodgers that he had discovered the secret of writing hits. "As I breathlessly awaited the magic formula, Porter leaned over and confided, 'I'll write Jewish tunes.' I laughed at what I took to be a joke but not only was Cole dead serious, he eventually did exactly that."[4]

And Rodgers, suggesting we hum the melodies that go with "Only you beneath the moon and under the sun" from "Night and Day," or any of "Begin the Beguine," or "Love for Sale," or "My Heart Belongs to Daddy," or "I Love Paris," goes on to comment, "It's surely one of the ironies of the musical theatre that, despite the abundance of Jewish composers, the one who has written the most enduring 'Jewish' music should be an Episcopalian millionaire who was born on a farm in Peru, Indiana."[5]

It may well be that the polarity between his witty, suggestive lyrics and the throbbing, charged "Eastern Mediterranean" melodies, as Rodgers characterized some of them, gives Porter's songs a quality that prevents them from palling and that elicits the contrasting interpretations accorded them by singers as diverse as Ethel Merman, Ella Fitzgerald, and Frank Sinatra. Porter's songs were clearly as much an expression of his ambivalent personality as they were the embodiment of a dislocated era of high living and romantic disillusion. Unquestionably, however, his most peaceful and his most relaxed hours were those he spent writing the songs that generations will go on singing and listening to. "If we listen to his early efforts," Stanley Green has said, "and compare them with his most recent songs [1960], we find little change in his basic attitudes. There is still something of the glittering Twenties about even his most recent compositions."[6]

Epilogue

In 1929 Ernest Hemingway bade *A Farewell to Arms,* while Harry Crosby, another American expatriate writer of "the lost generation," bade farewell to life.

"Henry Grew Crosby, 32 years old, of a socially prominent Boston family," the *New York Times* reported on December 11, 1929, "and Mrs. Josephine Rotch Bigelow, 22 years old, the wife of Albert S. Bigelow, a postgraduate student at Harvard, were found dead about ten o'clock last night, each with a bullet wound in the head, in the apartment of Crosby's friend, Stanley Mortimer, Jr., a portrait painter, on the ninth floor of the Hotel des Artistes, 1 West 67th Street.

"The couple had died in what Dr. Charles Norris, Medical Examiner, described as a suicide compact. . . . There were no notes, and the authorities were unable to obtain information pointing to a motive for the deaths."[1] The *Herald-Tribune* added the cogent detail that the two lay in bed fully clothed.[2]

Malcolm Cowley, who tried to explain Crosby's suicide in the terminal chapter of *Exile's Return* and traced it to the bankruptcy of the "religion of art," described the atmosphere of the time in the following evocative terms.

"Always, everywhere, there was jazz; everything that year was enveloped in the hard bright mist of it. There were black orchestras wailing in cafes and *boites de nuit,* radios carrying the music of the

Savoy ballroom in London, new phonograph records from Harlem and Tin Pan Alley played over and over again, *Organ Grinder, Empty Bed Blues, Limehouse Blues, Vagabond Lover, Broadway Melody.* . . . In the morning there would be more jazz—"[3]

"We play (taking turns at winding the gramophone)," Crosby wrote in his diary, "the *Broadway Melody* from before breakfast till after supper (over a hundred times in all)."[4] "And when the records wore out," Cowley continued, "there were new ones to take their places, new orchestras hot and sweet, jazz omnipresent and always carrying the same message of violent escape toward Mandalay, Michigan, Carolina in the morning, one's childhood, love, a new day. Everywhere was the atmosphere of a long debauch that had to end; the orchestra played too fast, the stakes were too high at gambling tables, the players were so empty, so tired, secretly hoping to vanish together into sleep and . . . maybe wake on a very distant morning and hear nothing whatsoever, no shouting or crooning, find all things changed.

"Everybody had money that year and was spending it. Harry Crosby had money too, but was living far beyond his comfortable Back Bay income."[5]

On July 19, Crosby wrote, "After innumerable sherry cobblers we stopped at the post office and sent the following cable to the family, 'Please sell $10,000 worth of stock—we have decided to lead a mad and extravagant life.' "[6] When the family sent a heartbroken cable instead of complying, Crosby replied in a letter that "for the poet there is love and there is death and infinity and for other things to assume such vital importance is out of the question and that is why I refuse to take the question of money seriously."[7] Cowley's comment: "Yet he took the getting and spending of it seriously enough. Eternal and infinite things were being forgotten in the general demoralization of the age."[8]

And so came the afternoon of December 10, 1929. In a life that demanded more and more sensations and stimulants to make it livable, death was as inevitable and as inescapable as the crash of October 1929 that served as a culmination of the era's uncontrolled psychological and economic profligacy.

Yet it was in the extravagant twenties that the Broadway theatre glowed brightly, with a plethora of revues, operettas, and musical comedies bringing to the fore a flock of gemlike show composers. Lyrics rose to a new level of literacy, wit, and sophistication, contrasting markedly with the clichés of Tin Pan Alley plug songs. Numerous hits became million-copy sellers, enriching an expanding group of popular music publishers and songwriters. The nation danced to the music of a thousand bands. Black creativity made Harlem a center of New York night life and introduced novel dances, tempi, and sounds to the musical theatre and the hit parade. With the infiltration of blues and jazz—the syncopated rhythms, new tonalities, fresh, offbeat harmonies, and improvisation—popular music acquired a unique American sound. The speakeasy world of the twenties may have been rowdy, boisterous, extravagant, cynical, and violent, but it produced *Show Boat*, Bix, "Tea for Two," Duke Ellington, Bessie Smith, *Rhapsody in Blue*, Louis Armstrong, and "Star Dust."

Notes

1: "FLAPPERS ARE WE"

1. Nancy Milford, *Zelda* (New York: Avon Books, 1971), 92.
2. Louis Untermeyer, *Makers of the Modern World* (New York: Simon and Schuster, 1955), 695.
3. Nat Shapiro and Nat Hentoff, eds., *Hear Me Talkin' to Ya* (New York: Rinehart, 1955), 276.
4. Lehman Engel, *The American Musical Theater* (New York: Collier Books, 1976), 78.
5. Hoagy Carmichael with Stephen Longstreet, *Sometimes I Wonder: The Story of Hoagy Carmichael* (New York: Farrar, Straus & Giroux, 1965), 43.
6. Milford, *Zelda*, 128.
7. Untermeyer, *Makers of the Modern World*, 694.
8. Ibid., 694.
9. Milford, *Zelda*, 92.
10. Walter Clemons, *Newsweek* (July 28, 1986), 65. *Benchley at the Theatre* (Ipswich, 1986) collects more than 80 of his pieces (plus, mysteriously, Ring Lardner's famous radio column parodying the lyrics of *Night and Day*, which the editor seems to think Benchley wrote).
11. Andrew Turnbull, ed., *The Letters of F. Scott Fitzgerald* (New York, Dell, 1963), 333.
12. Milford, *Zelda*, 131.
13. Ibid., 160.
14. Turnbull, *Letters of F. Scott Fitzgerald*, 165.
15. Ibid., 177–78.
16. May 21, 1920.

17. Marjorie Longley, Louis Silverstein, Samuel A. Tower, *America's Taste, 1851–1959* (New York: Simon and Schuster, 1960), 196.
18. Vincent Lopez, *Lopez Speaking* (New York: Citadel Press, 1964), 76.
19. Edward B. Marks as Told to Abbott J. Liebling, *They All Sang, From Tony Pastor to Rudy Vallee* (New York: Viking Press, 1935), 199.
20. When I was growing up in a middle-class neighborhood of Manhattan, it was a family custom to retire after dinner to the music room and listen to records by these classical artists.
21. Marks, *They All Sang*, 207.

2: KING OLIVER, JELLY ROLL, AND SATCHMO

1. Turnbull, ed., *The Letters of F. Scott Fitzgerald*, 249.
2. Lopez, *Lopez Speaking*, 76.
3. Ibid.
4. Shapiro and Hentoff, *Hear Me Talkin' to Ya*, 81.
5. Marshall W. Stearns, *The Story of Jazz* (New York: Oxford Univ. Press, 1956), 154.
6. Orrin Keepnews and Bill Grauer, Jr., *A Pictorial History of Jazz: People and Places from New Orleans to Modern Jazz* (New York: Crown, 1955), 22.
7. Barry Ulanov, *A History of Jazz in America* (New York: Viking Press, 1954), 82–83.
8. *Variety*, Nov. 23, 1921.
9. Ibid.
10. Shapiro and Hentoff, *Hear Me Talkin' to Ya*, 42.
11. Carmichael, *Sometimes I Wonder*, 101–12. Armstrong was quite partial to Carmichael's songs, recording, among others, "Rockin' Chair," "Bessie Couldn't Help It," "Star Dust," "Georgia on My Mind," "Lazy River," "Snow Ball," "Lyin' to Myself," "Ev'ntide," "Jubilee," and "Poor Old Joe." Only Jimmy McHugh, among white songwriters, approached the number of Carmichael titles recorded by Armstrong: "I Can't Give You Anything But Love," "I Can't Believe That You're in Love with Me," "Exactly Like You," "On the Sunny Side of the Street," "Blue Again," "I'm in the Mood for Love," and "I've Got My Fingers Crossed," among others.
12. Shapiro and Hentoff, *Hear Me Talkin' to Ya*, 103.
13. James Lincoln Collier, *The Making of Jazz* (Boston: Houghton Mifflin Co., 1978), 90.
14. Shapiro and Hentoff, *Hear Me Talkin' to Ya*, 42.
15. Ibid., 96.
16. Ibid., 99.

17. Ibid., 104.
18. Ibid., 188.
19. Ulanov, *History of Jazz in America*, 72.
20. Ibid., 78.
21. Stearns, *The Story of Jazz*, 176.
22. Shapiro and Hentoff, *Hear Me Talkin' to Ya*, 103–4.
23. Stearns, *The Story of Jazz*, 176.
24. Shapiro and Hentoff, *Hear Me Talkin' to Ya*, 43.
25. Ibid., 48.
26. Ibid., 49.
27. Albert McCarthy, Alun Morgan, Paul Oliver, Max Harrison, *Jazz on Record* (London: Hanover Books, 1968), 7.
28. Louis Armstrong, *Swing That Music* (London, New York: Longmans, Green, 1936), viii–ix.
29. *Jazz on Record*, 7.
30. Collier, *The Making of Jazz*, 141.
31. Dan Morganstern, "Louis Armstrong and the Transformation of the Jazz Repertory," paper read at the IASPM Conference, Univ. of Nevada, May 11, 1984.
32. Collier, *The Making of Jazz*, 85.
33. Ibid., 99.
34. *Jazz on Record*, 206.
35. Collier, *The Making of Jazz*, 107.

3: BIX, AUSTIN HIGH, AND CHICAGO STYLE

1. Shapiro and Hentoff, *Hear Me Talkin' to Ya*, 123.
2. Ibid., 119.
3. Ibid., 121.
4. Ibid.
5. Ibid., 125.
6. Ibid., 129.
7. Ibid., 123.
8. *The New Republic* (June 8, 1938), 136.
9. Ibid.
10. Shapiro and Hentoff, *Hear Me Talkin' to Ya*, 151.
11. Ibid., 158.
12. Ibid., 160.
13. Ibid., 274.
14. Philip Larkin, *All What Jazz, A Record Diary, 1961–1971* (New York: Farrar, Straus & Giroux, 1981).
15. Collier, *The Making of Jazz*, 171.

16. Shapiro and Hentoff, *Hear Me Talkin' to Ya*, 157.
17. Richard Hadlock, *Jazz Masters of the 20s* (New York: Macmillan, 1965), 89.
18. Ibid., 90.
19. Ibid.
20. Carmichael, *Sometimes I Wonder*, 115.
21. Hadlock, *Jazz Masters of the 20s*, 104.
22. Carmichael, *Sometimes I Wonder*, 108.
23. Hadlock, *Jazz Masters of the 20s*, 76.
24. Ibid., 102.
25. Shapiro and Hentoff, *Hear Me Talkin' to Ya*, 163.
26. Collier, *The Making of Jazz*, 162–63.

4: POPS AND SMACK

1. *Gene Lees Newsletter*, Mar. 1984, 1.
2. Stearns, *The Story of Jazz*, 165.
3. At the major companies, different budgets are allotted to records in different fields, based on anticipated sales and the size of the market. Jazz records received a smaller budget than pop.
4. Isaac Goldberg, supp. by Edith Garson, *George Gershwin* (New York: Frederick Ungar, 1958), 137.
5. Ibid., 136.
6. Bill Zakariasen, *New York Post* (Feb. 13, 1984).
7. *The New Yorker* (Apr. 16, 1984), 137.
8. Goldberg, *George Gershwin*, 151.
9. Ibid.
10. Ibid., 152.
11. Ibid.
12. Edward Jablonski and Lawrence D. Stewart, *The Gershwin Years* (New York: Doubleday, 1958), 86.
13. Ibid., 86–87.
14. Goldberg, *George Gershwin*, 139.
15. Ibid.
16. Ibid., 140.
17. Jablonski and Stewart, *The Gershwin Years*, 83.
18. David Ewen, *All the Years of American Popular Music* (Englewood Cliffs, N.J.: Prentice-Hall, 1977), 262.

5: DUKE, ETHEL, AND THE HARLEM SCENE

1. Langston Hughes, *The Big Sea* (New York: Thunder's Mouth Press, 1986), 81.

2. Ibid., 240.

3. *Freedomways*, Summer, 1963, vol. 3, no. 3, 314.

4. Liner notes, *The Sound of Harlem*, Jazz Odyssey, vol. III, Columbia C3L 33.

5. James Weldon Johnson, *Black Manhattan* (New York: Arno Press and New York Times, 1968), 260.

6. Frank Driggs, *The Sound of Harlem*, booklet with Columbia recording C3L 33.

7. Stanley Dance, *The World of Duke Ellington* (New York: Charles Scribner's Sons, 1970), 68.

8. Quoted in Frank Driggs, liner note, *Ethel Waters: Greatest Years*, Columbia KG 31571.

9. Ibid.

10. Ibid.

11. Henry Pleasants, *The Great American Popular Singers* (New York: Simon and Schuster, 1974), 86.

12. Ibid., 9.

13. Shapiro and Hentoff, *Hear Me Talkin' to Ya*, 224–25.

6: "THE BIRTH OF THE BLUES"

1. Ewen, *All the Years of American Popular Music*.

2. W. C. Handy with Abbe Niles, *A Treasury of the Blues* (New York: Boni, 1949).

3. OKeh's 8000 series soon had competition from Paramount's 12000 series (1921), Columbia's 14000 D series (1922), Vocalion's 1000 series (1925), Perfect's 100 series (1925), Brunswick's 7000 series (1926), and Victor's V38500 series (1927). Most of these were decimated, dropped, or phased out during the Depression.

4. Robert Dixon and John Godrich, *Recording the Blues* (New York: Stein and Day, 1970), 99.

5. Shapiro and Hentoff, *Hear Me Talkin' to Ya*, 248.

6. Dixon and Godrich, *Recording the Blues*, 24.

7. Ibid.

8. But presumably the most famous version of the song is Louis Armstrong's.

9. Chris Albertson, liner note, *Bessie Smith, The World's Greatest Blues Singer*, Columbia GP 33.

10. Ibid.

11. Shapiro and Hentoff, *Hear Me Talkin' to Ya*, 247.

12. Ibid., 240–41.

13. John Chilton, *Who's Who in Jazz, Storyville to Swing Street* (New

York: Time-Life Records Special Edition, 1978), 302–3. Bessie was given first aid by a passing physician and an ambulance took her to the Afro-American Hospital in Clarksdale. She was operated on and died "from a combination of shock and severe injuries."

14. Liner Note, *Bessie Smith, The World's Greatest Blues Singer*, Columbia GP 33.

15. Alec Wilder, *American Popular Song: The Great Innovators 1900–1950* (New York: Oxford University Press, 1972), 26–27.

16. Kay Shirley, ed., *The Book of the Blues* (New York: Leeds Music, 1963), 24.

17. The years with the largest number of such titles were 1923 (46), 1924 (34), and 1928 (33). There was no year without at least a dozen titles.

18. Wilder, *American Popular Song*, 21.

7: "KITTEN ON THE KEYS"

1. Shapiro and Hentoff, *Hear Me Talkin' to Ya*, 228.
2. Ibid., 228–29.
3. Driggs, *The Sound of Harlem*, Columbia C3L 33.
4. Shapiro and Hentoff, *Hear Me Talkin' to Ya*, 169.
5. Quoted by Whitney Balliett, *The New Yorker* (Sept. 9, 1985), 93.

8: SHUFFLE ALONG

1. *Newsweek*, May 26, 1980, 84.
2. Ibid.
3. Driggs, *The Sound of Harlem*, Columbia 3L 33.
4. *Variety*, Nov. 25, 1921.
5. Gerald Bordman, *American Musical Theatre* (New York: Oxford Univ. Press, 1978), 391.
6. Ibid.
7. Ibid., 382.
8. Ibid.
9. Ibid., 417.
10. Ibid., 452.
11. Ibid.
12. Langston Hughes, *The Big Sea* (New York: Thunder's Mouth Press, 1986), 223, 224.

9: "DARDANELLA" (1920)

1. *New York Times,* Jan. 1, 1920, 1.
2. Stanley Walker, *The Night Club Era* (New York: Frederick A. Stokes, 1933), 2.
3. Douglas Gilbert, *Lost Chords* (New York: Doubleday, Doran, 1942), 331.
4. Sigmund Spaeth, *A History of Popular Music in America* (New York: Random House, 1948), 412.
5. Bordman, *American Musical Theatre,* 341, states that Ted Lewis introduced "When My Baby Smiles at Me" in the first *Greenwich Village Follies,* which opened on July 15, 1919. There is no indication of precisely when the song was first interpolated in the revue. But Von Tilzer's claim that he improvised the words of the chorus in September and suggested the title does not square with the writer credits: (words) Andrew B. Sterling and Ted Lewis, (music) Bill Munro.
6. Mel Gussow, *New York Times* (May 11, 1986).
7. Wilder, *American Popular Song,* 120.
8. Max Wilk, *They're Playing Our Song* (New York: Atheneum, 1973), 27–28.
9. Ibid., 42.
10. *Variety,* Jan. 2, 1920.

10: "THE SHEIK OF ARABY" (1921)

1. Frederick Lewis Allen, *Only Yesterday: An Informal History of the Nineteen-Twenties* (New York: Bantam Books, 1986, repr. of 1931 ed.), 150.
2. Ibid., 150–51.
3. Bordman, *American Musical Theatre,* 365.

11: "THREE O'CLOCK IN THE MORNING" (1922)

1. Marks, *They All Sang,* 203.
2. *Los Angeles Times* (June 1, 1986), "Calendar," 3.
3. Bordman, *American Musical Theatre,* 375.
4. Isidore Witmark and Isaac Goldberg, *From Ragtime to Swingtime* (New York: Lee Furman, 1939), 344.
5. Bordman, *American Musical Theatre.*
6. Richard Rodgers, *Musical Stages* (New York: Random House, 1975), 172.

7. Quoted in Henry T. Sampson, *Blacks in Blackface* (Metuchen, N.J.: Scarecrow Press, 1978), 91.
8. Ted Fox, *Showtime at the Apollo* (New York: Holt, Rinehart and Winston, 1983), 26.

12: "YES, WE HAVE NO BANANAS"/"CHARLESTON" (1923)

1. Douglas Gilbert, *Lost Chords* (New York: Doubleday, Doran, 1942), 335.
2. Sigmund Spaeth, *A History of Popular Music in America* (New York: Random House, 1948), 437.
3. Gilbert, *Lost Chords*, 335.
4. Spaeth, *History*, 437.
5. Milford, *Zelda*, 147.
6. Bordman, *American Musical Theatre*, 382.
7. *Variety* (Sept. 13, 1923).
8. Ibid. (Sept. 27, 1923).
9. Ibid. (Aug. 23, 1923), 16.
10. Max Wilk, *They're Playing Our Song* (New York: Atheneum, 1973), 26.
11. Ibid.
12. *Insight* (Oct. 13, 1986), 67.

13: "RHAPSODY AND ROMANCE IN BLUE" (1924)

1. Fred Astaire, *Steps in Time* (New York: Harper and Brothers, 1969), 134–35.
2. Ibid., 129.
3. Ira Gershwin, *Lyrics on Several Occasions* (New York: Alfred A. Knopf, 1959), 174.
4. Kahn's first published song came in 1906, "My Dreamy Lady." His first hit was "Memories" (1915), followed by "Pretty Baby" (1916); "I'll Say She Does" in *Sinbad* (1918); "Ain't We Got Fun" (1921); "Carolina in the Morning," "My Buddy," and "Toot, Toot, Tootsie," all in *The Passing Show* of 1922; "Charley My Boy," "I'll See You in My Dreams," "Spain," "It Had to Be You," "Nobody's Sweetheart," all in 1924; "Ukulele Lady" and "Yes, Sir, That's My Baby" (1925); "Chloe" (1927); "Makin' Whoopee," "Love Me or Leave Me," and "My Baby Just Cares for Me," all in *Whoopee* (1928); plus hits in the 30s and "You Stepped Out of a Dream" in the film, *The Ziegfeld Girl* (1941), the year of his death.
5. Spaeth, *A History of Popular Music in America*, 445.

6. Ibid.
7. Stearns, *The Story of Jazz*, 171.
8. Ibid., 173.
9. Hoagy Carmichael, *The Stardust Road* (New York: Rinehart, 1946), 42.
10. Lopez, *Lopez Speaking*, 182.
11. Ibid., 186.
12. Ibid., 187.
13. Ibid., 184.
14. Ibid., 190.
15. Ibid., 190.

14: "TEA FOR TWO" (1925)

1. Bordman, *American Musical Theatre*, 404.
2. Ibid., 403.
3. Ewen, *American Popular Songs*, 453.
4. Patricia Dubin McGuire, *Lullaby of Broadway: Life and Times of Al Dubin* (Secaucus, N.J.: Citadel Press, 1983), 9.
5. Ibid., 94.
6. Marks, *They All Sang*, 210.
7. Ibid.
8. Astaire, *Steps in Time*, 125.

15: "THE BLACK BOTTOM" (1926)

1. Shapiro and Hentoff, *Hear Me Talkin' to Ya*, 111.
2. Gershwin, *Lyrics on Several Occasions*, 261.
3. Spaeth, *A History of Popular Music in America*, 455.
4. *Variety* (Feb. 10, 1926), 1.
5. Wilder, *American Popular Song*, 14.

16: "TALKIES" AND THEME SONGS (1927)

1. Charles Hamm, *Yesterdays, Popular Song in America* (New York: W. W. Norton, 1979), 334.
2. Andrew Sarris, "The Cultural Guilt of Musical Movies: The Jazz Singer 50 Years After," *Film Comment* (Sept.–Oct. 1977), 41.
3. Ibid., 39.
4. In 1983 Hans Fantel, writing in the *New York Times*, reported, "A search in the archives of the Swedish Radio Company in Stockholm and at the Edison National Historic Site in West Orange, N.J., re-

cently led to the rediscovery of the astounding fact that early in 1913 Edison linked two of his inventions, the phonograph and the motion picture—to produce a film in which the characters talked and sang in sync and with surprising clarity. . . . Known as the "Great Electrician," Edison ignored all possibilities of synchronizing by means of electric signals and relied on ingenious mechanical devices. . . . On Feb. 17, 1913, when Edison's *Kinetophone* opened to a fanfare of publicity at the Colonial Theatre in Manhattan—part of the Orpheum vaudeville chain that later became RKO—the belts slipped and stretched. As a result, the sound lagged behind, as sourly noted in this newspaper the next day by an anonymous reporter who must have been one of the first film critics. . . ." (Jan. 9, 1983).

5. *Variety* (Mar. 21, 1928).
6. Ibid.
7. Preston J. Hubbard, "Synchronized Sound and Movie-House Musicians, 1926–29," *American Music* (Winter 1985), 439.
8. Abel Green and Joe Laurie, Jr., *Showbiz: From Vaudie to Video* (New York: Henry Holt, 1951), 271.
9. Bordman, *American Musical Theatre*, 422.
10. Leonard Feather, *Los Angeles Times* (Apr. 28, 1985), "Calendar."
11. Marshall and Jean Stearns, *Jazz Dance* (New York: Macmillan, 1968), 315–16, 323.
12. Wilk, *They're Playing Our Song*, 281–82.
13. Ibid., 282.
14. Ibid., 282.
15. *Variety* (Nov. 11, 1927).
16. Ibid.

17: "THE SINGING FOOL" (1928)

1. Charles Chaplin, *Autobiography* (New York: Simon and Schuster, 1964), 260.
2. Ewen, *American Popular Songs*, 454.
3. Sophie Tucker with Dorothy Giles, *Some of These Days* (New York: Doubleday, 1945), 260.
4. Arnold Shaw, *52nd St.: The Street of Jazz* (New York: Da Capo Press, 1971), 214.
5. Ibid., 214–15.
6. Marjorie Farnsworth, *The Ziegfeld Follies* (New York: Bonanza Books, 1956), 146.
7. Ibid.
8. *Variety* (Jan. 18, 1928), 54.

9. *Variety* (Feb. 15, 1928).
10. Liner note, *The Symphonic Jazz of James P. Johnson,* MMD stereo recording 20066.

18: CALIFORNIA GOLD RUSH (1929)

1. Pauline Kael, *I Lost It at the Movies* (Boston: Little, Brown, 1954), 142.
2. Jerry Hoffman, "Westward the Course of Tin-Pan Alley," *Photoplay* (Sept. 1929), 39.
3. Ibid.
4. Douglas Gilbert, *Lost Chords* (Garden City, N.Y.: Doubleday, Doran, 1942), 329–30.
5. Quoted in Ewen, *American Popular Songs,* 366–67.
6. Ibid., 7.
7. Spaeth, *A History of Popular Music in America,* 372.
8. Hughes, *The Big Sea,* 334.
9. *Variety* (Oct. 30, 1929).
10. Ewen, *American Popular Songs,* 135.

19: THE MUSICAL REVUE

1. Gerald Bordman, *American Musical Revue* (New York: Oxford University Press, 1985), 51.
2. In a 1908 production, Anna Held, "married" to and produced by Ziegfeld, disrobed on stage, but did so innocently behind a screen.
3. Wilk, *They're Playing Our Song,* 55.
4. Bordman, *American Musical Theatre,* 230.
5. Ibid., 341.
6. Ibid., 389.
7. Robert Baral, *Revue, The Great Broadway Period* (New York: Fleet Press, 1962), 89.
8. Bordman, *American Musical Theatre,* 427.
9. Baral, *Revue,* 33.
10. Ibid., 101.
11. Ibid., 339.
12. Ibid., 139.
13. Ibid., 119–21.
14. Ibid., 122.
15. Ibid., 123.
16. Bordman, *American Musical Theatre,* 393.
17. Ibid., 438.

18. Baral, *Revue*, 117.
19. Wilder, *American Popular Song*, 120. Born in 1888, Berlin has out-lived all his contemporaries and some writers of the next generation.
20. Bordman, *American Musical Theatre*, 365.
21. Baral, *Revue*, 161.
22. Ibid., 105.
23. Ibid., 115.
24. Bordman, *American Musical Theatre*, 275.
25. Baral, *Revue*, 174.
26. Ibid., 186.
27. Ibid.
28. Rodgers, *Musical Stages*, 65.
29. Ibid., 74.
30. Ibid., 83.

20: THE GOLDEN COTERIE

1. Wilder, *American Popular Song*, 31.
2. Wilk, *They're Playing Our Song*, 12.
3. Milton Babbitt, "Jerome Kern," *Newsletter*, Institute for Studies in American Music, May 1985, pp. 8–9.
4. Wilder, *American Popular Song*, 48–49.
5. Ewen, *American Popular Songs*, 209–10.
6. David Ewen, *Complete Book of the American Musical Theatre* (New York: Holt, Rinehart and Winston, 1958, 1959), 174–75.
7. Edna Ferber, *A Peculiar Treasure* (New York: Doubleday, 1960), 306.
8. Ewen, *American Popular Songs*, 41.
9. Wilder, *American Popular Song*, 163.
10. Rodgers, *Musical Stages*, 55–56.
11. Ibid., 55–6.
12. Wilder, *American Popular Song*, 169.
13. Bordman, *American Musical Theatre*, 442.
14. Ibid.
15. Ewen, *American Popular Songs*, 336.
16. Vincent Youmans: Liner Note, *Through the Years 1921–1933* Monmouth/Evergreen MES 7086–87.
17. Max Wilk, *They're Playing Our Song*, 39.
18. Ibid.
19. Bordman, *American Musical Theatre*, 377.
20. Ibid.
21. Ibid., 403.

22. Ewen, *American Popular Songs*, 340.
23. Wilder, *American Popular Song*, 297, describes the syncopation as the result of an "accented fourth best being tied to at least half a note in the next measure."
24. I happened to see a performance of the short-lived work, and the memory has never faded. It was a musical with great songs that looked like an amateur show.
25. Wilder, *American Popular Song*, 304.
26. Bordman, *American Musical Theatre*, 339.
27. Ibid.
28. Ibid., 395.
29. Ewen, *American Popular Songs*, cit. by, 106.
30. Astaire, *Steps in Time*, 134–35.
31. Ewen, *American Musical Theatre*, cited by, 105.
32. Gershwin, *Lyrics on Several Occasions*, 214.
33. Ewen, *American Popular Songs*, 68.

21: THE OPERETTA REVIVAL

1. Bordman, *American Musical Theatre*, 121.
2. Ibid., 78.
3. Ibid., 79.
4. Ibid., 283.
5. Ibid., 416.
6. Ibid., 442.

22: SONG LAUREATE OF THE ROARING TWENTIES

1. Stanley Green, *The World of Musical Comedy* (New York: Grosset and Dunlap, 1960), 168.
2. Cecil Smith, *Musical Comedy in America* (New York: Theatre Art Books, 1950), 308.
3. Rodgers, *Musical Stages*, 88.
4. Ibid.
5. Ibid.
6. Green, *World of Musical Comedy*, 180.

EPILOGUE

1. Cited in Malcolm Cowley, *Exile's Return: A Narrative in Ideas* (New York: W. W. Norton, 1934), 282.
2. Ibid., 283.

3. Ibid., 279.
4. Ibid.
5. Ibid., 289.
6. Ibid.
7. Ibid.
8. Ibid.

Bibliography

Albertson, Chris. *Bessie*. New York: Stein and Day, 1972.

Allen, Frederick Lewis. *Only Yesterday: An Informal History of the Nineteen-Twenties*. New York: Bantam Books, repr. 1931.

Armitage, Merle. *George Gershwin, Man and Legend*. New York: Duell, Sloan and Pearce, 1958.

ASCAP Biographical Dictionary. New York and London: Jacques Cattell Press, R. R. Bowker Company, 1980.

Baral, Robert. *Revue, The Great Broadway Period*. New York and London: Fleet Press, 1962.

Bordman, Gerald. *American Musical Theatre: A Chronicle*. New York: Oxford University Press, 1978.

———. *American Musical Comedy: From Adonis to Dreamgirls*. New York: Oxford University Press, 1982.

———. *American Musical Revue: From the Passing Show to Sugar Babies*. New York: Oxford University Press, 1985.

———. *American Operetta: From H.M.S. Pinafore to Sweeney Todd*. New York: Oxford University Press, 1981.

Burton, Jack. *The Blue Book of Broadway Musicals*. Watkins Glen, N.Y.: Century House, 1952.

———. *The Blue Book of Hollywood Musicals*. Watkins Glen, N.Y.: Century House, 1953.

———. *The Blue Book of Tin Pan Alley*. Watkins Glen, N.Y.: Century House, 1965, rev. ed.

Brunn, H. O. *The Story of the Original Dixieland Jazz Band*. New York: Da Capo Press, 1977.

Cahn, William. *Good Night, Mrs. Calabash: The Secret of Jimmy Durante*. New York: Duell, Sloan and Pearce, 1963.

Carmichael, Hoagy, with Stephen Longstreet. *Sometimes I Wonder.* New York: Farrar, Straus and Giroux, 1965.

——. *The Stardust Road.* New York: Rinehart, 1946.

Cohan, George M. *Twenty Years on Broadway.* New York and London: Harper and Brothers, 1924.

Collier, James Lincoln. *Louis Armstrong: An American Genius.* New York: Oxford University Press, 1983.

——. *The Making of Jazz: A Comprehensive History.* Boston: Houghton Mifflin, 1978.

Coward, Noel. *Present Indicative: An Autobiography.* New York: Da Capo Press, 1980.

Cantor, Eddie. *As I Remember Them.* New York: Duell, Sloan and Pearce, 1963.

—— with Jane Kean Ardmore. *Take My Life.* Garden City, N.Y.: Doubleday, 1957.

——. *The Way I See It.* Phyllis Rosenteur, ed. Englewood Cliffs, N.J.: Prentice-Hall, 1959.

Charters, Ann. *Nobody: The Story of Bert Williams.* New York: Da Capo Press, 1983.

Chilton, John. *Who's Who of Jazz, Storyville to Swing Street.* New York: Da Capo Press, 4th rev. ed.

Cowley, Malcolm. *Exile's Return: A Narrative of Ideas.* New York: W. W. Norton, 1934.

Crichton, Kyle. *The Marx Brothers.* Garden City, N.Y.: Doubleday, 1950.

Dance, Stanley. *The World of Duke Ellington.* New York: Charles Scribner's Sons, 1970.

Dimeglio, John E. *Vaudeville U.S.A.* Bowling Green, Ohio: Bowling Green University Popular Press, 1973.

Dixon, Robert, and John Godrich. *Recording the Blues.* New York: Stein and Day, 1970.

Drennan, Robert E., ed. *The Algonquin Wits.* Secaucus, N.J.: The Citadel Press, 1985.

Eells, George. *The Life That Late He Led: A Biography of Cole Porter.* New York: G. P. Putnam's Sons, 1967.

Ellington, Duke. *Music Is My Mistress.* New York: Da Capo Press, 1976.

Engel, Lehman. *The American Musical Theater.* New York: Collier Books, 1967.

——. *Their Words Are Music: The Great Theatre Lyricists and Their Lyrics.* New York: Crown, 1975.

Ewen, David. *All the Years of American Popular Music.* Englewood Cliffs, N.J.: Prentice-Hall, 1977.

————. *American Popular Songs, From the Revolutionary War to the Present.* New York: Random House, 1966.

————. *Complete Book of the American Musical Theater.* New York: Holt, Rinehart and Winston, rev. ed., 1959.

————. *The Life and Death of Tin Pan Alley: The Golden Age of American Popular Music.* New York: Funk and Wagnalls, 1964.

Farnsworth, Marjorie. *The Ziegfeld Follies.* New York: Bonanza Books, 1956.

Fitzgerald, F. Scott. *All the Sad Young Men.* New York: Charles Scribner's Sons, 1926.

————. *Flappers and Philosophers.* New York: Charles Scribner's Sons, 1921.

————. *The Great Gatsby.* New York: Charles Scribner's Sons, 1925.

————. *Tales of the Jazz Age.* New York: Charles Scribner's Sons, 1922.

————. *This Side of Paradise.* New York: Charles Scribner's Sons, 1920.

Fowler, Gene. *Schnozzola: The Story of Jimmy Durante.* Garden City, N.Y.: Permabooks, 1953.

Freedland, Michael. *Irving Berlin.* New York: Stein and Day, 1974.

————. *Jerome Kern.* New York: Stein and Day, 1981.

Gammond, Peter, ed. *Duke Ellington, His Life and His Music.* New York: Da Capo Press, 1977.

Gershwin, George. *George Gershwin's Songbook.* New York: Simon and Schuster, 1932.

————. *Gershwin Years in Song.* New York: Quadrangle/New York Times Book, 1973.

Gershwin, Ira. *Lyrics on Several Occasions.* New York: Alfred A. Knopf, 1959.

Gilbert, Douglas. *Lost Chords: The Diverting Story of American Popular Songs.* New York: Doubleday, Doran, 1942.

Goldberg, Isaac. *George Gershwin: A Study in American Music.* New York: Simon and Schuster, 1931.

————. *Tin Pan Alley: A Chronicle of the American Popular Music Racket.* New York: John Day, 1930.

Goffin, Robert. *Horn of Plenty: The Story of Louis Armstrong.* New York: Da Capo Press, 1977.

Green, Stanley. *Encyclopedia of the Musical Theatre.* New York: Da Capo Press, 1980.

————. *The World of Musical Comedy.* New York: Da Capo Press, 1984.

Hadlock, Richard. *Jazz Masters of the 20s.* New York: Macmillan, 1965.

Hamm, Charles. *Yesterdays: Popular Song in America.* New York and London: W. W. Norton, 1979.

Handy, W. C. *Father of the Blues: An Autobiography.* London: Sidgwick and Jackson, 1957.

Harris, Sheldon. *Blues Who's Who: A Biographical Dictionary of Blues Singers.* New Rochelle, N.Y.: Arlington House, 1979.

Hart, Dorothy. *Thou Swell, Thou Witty.* New York: Harper and Row, 1976.

Hirschhorn, Clive. *The Hollywood Musical: Every Hollywood Musical from 1927 to the Present Day.* New York: Crown Publishers, 1981.

Huggins, Nathan Irvin. *Harlem Renaissance.* New York: Oxford University Press, 1971.

Hughes, Langston. *The Big Sea.* New York: Thunder's Mouth Press, 1986.

Jablonski, Edward and Lawrence D. Stewart. *The Gershwin Years.* Garden City, N.Y.: Doubleday, 1958.

Jay, Dave. *The Irving Berlin Songography 1907–1966.* New Rochelle, N.Y.: Arlington House, 1969.

Jessel, George. *Elegy in Manhattan.* New York: Holt, Rinehart and Winston, 1961.

———. *So Help Me: The Autobiography of George Jessel.* New York: Random House, 1943.

———. *This Way, Miss.* New York: Henry Holt, 1955.

Jewell, Derek. *Duke: A Portrait of Duke Ellington.* New York: W. W. Norton, 1977.

Johnson, James Weldon, and J. Rosamond Johnson. *The Book of American Negro Spirituals.* New York: Da Capo Press, 1977.

Johnson, James Weldon. *Along This Way: The Autobiography of James Weldon Johnson.* New York: Viking Press, 1968.

———. *Black Manhattan.* New York: Arno Press and the New York Times, 1968.

Katkov, Norman. *The Fabulous Fanny: The Story of Fanny Brice.* New York: Alfred A. Knopf, 1953.

Kimball, Robert, and Alfred Simon. *The Gershwins.* New York: Atheneum, 1973.

Kimball, Robert, ed. *Music and Lyrics of Cole Porter: A Treasury of Cole Porter.* New York: Random House and Chappell, n.d.

Kiner, Larry F. *The Rudy Vallee Discography.* Westport, Conn.: Greenwood Press, 1985.

Kinkle, Roger D. *The Complete Encyclopedia of Popular Music and Jazz, 1900–1950.* 4 vols. New Rochelle, N.Y.: Arlington House, 1974.

Kirkeby, Ed. *Ain't Misbehavin': The Story of Fats Waller.* New York: Da Capo Press, 1975.

Kreuger, Miles. *Show Boat: The Story of a Classic American Musical*. New York: Oxford University Press, 1977.

Lahr, John. *Notes on a Cowardly Lion: The Biography of Bert Lahr*. New York: Alfred A. Knopf, 1969.

Lee, Claire. *Victor Herbert, American Music Master*. New York: Pantheon Books, 1976.

Lomax, Alan. *Mister Jelly Roll: The Fortunes of Jelly Roll Morton, New Orleans Creole and "Inventor of Jazz."* New York: Duell, Sloan and Pearce, 1950.

Lesley, Cole, Graham Payn, and Sheridan Morley. *Noel Coward and His Friends*. New York: William Morrow, 1979.

Lopez, Vincent. *Lopez Speaking*. New York: Citadel Press, 1964.

Levant, Oscar. *The Memoirs of an Amnesiac*. New York: Bantam Books, 1966.

———. *The Unimportance of Being Oscar*. New York: G. P. Putnam's Sons, 1968.

Marks, Edward B. *They All Sang, From Tony Pastor to Rudy Vallee*, as Told to Abbott J. Liebling. New York: The Viking Press, 1935.

Marx, Arthur. *Life with Groucho*. New York: Simon and Schuster, 1954.

Marx, Groucho. *Groucho and Me*. New York: Dell, 1959.

Marx, Harpo with Rowland Barber. *Harpo Speaks!* New York: Bernard Geis Associates, 1961.

Mattfeld, Julius. *Variety Music Cavalcade 1620–1950, A Chronology of Vocal and Instrumental Music Popular in the United States*. New York: Prentice-Hall, 1952.

Maxwell, Gilbert. *Helen Morgan, Her Life and Legend*. New York: Hawthorn Books, 1974.

McGuire, Patricia Dubin. *Lullaby of Broadway: A Biography of Al Dubin*. Secaucus, N.J.: Citadel Press, 1983.

Milford, Nancy. *Zelda*. New York: Avon Books, 1971.

Murrells, Joseph. *The Book of Golden Discs*. London: Barrie & Jenkins, 1978.

Oliver, Paul. *The Meaning of the Blues*. New York: Collier Books, 1963.

———. *Bessie Smith*. New York: A. S. Barnes, 1961.

———. *The Story of the Blues*. Philadelphia: Chilton, 1969.

Pearsall, Ronald. *Popular Music of the Twenties*. London: David & Charles, 1976.

Perry, Hamilton Darby. *Libby Holman, Body and Soul*. Boston: Little, Brown, 1983.

Pleasants, Henry. *The Great American Popular Singers*. New York: Simon and Schuster, 1974.

Richman, Harry with Richard Gehman. *A Hell of a Life.* New York: Duell, Sloan and Pearce, 1966.

Roth, Lillian, with Mike Connolly and Gerold Frank. *I'll Cry Tomorrow.* New York: Frederick Fell, 1954.

Rowland, Mabel, ed. *Bert Williams, Son of Laughter.* New York: English Crafters, 1923.

Sann, Paul. *The Lawless Decade.* New York: Bonanza Books, 1957.

Schwartz, Charles. *Gershwin, His Life and Music.* Indianapolis/New York: Bobbs-Merrill, 1973.

———. *Cole Porter.* London: W. H. Allen, 1978.

Shapiro, Nat. *Popular Music, An Annotated Index of American Popular Song,* Vol. 5, *1920–1929.* New York: Adrian Press, 1969.

Shapiro, Nat, and Nat Hentoff. *Hear Me Talkin' to Ya.* New York: Rinehart, 1955.

Spaeth, Sigmund. *A History of Popular Music in America.* New York: Random House, 1948.

Spitzer, Marian. *The Palace.* New York: Atheneum, 1969.

Stambler, Irwin. *Encyclopedia of Popular Music.* New York: St. Martin's Press, 1965.

Stearns, Marshall W. *The Story of Jazz.* New York: Oxford University Press, 1956.

Stearns, Marshall, and Jean. *Jazz Dance.* New York: Macmillan, 1968.

Stein, Charles W., ed. *American Vaudeville as Seen by Its Contemporaries.* New York: Alfred A. Knopf, 1984; Da Capo Press, 1985.

Stewart-Baxter, Derrick. *Ma Rainey and the Classic Blues Singers.* New York: Stein and Day, 1970.

Thomas, Tony. *Harry Warren and the Hollywood Musical.* Secaucus, N.J.: Citadel, 1975.

Tucker, Sophie with Dorothy Giles. *Some of These Days.* New York: Doubleday, 1945.

Turnbull, Andrew, ed. *The Letters of F. Scott Fitzgerald.* New York: Dell, 1966.

Ulanov, Barry. *Duke Ellington.* New York: Da Capo Press, 1975.

———. *A History of Jazz in America.* New York: The Viking Press, 1954.

Vallee, Rudy, and Gil McKean. *My Time Is Your Time.* New York: Ivan Obolensky, 1962.

Vallee, Rudy. *Vagabond Dreams Come True.* New York: Grossett & Dunlap, 1930.

Walker, Stanley. *The Night Club Era.* New York: Frederick A. Stokes, 1933.

Waller, Maurice, and Anthony Calabrese. *Fats Waller.* New York: Schirmer Books, 1977.

Waters, Ethel with Charles Samuels. *His Eye Is on the Sparrow, An Autobiography.* New York: Bantam Books, 1952.

Whitcomb, Ian. *Tin Pan Alley, A Pictorial History, 1919–1939.* New York, Two Continents, 1975.

Whiteman, Paul, and Mary Margaret McBride. *Jazz.* New York: J.H. Sears, 1926.

Wilder, Alec. *American Popular Song, The Great Innovators 1900–1950.* New York: Oxford University Press, 1972.

Wilk, Max. *They're Playing Our Song.* New York: Atheneum, 1973.

Wilson, Edmund. *The Twenties, from Notebooks and Diaries of the Period.* New York: Bantam Books, 1975.

Witmark, Isidore, and Isaac Goldberg. *From Ragtime to Swingtime, The Story of the House of Witmark.* New York: Lee Furman, 1939.

Woollcott, Alexander. *The Story of Irving Berlin.* New York and London: G.P. Putnam's Sons, 1925.

Discography

PERFORMERS AND COMPOSERS

Louis Armstrong and His Hot Five, Vol. 1, Columbia ML 54383
Louis Armstrong and His Hot Seven, Vol. 2, Columbia ML 54384
Louis Armstrong, Genius Of, Vol. 1 (1923–1933), 2 Columbia CG 30416
Louis and the Big Bands (1923–30), Swing SW 8450
Louis Armstrong & King Oliver (1923–24), 2 Milestone 47017
Bix Beiderbecke 1924, Olympic 7130
The Bix Beiderbecke Legend, RCA Victor LPM 2323
Bix Beiderbecke and Chicago Cornets (1924), 2 Milestone 47019
Bix Beiderbecke (1924–30), Archive of Folk and Jazz Music 317
The Bix Beiderbecke Story, Vol. 1: *And His Gang* Columbia, CL 844
      Vol. 2: *And Tram,* with Frankie Trumbauer, Columbia CL 845
      Vol. 3: *Whiteman Days* Columbia, CL 846
Irving Berlin, *And Then I Wrote,* Time Records S/2113
      The Music Of, Al Goodman and Orchestra, Columbia C 78
      Melodies, Wayne King and His Orchestra, Victor P-159
Eubie Blake, *Early Rare Recordings with Sissle,* EBM 4
      Vol. 2: *With Noble Sissle,* EBM 7
The Perry Bradford Story, Crispus-Attucks PB 101 B
Nat Brandwynne and Orchestra, *Songs of Our Times: Hits of 1920,* Coral
      20081E
Fannie Brice, *Songs She Made Famous,* Audio Fidelity 707
      See *Legends of the Musical Stage,* Take Two Records TT104
Eddie Cantor, *Date With,* Audio Fidelity 702
      Memories, MCA 1506E
      Rare Early Recordings, Bio 10254
      See *Legends of the Musical Stage,* Take Two Records TT 104

Hoagy Carmichael, *From "Star Dust" to "Ole Buttermilk Sky,"* Book-of-the-Month Records 61–5450, 3 LP's.
>*Hoagy Sings Carmichael with Art Pepper, Jimmy Rowles,* et al., Pausa 9006E
>*Stardust* (1927–30), Bio 37
>*Stardust Road,* MCA 1507E
>*In Hoagland:* Georgie Fame, Annie Ross, Hoagy Carmichael, DRG Records

Dixieland with Eddie Condon, Vol. 1, Jazz Panorama 1805

The Chicagoans: Muggsy, Tesch and the Chicagoans, Riverside 1004

Zez Confrey, *Novelty Rag (1918–24),* Folkways RF 28

Kitten on the Keys: The Music of Zez Confrey, Dick Hyman, Piano, RCA XRL 1–4746

Cotton Club Stars, Cab Calloway and the Cotton Club Orchestra, Stash ST 124

Noel Coward, *Album,* 2 Columbia MG 30088
>*We Were Dancing with Gertrude Lawrence,* Monmouth-Evergreen 7042E
>*The Golden Age of Noel Coward,* EMI GX 2502

Vernon Dalhart, *First Recorded Railroad Songs,* Mark 56 794
>*First Singing Cowboy,* Mark 56 793

Dancing Twenties (Carle, Confrey, et al.), Folkways RBF 27

The Legend of Jimmy Durante, Narrated by Walter Winchell, Collectors Edition

Duke Ellington, *The Beginning (1926–28),* MCA 1358
>*Hot in Harlem (1928–29),* MCA 1359
>*Music of Ellington (1928–49),* Columbia Special Products JCL 558
>*Rockin' in Rhythm (1929–31),* MCA 1360
>*This Is (1927–45),* 2 RCA VPM 6042
>*This Is,* Vol. 2: Early Years, Archive of Folk Jazz Music 249E

Ruth Etting, *Original Recordings,* Columbia ML 5050
>*1926–31,* Biograph C 11

Georgia Blues, 1927–33, Yazoo 10126

George Gershwin, *From Tin Pan Alley to Broadway* (piano rolls), 2 Mark 56 680
>*Plays Gershwin and Kern,* Klavier 122E

Golden Twenties, Longines Symphonette Recording Society

Benny Goodman, *Boys with Jim (Dorsey) and Glenn (Miller) 1928–29,* Sunbeam 141
>*Great Soloist, 1929–33,* Biograph C 1
>*Hotsy Totsy Gang 1928–29 with Teagarden,* Sunbeam 113
>*Rare Benny Goodman,* Sunbeam 112

Whoopee Makers 1928–29, Pausa 9031

The Great Gatsby Era, Music From, The St. Valentine's Day Mob Singers and Orchestra, Ambassador Records S 98105

Harlem Comes to London, DRG Records
(Includes Plantation Orchestra, Dec. 1, 1926; Noble Sissle and His Orchestra, Sept. 10, 1929).

The Sound of Harlem, Jazz Odyssey, Vol. 3, Columbia C 3L 33

Fletcher Henderson, *First Impressions* (1927–31), MCA 1310
 1924–41, Biograph C 12
 1923–27, Biograph 12039
 and the Dixie Stompers 1925–1928, DRG SW 8445/6
 A Study in Frustration, Columbia C4L 19

Libby Holman, *Legendary: The Torch Songs*, Monmouth MRS 6501
 To Remember Her By, Monmouth/Evergreen 7067

Albert Hunter, Young, *Original Blues & Jazz Vocals* (1921–1929), Stash 123

Mississippi John Hurt, *Best* 2 Vanguard T 19/20
 In 1928, Yazoo 1065
 1928, Biograph C 4

Blind Lemon Jefferson, *Black Snake Moan*, Milestone 2013
 1926–29, 2-Milestone 47022
 Immortal, Vols. 1 and 2, 2-Milestone 2004/7
 Master of Blues, Biograph 12015
 1926–1929, Biograph 12000

James P. Johnson, *New York Jazz*, Stinson 21
 Rare Piano Rolls 1917–21, Biograph 10030
 1921–1926, Olympic 7132
 Rare Piano Rolls, Vol. 2, Biograph 1009Q
 The Symphonic Jazz Of, William Albright, piano, MMD Stereo 20066

Al Jolson, *Best*, 2-MCA 1002E
 California, Here I Come (*1911–1929*), Sunbeam 505
 Rock-A-Bye Your Baby, Decca DL 9035, MCA 27052E
 Steppin' Out (*1911–1929*), Sunbeam 503

Legends of the Musical Stage: Fanny Brice, Eddie Cantor, Al Jolson, Nick Lucas, Ethel Merman, Marilyn Miller, Harry Richman, Sophie Tucker, Take Two Records TT 104

Ted Lewis, *Best*, 2-MCA 4101E
 Greatest Hits, MCA 258E
 1928–32, Biograph C 8

Nick Lucas, See *Legends of the Musical Stage*

McKinney's Cotton Pickers, Victor HJ5

Mabel Mercer, *Merely Marvelous*, Atlantic SD 1322
  MCA 1516E
  Art Of, 2 Atlantic 602
Marilyn Miller, See *Legends of the Musical Stage*
Helen Morgan/Nelson Eddy, *The Torch Singer and the Mountie*, Trisklog
  HMNE 4
Ferdinand "Jelly Roll" Morton, *Classic Piano Solos 1923–24*, 12 River-
  side 12–111, Folkways 47
  New Orleans Memories, Commodore XLF 14942
  The King of New Orleans Jazz 1926–28, 12 RCA LPM 1649
  1923–24, 2-Milestone 47018
  1924–26: Rare Piano Rolls, Biograph 1004Q
  The Incomparable, 1923–1926, Milestone MLP 2003
New Orleans Rhythm Kings, *NORK (1922–23) with Morton*, 2-Milestone
  47020
  (Mannone-Arodin), Brunswick BL 58011
  12", Folkways FP 57
Red Nichols and His 5 Pennies, *1929–31 with Goodman*, Sunbeam 137
  Popular Concert 1928–32, 2-Sunbeam 12
  Rareset Brunswick Masters (1926–31), MCA 1518E
King (Joe) Oliver, *Immortal with Armstrong*, Milestone 2006
  Zulus Ball/Working Man Blues, 1923, Herwin 106
  Vol. 1, Brunswick BL 58020
  Lincoln Gardens, 12" Jazz Panorama 1205
  Plays the Blues, Riverside 1007
Original Dixieland Jazz Band, Commodore 20003
  In England 1919–20, 10" Columbia 33S 1087
Ma Rainey, *Blame It on the Blues*, Aircheck 20
  Down in the Basement, Biograph 12001
  Immortal, Milestone 2017
  Ma Rainey, 2-Milestone 47021
  Oh My Baby Blues, Biograph 12011
  Queen of the Blues, Biograph 12032
Harry Richman, See *Legends of the Musical Stage*
The Original Roaring 20's, Enoch Light, Charleston City All Stars, Vol.
  3, Grand Award GA 229SD
The Roaring 20's, Music from Warner Bros., WS 1394
The Roaring 20's, Hal McShay and His Old-Time Charleston Band, Vol.
  2, Tops L 1630
Paul Robeson, *The Historic*, Everest FS 345
Jimmie Rodgers, *Best of Legendary*, RCA AHL 1–3315E
  My Rough and Rowdy Ways, RCA ANLI–1209E

This Is, RCA VPS 6091E

Sissle & Blake, *Early Rare Recordings*, Vol. 1: Eubie Blake, EBM 4

Bessie Smith Story, Vol. 1: *With Louis Armstrong*, Columbia CL 855

      Vol. 2: *Blues to Barrelhouse*, Columbia CL 856

      Vol. 3: *With Joe Smith and Fletcher Henderson's Hot Six*, Columbia CL 857

      Vol. 4: *With James P. Johnson and Charlie Green*, Columbia CL 858

      World's Greatest Blues Singer, Columbia GP 33

Miss Kate Smith 1926–1931, Sunbeam 12

Willie "The Lion" Smith, *The Legend Of*, Grand Award GA 33–368

      Pork and Beans, Black Lion BL 156

Song Hits of Our Times—1920, Coral 20081

      1922–24, Coral 20046, 20047, 20083

      1925, Vocalion 3837

      1926–28, Coral 20048, 20049, 20050

      1929–31, Vocalion 3641, 3642, 3643

Songs of the Railroad (1924–34), Vetco 103

Stars of Grand Ole Opry 1926–1974, 2-RCA CPL2-0466

Kay Swift, *Fine and Dandy*, 2-Mark 56/700

Frank Teschemacher, *Tesch*, Brunswick BL 58017

      Muggsy, Tesch and the Chicagoans, Riverside RLP 1004

Bob Thiele and His New Happy Times Orchestra, *The 20s Score Again*, Doctor Jazz FW 39876

Frankie Trumbauer and His Orchestra, Columbia SEG 7577 (Released in England)

Sophie Tucker, *Greatest Hits*, MCA 263

      Vintage Show Biz Greats, with Jimmy Durante, Ted Lewis, Folkways 603

      and Ted Lewis, Soted 1200

      Cabaret Days, Mercury MG 20046

Rudy Vallee, and the Coast Guard Band, Mark 56/714

      Evening with, 2 Mark 56/681

Joe Venuti, *Violin Jazz*, with Eddie Lang, Adrian Rollini, Yazoo 1062

      and Eddie Lang, *Stringing the Blues, 1927–32*, 2-CSP JC2L-24

Fats Waller, *Ain't Misbehavin'*, RCA LPM 1246

      Ain't Misbehavin', Archives of Folk and Jazz Music 337

      In London (1922–39), 2-Swing SW 8442/3

      Legendary (1929–38), RCA CPL 1-2904E

      Piano Solos (1929–41), 2-Bluebird AXM 2–5518

      Rediscovered Solos (from player piano rolls, 1923 and 1926), Riverside 1010

Ethel Waters, *Greatest Years*, Columbia KG 31571
    Miss, Monmouth/Evergreen MES 6812
    1921–4, Biograph 12022
    On Stage and Screen, (1925–40), CSP CCL 2792
Paul Whiteman, *Concert 1927–32*, Sunbeam 18
    Tribute to Gershwin 1936, Mark 56/761
    With Bing Crosby, Columbia CL 2830
*The New Paul Whiteman Orchestra, Playing the Classic Arrangements
    of Bill Challis, Tom Satterfield and Lennie Hayton*, Monmouth
    Evergreen MES/7074
Clarence Williams, *Vol. 1: 1927–29*, Biograph 12006
    Vol. 2: 1927–28, Biograph 12038

MUSICALS

Ain't Misbehavin' (OC), RCA CBL2–2965
Anything Goes (1962 OC), Epic FLS 15100
Irving Berlin Revisited, Painted Smiles 1356
Music of Irving Berlin, Heritage of Broadway Bainbridge 1017
Noel Coward Revisited, Painted Smiles 1355
De Sylva, Brown and Henderson (Bagley), Painted Smiles 1351
Desert Song, Angel S 37319
Eubie (OC), Warner Brothers HS 3267
Funny Face (OST/Paramount), Verve MGV 15001
George Gershwin Revisited, Painted Smiles 1357
George Gershwin Plays Gershwin & Kern (Show tunes of the 20s),
    Klavier KS 122
Music of George Gershwin, Heritage of Broadway Bainbridge 1912
Ira Gershwin Revisited (Bagley), Painted Smiles 1353
Oscar Hammerstein Revisited (Bagley), Painted Smiles 1365
Hit the Deck (OST MGM), MGM E3163
Jerome Kern Revisited (Bagley), Painted Smiles 1363
Jerome Kern in London (OC Recordings), Monmouth/Evergreen MES
    7061
Music of Jerome Kern, Heritage of Broadway Bainbridge 1011
New Moon, Angel S 37320
Oh Kay! (1960 Off Broadway), Stet DS 15017
Oh, Kay! (Goddard Lieberson, Prod.), Columbia ACL 1050
No, No, Nanette (The New 1925 Musical), Columbia S 30563
No, No. Nanette, Music from, RCA Victor LSP 4504
No, No Nanette/Sunny (Only OC Album), Stanyan 10035

Cole (London OC), 2 RCA CRL2–5054
Cole Porter, Music Of, Heritage of Broadway Bainbridge 1014
Cole Porter Revisited (Bagley), Painted Smiles 1340
Cole Porter, Vol. III (Bagley), Painted Smiles 1370
Cole Porter, Vol. IV, Painted Smiles 1371
Rodgers & Hart, Music Of, Heritage of Broadway Bainbridge 1015
Rodgers & Hart Revisited (Bagley) Vols. 1 and 2, 2 Painted Smiles
    1341, 3
Rodgers & Hart Revisited, Vol. 3, Painted Smiles 1366
Rodgers & Hart Revisited, Vol. 4, Painted Smiles 1367
Arthur Schwartz Revisited (Bagley), Painted Smiles 1350
Show Boat (Allers Orch, 1966), RCA LSO 1126
Show Boat (Prod. and Cond. by Lehman Engel), RCA LM 2008
Show Boat (OC, 1946 Broadway Revival), Columbia OL 4058
Show Boat (OC London 1972 Revival), Stanyan 10048
Show Boat, Shirley Bassey in (London cast), Stanyan SR 10036
Show Boat, Magic Violins, Diplomat 2515
Student Prince (Lanza), RCA LSC 2339
Sunny/No No Nanette (OC, London Hippodrome), Stanyan SR 10035
Vincent Youmans, *Through the Years with* (*1921–1933*), Monmouth/
    Evergreen MES/7086–87
Vincent Youmans, *Through the Years with* (*36 songs*), Monmouth MRS
    6401/2
Vincent Youmans Revisited (Bagley), Painted Smiles 1352

BIOPICS

Nora Bayes: *Shine on Harvest Moon* (WB, 1944)
Bix Beiderbecke: *Young Man with a Horn* (WB, 1950)
Fanny Brice: *Rose of Washington Square* (20th Cent.-Fox, 1939)
De Sylva, Brown and Henderson: *The Best Things in Life Are Free*
    (20th Cent.-Fox, 1956)
Ruth Etting: *Love Me or Leave Me* (MGM, 1955)
Fred Fisher: *Oh, You Beautiful Doll* (TCF, 1949)
Jane Froman: *With a Song in My Heart* (20th. Cent.-Fox, 1952)
George Gershwin: *Rhapsody in Blue* (WB, 1945)
Benny Goodman: *The Benny Goodman Story* (Universal, 1936)
W. C. Handy: *St. Louis Blues* (Paramount, 1958)
Gus Kahn: *I'll See You in My Dreams* (WB, 1951/2)
Kalmar and Ruby: *Three Little Words* (MGM, 1950)
Jerome Kern: *Till the Clouds Roll By* (MGM, 1945)

Ted Lewis: *Is Everybody Happy?* (Col., 1943)
Cole Porter: *Night and Day* (W.B, 1946)
Rodgers & Hart: *Words and Music* (MGM, 1948)
Sigmund Romberg: *Deep in My Heart* (MGM, 1954)
Lillian Roth: *I'll Cry Tomorrow* (MGM, 1955)
Blossom Seeley & Benny Fields: *Somebody Loves Me* (Paramount, 1952)

Variety's "Golden 100 Tin Pan Alley Songs"
Songs of the Twenties

"All Alone"—words and music, Irving Berlin (1924)

"Always"—words and music, Irving Berlin (1925)

"April Showers"—words, B. G. De Sylva; music, Louis Silvers (1921)

"Chicago"—words and music Fred Fisher (1922)

"Dinah"—words, Sam M. Lewis and Joe Young; music, Harry Akst (1925)

"Great Day"—words, William Rose and Edward Eliscu; music, Vincent Youmans (1929)

"Happy Days Are Here Again"—words, Jack Yellen; music, Milton Ager (1929)

"I Can't Give You Anything But Love"—words, Dorothy Fields; music, Jimmy McHugh (1928)

"I'll See You in My Dreams"—words, Gus Kahn; music, Isham Jones (1924)

"Love Me or Leave Me"—words, Gus Kahn; music, Walter Donaldson (1928)

"Lover Come Back to Me"—words, Oscar Hammerstein II; music, Sigmund Romberg (1928)

"Marie"—words and music, Irving Berlin (1928)

"My Blue Heaven"—words, George Whiting; music, Walter Donaldson (1927)

"My Heart Stood Still"—words, Lorenz Hart; music, Richard Rodgers (1927)

"Ol' Man River"—words, Oscar Hammerstein II; music, Jerome Kern (1927)

"Somebody Loves Me"—words, Ballard MacDonald and B. G. De Sylva; music, George Gershwin (1924)

"Sometimes I'm Happy"—words, Irving Caesar; music, Vincent Youmans (1927)

"Stardust"—words, Mitchell Parish; music, Hoagy Carmichael (1929)

"Sweet Sue"—words, Will J. Harris; music, Victor Young (1928)

" 'S Wonderful"—words, Ira Gershwin; music, George Gershwin (1927)

"Tea for Two"—words, Irving Caesar; music, Vincent Youmans (1924)

"The Birth of the Blues"—words, B. G. De Sylva and Lew Brown; music, Ray Henderson (1926)

"The Man I Love"—words, Ira Gershwin; music, George Gershwin (1924)

"With a Song in My Heart"—words, Lorenz Hart; music, Richard Rodgers (1929)

"Without a Song"—words, William Rose and Edward Eliscu; music, Vincent Youmans (1929)

Index

Song Index